a primer of

COMPLEX VARIABLES

with an introduction to
advanced techniques

CONTEMPORARY
UNDERGRADUATE
MATHEMATICS
SERIES

Robert J. Wisner,
editor

A PRIMER OF COMPLEX VARIABLES WITH AN INTRODUCTION TO
ADVANCED TECHNIQUES
Hugh J. Hamilton, Pomona College

MODERN MATHEMATICS: AN ELEMENTARY APPROACH
Ruric E. Wheeler, Samford University

to E. R. Hedrick and C. R. Adams

Brooks/Cole Publishing Company
A Division of Wadsworth Publishing Company, Inc.,
Belmont, California

L. C. Cat. Card No.: 66-12865
Printed in the United States of America

a primer of
COMPLEX VARIABLES
with an introduction to
advanced techniques

HUGH J. HAMILTON
Pomona College

Brooks/Cole Publishing Company, Belmont, California
A Division of Wadsworth Publishing Company, Inc.

Preface

Chapters 1 through 8 of this book are based on the belief that a substantial amount of elementary complex variable theory can be taught successfully without using techniques beyond those already familiar to the student who has passed an introductory course in partial differentiation, multiple integration, and infinite series. (What has been done here is not merely to forego the traditional advanced calculus prerequisite but to proceed *without developing along the way* those techniques of advanced calculus that are usually supposed to be necessary even in an elementary course in complex variables.)

The material in these opening chapters should be intelligible to all mathematics majors by the second half of their junior year—to some a semester or a year earlier—and to most physical science majors while they are still undergraduates. Also, it is hoped that, by maintaining a medium level of mathematical sophistication in the theoretical developments in these chapters, the book will enable many students to gain significant appreciation of a useful and delightful field of mathematics that would otherwise be inaccessible to them. Such students would include, in particular, a large proportion of prospective teachers of secondary mathematics and a number of laboratory and non-physical scientists.

It has been possible to keep to a remarkably satisfactory minimum the number of appeals in Chapters 1 through 8 to the results of more advanced investigation (many of which are derived in the final chapters). Yet almost all of the results obtained in the earlier chapters are very close approximations to the sharpest results customarily obtained by means of advanced techniques.

The instructor may present the material in Chapters 1 through 8 with greater or less emphasis on ϵ-δ techniques, according to his students' background. This background may also be used to decide whether to treat the material on complex algebra in Chapter 1 and the elements of line integration in Chapter 4 as new or as review.

Chapters 9 through 11 develop and use the more advanced techniques and may therefore be regarded as sections of an appendix. However, they should be used as parts of the course, in sequence, for those classes that cover the earlier chapters in less than a full semester. Chapter 9 begins with a thorough discussion of ϵ-δ techniques, proceeds to develop a considerable amount of point set topology, and concludes with a "Goursat-type" proof of continuity of the derivative. Chapter 10 is largely devoted to uniform convergence, and Chapter 11 is a short essay on connectedness (including, for completeness, some remarks on connectedness of closed sets).

The book will be optimally effective if the several topics are taken up in the order in which they are presented, even for students who have already had advanced calculus. However, an instructor can bring the course into line with the "classical" approach by dipping from time to time into various parts of the last three chapters in the course of presenting the first eight. And if his students have not had advanced calculus and he still feels that some particular concept deferred to the later chapters deserves an earlier billing, he will probably find it easy to arrange whatever sequence he desires. Thus an early acquaintance with the idea of uniform convergence (though the text has been carefully designed to make this unnecessary) can be achieved by taking a short detour through §10-3 immediately following §3-4, with appropriate limitations in the assignment of problems along the way.

Certain relevant matters whose detailed consideration belongs properly to the field of advanced calculus are for the most part not critically examined in this book; these matters are those of which the intermediate calculus student may be assumed to have an adequate working knowledge. For example, the line integrals of Chapter 4 are unhesitatingly interpreted as areas, and Fubini's theorem is assumed without mention of the fact. It should also be noted at this point that the concept of "set"—in spite of the logical complications at deep levels—is taken as undefined.

All problems marked with an asterisk should be assigned, since their solution is presupposed elsewhere in the text or in other sets of problems. Certain extensions of the theory, often developed in the bodies of other textbooks, will be found among the problems. The bibliography has been placed at the end, since the amplifications available in these references for the most part require some familiarity with the material covered in Chapters 9 and 10.

Grateful acknowledgement is hereby made to S. G. Tellman of the University of Arizona, who taught the course from an early version of the manuscript; to Jeffrey D. Scargle of the California Institute of Technology, who made helpful suggestions, read proof, and prepared the bibliography; to Elmer Tolsted of Pomona College, who read proof; and to John S. Maybee of Purdue University and Robert J. Wisner of New Mexico State University, who provided useful comments in the manuscript stage.

CONTENTS

Chapter 1   Elementary Concepts

1-1   A Historical Note   *1*

1-2   Complex Numbers.   Complex Algebra   *2*

1-3   Problems   *4*

1-4   Complex Real Numbers   *5*

1-5   Quadratic Equations   *5*

1-6   The Simplified Notation   *6*

1-7   Problems   *7*

1-8   The Complex Plane and the Complex Sphere   *8*

1-9   Problems   *11*

1-10 The Conjugate   *13*

1-11 Descriptions of Certain Loci   *13*

1-12 The Triangle Inequality   *13*

1-13 Problems   *15*

Chapter 2   Differentiability.   The Elementary Functions

2-1   Variables.   Constants.   Functions   *18*

2-2   Limits of Variables   *19*

2-3   Problems   *23*

2-4   Continuity and Differentiability   *25*
2-5   Problems   *26*
2-6   Conditions for Differentiability.   The Cauchy-Riemann Equations   *28*
2-7   Problems   *31*
2-8   Identical Vanishing of the Derivative   *33*
2-9   The Functions e^z and ln z *33*
2-10   Problems   *35*
2-11   The Elementary Functions   *38*
2-12   Problems   *39*

Chapter 3   Infinite Series

3-1   Sequences   *41*
3-2   Series   *42*
3-3   Absolute Convergence.   Product Series   *43*
3-4   Power Series   *46*
3-5   Circle and Radius of Convergence   *46*
3-6   Problems   *48*
3-7   Termwise Differentiation of Power Series.   A Uniqueness Theorem   *50*
3-8   Problems   *54*

Chapter 4   Integration

4-1   Simple Curves of Class C_1 *56*
4-2   Definite Integral of a Continuous Function.   Line Integrals   *57*
4-3   Evaluation of the Integral   *58*
4-4   Some General Properties of the Integral.   A Bounding Theorem   *59*
4-5   Problems   *60*
4-6   Open Region.   Connected and Simply Connected Open Regions   *61*
4-7   Problems   *62*
4-8   Line Integrals Independent of the Path   *63*
4-9   Problems   *69*
4-10   Integrals of Regular Functions.   Cauchy's and Morera's Theorems   *71*

4-11   Evaluation of Definite Integrals of Regular Functions   *73*
4-12   Problems   *74*

Chapter 5   The Taylor Expansion

5-1   Equivalent Paths of Integration   *77*
5-2   Cauchy's Integral Formula   *78*
5-3   Taylor's Series   *80*
5-4   Problems   *83*
5-5   Identity Theorems   *86*
5-6   The Algebra of Power Series   *87*
5-7   The Maximum Modulus Principle   *89*
5-8   Problems   *90*
5-9   Entire Functions.   Liouville's Theorem   *91*
5-10   The Fundamental Theorem of Algebra   *93*
5-11   Problems   *93*
5-12   The Casorati-Weierstrass Theorem for Transcendental Entire Functions   *95*
5-13   Problems   *97*

Chapter 6   The Laurent Expansion

6-1   Neighborhoods   *99*
6-2   Limit Points of Sets and of Sequences   *99*
6-3   Problems   *100*
6-4   Singular Points   *101*
6-5   Problems   *102*
6-6   The Laurent Expansion   *102*
6-7   Uniqueness of the Laurent Expansion   *105*
6-8   Problems   *108*
6-9   Analysis of Isolated Singular Points.   Decomposition of Rational Functions into Partial Fractions   *109*
6-10   The Point at Infinity   *111*
6-11   Problems   *113*
6-12   Zeros   *115*
6-13   Problems   *117*
6-14   Residues   *119*
6-15   Problems   *120*

6-16 The Residue Theorem. The Principle of the Argument. Rouché's Theorem *121*

6-17 Problems *123*

6-18 Residue Theory in the Evaluation of Certain Real Integrals *125*

6-19 Problems *129*

6-20 Inverse Functions *129*

6-21 Problems *133*

Chapter 7 Analytic Continuation

7-1 Analytic Continuation from Open Regions *134*

7-2 An Analytic Function with a Natural Boundary *135*

7-3 Generation of an Analytic Function from an Element *135*

7-4 Problems *137*

7-5 Multi-valued Analytic Functions *138*

7-6 Riemann Surfaces *140*

7-7 Problems *141*

7-8 Analytic Continuation from a Line Segment *143*

7-9 Problems *143*

7-10 Persistence of Functional Relationships *144*

7-11 Problems *145*

Chapter 8 Conformal Mapping

8-1 Mappings or Transformations *147*

8-2 Problems *148*

8-3 Mappings or Transformations, Continued *149*

8-4 Conformal Mapping *150*

8-5 Problems *154*

8-6 Streamlines for Harmonic Equipotential Curves *155*

8-7 Problems *157*

8-8 The General Bilinear Transformation *158*

8-9 Problems *160*

8-10 Fixed Points of the General Bilinear Transformation *161*

8-11 Problems *162*

8-12 Other Mappings by Analytic Functions *162*

8-13 Problems *165*

Chapter 9 Some Techniques for More Penetrating Analysis

9-1   Epsilon-Delta and Related Techniques   *166*
9-2   Problems   *170*
9-3   Closed, Null, and Bounded Point Sets   *171*
9-4   Problems   *171*
9-5   Complementary Set. Isolated Points. Boundary Points.
      Interior Points   *172*
9-6   Problems   *173*
9-7   The Elementary Algebra of Sets   *174*
9-8   Problems   *175*
9-9   The Elementary Algebra of Sets, Continued   *176*
9-10 Problems   *177*
9-11 Extreme Bounds on Real Sets   *177*
9-12 Problems   *178*
9-13 The Axiom of Continuity   *179*
9-14 Problems   *181*
9-15 Nests of Intervals.   The Bolzano-Weierstrass Theorem   *181*
9-16 Extreme Limit Points of Real, Infinite Sets   *182*
9-17 Extreme Limit Points of Real Sequences   *183*
9-18 Problems   *184*
9-19 The Bolzano-Weierstrass Theorem for Plane Sets   *185*
9-20 Problems   *188*
9-21 Nests of Plane Sets   *191*
9-22 The Heine-Borel Theorem.   The Maximum Modulus
      Theorem   *191*
9-23 Problems   *194*
9-24 The Continuous Differentiability of Regular Functions   *195*
9-25 Problems   *199*

Chapter 10 Some General Theorems Concerning Series

10-1 Cauchy's Convergence Criterion   *200*
10-2 A Formula for the Radius of Convergence of the General Power
      Series   *201*
10-3 Problems   *202*
10-4 Uniform Convergence   *204*
10-5 Problems   *205*

10-6 Applications of Uniform Convergence *207*

10-7 Problems *209*

Chapter 11 On Connectedness of Sets

11-1 Connectedness of Sets in General *211*

11-2 Problems *213*

11-3 Connectedness of Open and of Closed Sets *214*

11-4 Problems *216*

Bibliography *218*

Index *221*

Elementary Concepts

1

1-1. A Historical Note.

Historically, complex numbers made their appearance in connection with the solutions of quadratic equations.   If, in solving the equation

$$ax^2 + bx + c = 0,$$

the early mathematician was confronted by a negative discriminant, then either the "solutions"

$$x = \frac{-b \pm \sqrt{b^2 - 4ac}}{2a}$$

simply did not exist, or the existence of numbers whose squares were negative had to be admitted.   Thus the "imaginary unit" i was invented, for which $i^2 = -1$, and it was agreed to operate with "complex numbers" $a + bi$, where a and b were "real."   Keeping the definition of i in mind and otherwise working within the formal framework of established arithmetic, it was found that, for two complex numbers $a + bi$ and $c + di$, the equation $a + bi = c + di$ meant that both $a = c$ and $b = d$, and that

$$(a + bi) + (c + di) = (a + c) + (b + d)i,$$
$$(a + bi)(c + di) = (ac - bd) + (ad + bc)i.$$

This cavalier approach does not meet present standards of logical precision, which would ask, first, by what right may this number i be *invented*, and then, by what right may it be combined arithmetically with the numbers of ordinary arithmetic and subjected to the laws of that arithmetic.   A currently acceptable development of the theory of complex numbers will now be sketched.   (It is to be noted that the definitions are so formulated as to lead to the conclusions displayed above. There is nothing illogical in this; the ideas presented in those conclusions are not to be attacked but, rather, to be firmly attached to a logical structure built on definitions.)

1-2. Complex Numbers. Complex Algebra.

One begins by symbolizing and defining a *complex number* as an ordered pair of real numbers a and b, thus: (a, b). (The adjectives "real" and "imaginary," as applied to numbers, are unfortunate, but they are too firmly established by usage to be successfully replaced by less misleading terms. Imaginary numbers are no more lacking in mathematical reality than irrational numbers are lacking in mathematical good sense.) Next, one symbolizes and defines *equality* between two complex numbers (a, b) and (c, d) thus:

$$(a, b) = (c, d) \quad \text{means both} \quad a = c \quad \text{and} \quad b = d.$$

[Note that, in general, $(a, b) \neq (b, a)$.] The *sum* of two complex numbers is symbolized and defined thus:

$$(a, b) + (c, d) \equiv (a + c, b + d),$$

and the *product* thus:

$$(a, b)(c, d) \equiv (ac - bd, bc + ad).$$

It is to be observed that the *order* of the terms, in addition, and of the factors, in multiplication, is irrelevant; that is, these operations are *commutative*. It is shown in the problems of §1-3 that they are also *associative*, which means that

$$(a, b) + [(c, d) + (e, f)] = [(a, b) + (c, d)] + (e, f),$$
$$(a, b)[(c, d)(e, f)] = [(a, b)(c, d)](e, f).$$

It is also shown in the problems of §1-3 that multiplication is *distributive* with respect to addition; that is,

$$(a, b)[(c, d) + (e, f)] = (a, b)(c, d) + (a, b)(e, f).$$

The *difference* between two complex numbers (in the order given) is symbolized and defined thus:

$$(a, b) - (c, d) \equiv (x, y),$$

where

$$(a, b) = (c, d) + (x, y),$$

provided that such a number exists. Since solution of the defining equation above is equivalent to solution of the simultaneous real equations

$$a = c + x,$$
$$b = d + y,$$

the following result is obtained.

THEOREM 1-1.   *The difference between any two complex numbers* (a, b) *and* (c, d) *exists, is unique, and is given by*

$$(a, b) - (c, d) = (a - c, b - d).$$

The *complex zero*, (0, 0), is the next object for scrutiny. From the definitions of addition and multiplication and Theorem 1-1, it follows that addition of the complex zero to any complex number leaves that number unchanged, that the product of the complex zero by any complex number is the complex zero, and that the difference between any complex number and itself is the complex zero. The *negative* of a complex number (a, b) is symbolized and defined thus:

$$-(a, b) \equiv (0, 0) - (a, b).$$

The *quotient* of the complex number (a, b) by the complex number (c, d) is symbolized and defined thus:

$$\frac{(a, b)}{(c, d)} \equiv (x, y),$$

where

$$(a, b) = (c, d)(x, y),$$

provided that such a number exists. Since solution of the defining equation here is equivalent to solution of the simultaneous real equations

$$a = cx - dy,$$
$$b = cy + dx$$

and is therefore possible (and uniquely so) if and only if not both c and d are zero, the following result is obtained.

THEOREM 1-2.   *The quotient of any complex number* (a, b) *by any other complex number* (c, d) *exists, is unique, and is given by*

$$\frac{(a, b)}{(c, d)} = \left[\frac{(ac + bd)}{(c^2 + d^2)}, \frac{(bc - ad)}{(c^2 + d^2)} \right]$$

if the divisor is not the complex zero.

For reasons which will be established in the problems of §1-3, division by the complex zero is not defined.

Such terms as *addition, subtraction, multiplication, division,* and so on are used in complex algebra in the same ways that they are used in real algebra.

Just as there is a complex zero, there is a *complex one,* $(1, 0)$. It is easy to verify that $(a, b)(1, 0) = (a, b)$ for each complex number (a, b). The *reciprocal* of a complex number (a, b) is defined as the quotient of $(1, 0)$ by (a, b) and therefore exists and is unique if $(a, b) \neq (0, 0)$.

1-3. Problems.

1. How could the early mathematician (§1-1) "prove" that the equation $a + bi = c + di$ implies that $a = c$ and $b = d$? (Collect the "real" terms a and c on one side of the equation and the "pure imaginaries" bi and di on the other side. Then square.)

2. Evaluate $(a, b) * (c, d)$, where the symbol $*$ indicates, in succession, addition, subtraction, multiplication, and division, if
    (a) $a = 1, b = 2, c = 3, d = 4$;
    (b) $a = 2, b = -1, c = 4, d = -2$;
    (c) $a = 0, b = 2, c = 3, d = 0$.

*3. Prove that
    (a)   complex addition is associative,
    (b)   complex multiplication is associative,
    (c)   complex multiplication is distributive with respect to complex addition.

4. (a)   Write the negative of (a, b) in the form (c, d).
    (b)   Write the reciprocal of (a, b) in the form (c, d).
    (c)   Find the negative and the reciprocal of $(1, -2)$, of $(3, 0)$, of $(0, -4)$.

*5. (a)   Show that the difference between (a, b) and (c, d) equals the sum of (a, b) and the negative of (c, d).
    (b)   Show that the quotient of (a, b) by (c, d) equals the product of (a, b) and the reciprocal of (c, d).

6. Perform the indicated operations:
    (a) $(1, -2)[(3, 4) - (2, 0)]$,
    (b) $\dfrac{(-2, 1) + (0, 4)}{(3, 5) - (1, 3)}$,
    (c) $\dfrac{(-2, 1)}{(3, 5)} + \dfrac{(0, 4)}{(1, 3)}$.

7. Show that, if the definition of quotient assigns a value to
   (a) $(a, b)/(0, 0)$, then $(a, b) = (0, 0)$;
   (b) $(0, 0)/(0, 0)$, then the value is not unique.

*8. Prove that, if $(a, b)(c, d) = (0, 0)$, then either $(a, b) = (0, 0)$ or $(c, d) = (0, 0)$.

*9. Show that, if neither (c, d) nor (g, h) is the complex zero, then

$$\frac{(a, b)}{(c, d)} \cdot \frac{(e, f)}{(g, h)} = \frac{(a, b)(e, f)}{(c, d)(g, h)}.$$

1-4. Complex Real Numbers.

Complex numbers of the form $(a, 0)$ may be called *complex real numbers*, or *complex reals*. Examination of the definitions and theorems shows that the operations of addition, subtraction, multiplication, and division (where defined) with complex reals lead always to complex reals. If moreover each complex real $(a, 0)$ is imagined as set alongside its real *counterpart* a, it is seen that each of these operations, when applied to the complex reals and simultaneously to their real counterparts, leads to a complex real and to a real, respectively, such that the latter is the counterpart of the former. This correspondence between complex reals and their real counterparts is usually referred to as an *isomorphism* between complex reals and reals with respect to the operations of algebra.

1-5. Quadratic Equations.

A brief return to quadratic equations may be of interest at this point. Consider first the equation

$$x^2 - 3x + 2 = 0, \tag{1-1}$$

whose roots are 1 and 2. A corresponding complex equation is

$$(u, v)^2 - (3, 0)(u, v) + (2, 0) = (0, 0), \tag{1-2}$$

where (u, v) is the "unknown" and $(u, v)^2$ means $(u, v)(u, v)$. Now (1-2) is the same thing as

$$(u^2 - v^2, 2uv) - (3u, 3v) + (2, 0) = (0, 0),$$

or

$$(u^2 - v^2 - 3u + 2, 2uv - 3v) = (0, 0),$$

and the last equation is equivalent to the two simultaneous equations

$$u^2 - v^2 - 3u + 2 = 0, \tag{1-3}$$

$$2uv - 3v = 0. \tag{1-4}$$

From (1-4), either $v = 0$ or $u = 3/2$. Substitution of the first of these values in (1-3) leads to the equation

$$u^2 - 3u + 2 = 0,$$

with roots $u = 1$ or 2. Substitution of the second in (1-3) leads to the equation $v^2 = -\frac{1}{4}$, which is an impossible situation, since u and v are real. Thus the roots of (1-2) are—as might have been expected—the complex counterparts $(1, 0)$ and $(2, 0)$ of the (real) roots of (1-1).

On the other hand, the equation

$$x^2 - 2x + 2 = 0 \tag{1-5}$$

has, if any roots at all, these:

$$x = \frac{2 \pm \sqrt{4 - 8}}{2}.$$

That is, (1-5) has *no roots*, *unless* that equation is interpreted to mean

$$(u, v)^2 - (2, 0)(u, v) + (2, 0) = (0, 0), \tag{1-6}$$

with the unknown (u, v) identified with "x." But this leads one [by the procedure used in solving (1-2)] to the simultaneous equations

$$u^2 - v^2 - 2u + 2 = 0, \tag{1-7}$$

$$2uv - 2v = 0. \tag{1-8}$$

From (1-8) either $v = 0$ or $u = 1$. Substitution of $v = 0$ in (1-7) leads to the equation

$$u^2 - 2u + 2 = 0,$$

which is equivalent to (1-5) under the real interpretation and therefore has no roots; but substitution of $u = 1$ in (1-7) leads to the equation $v^2 = 1$. Hence (1-6) has the roots $(1, \pm 1)$, a circumstance perhaps foreseen in the earlier, logically meaningless expression $(2 \pm \sqrt{4 - 8})/2$ for the (by presumption, real) values of x.

1-6.   The Simplified Notation.

While in the preceding sections complex numbers have been freed from the overtones associated with the term "imaginary" and the logically important distinction between reals and complex reals has been made, the resulting notation is unnecessarily awkward. In order to see how this notation can be simplified, it is helpful to turn first to *real multiples* of complex numbers. One defines the multiple $a(c, d)$ or (c, d) by a as

$(a, 0)(c, d)$ and on occasion writes $(c, d)a$ to represent the same thing. It follows that

$$(a + b)(c, d) = a(c, d) + b(c, d),$$

and that

$$a(b, c)d(e, f) = (ad)[(b, c)(e, f)].$$

In particular, the general complex number (a, b) can be written thus:

$$(a, b) = (a, 0) + (0, b) = a(1, 0) + b(0, 1).$$

In this final expression, the coefficient of a is the complex one; the single letter $\mathcal{I}$ will be used to represent this number $(1, 0)$. Also, the single letter i will be used to represent the coefficient $(0, 1)$ of b. Thus

$$(a, b) = a\mathcal{I} + bi.$$

One calls a the *real part* or *real component*, and b the *imaginary part* or *imaginary component*, of (a, b). The interpretation (1-6) of (1-5), under which (1-5) has roots, can now be expressed in this way:

$$x^2 - 2x + 2\mathcal{I} = 0\mathcal{I},$$

where x represents $u\mathcal{I} + vi$ and u and v are unknown reals.

Now

$$\mathcal{I}^2 \equiv (1, 0)(1, 0) = (1, 0) \equiv \mathcal{I},$$
$$\mathcal{I}i \equiv (1, 0)(0, 1) = (0, 1) \equiv i,$$

and

$$i^2 \equiv (0, 1)(0, 1) = (-1, 0) \equiv -\mathcal{I}.$$

Hence

$$(a\mathcal{I} + bi) \pm (c\mathcal{I} + di) = (a \pm c)\mathcal{I} + (b \pm d)i,$$
$$(a\mathcal{I} + bi)(c\mathcal{I} + di) = (ac - bd)\mathcal{I} + (ad + bc)i,$$
$$\frac{a\mathcal{I} + bi}{c\mathcal{I} + di} = \frac{ac + bd}{c^2 + d^2}\mathcal{I} + \frac{bc - ad}{c^2 + d^2}i \quad (c, d) \neq (0, 0).$$

If alongside these results are set the results of the formal manipulations of $a + bi$ and $c + di$ mentioned in the first paragraph of §1-1, it can be seen that the formal manipulations are logically sound. They will be used henceforth in this book.

1-7. Problems.

1. Show by direct computation that the solutions of the real equation $x^2 - 2x - 3 = 0$ are the counterparts of the solutions of the complex equation

$$(u, v)^2 - (2, 0)(u, v) - (3, 0) = (0, 0).$$

2. Repeat problem 1 for the real equation $x^2 - x - 2 = 0$.

3. Show that the real equation $x^2 - 2x + 5 = 0$ has no solution, and find by direct computation the roots of the complex equation $(u, v)^2 - (2, 0)(u, v) + (5, 0) = (0, 0)$.

4. Repeat problem 3 for the real equation $5x^2 + 6x + 5 = 0$.

5. Solve the general quadratic equation with "real coefficients," $(a, 0)(u, v)^2 + (b, 0)(u, v) + (c, 0) = (0, 0)$.

6. Show that
    (a) $(ab)(c, d) = a[b(c, d)]$,
    (b) $a[(c, d) + (e, f)] = a(c, d) + a(e, f)$.

7. Write the complex numbers in problem 6 of §1-3 in the form $a + bi$ and perform the operations indicated there by using the "formal manipulations."

*8. (a) Show that $\sqrt{2i}$ exists and has two values. (Set $\sqrt{2i} = x + iy$ and square.)
     (b) Show that $\sqrt{u + iv}$ in general exists, and that it has two values unless $u = v = 0$.
     (c) Using part (b), show that the familiar "quadratic formula" provides the solutions of the general quadratic equation (with complex coefficients and complex unknown).

*9. Show that
     (a) $(\cos \theta + i \sin \theta)(\cos \varphi + i \sin \varphi) = \cos (\theta + \varphi) + i \sin (\theta + \varphi)$,
     (b) $(\cos \theta + i \sin \theta)/(\cos \varphi + i \sin \varphi) = \cos (\theta - \varphi) + i \sin (\theta - \varphi)$.

*10. Using problem 9(a) with $\varphi = \theta$ and then applying mathematical induction, show that $(\cos \theta + i \sin \theta)^n = \cos n\theta + i \sin n\theta$ for every positive integer n.

1-8. The Complex Plane and the Complex Sphere.

Henceforth the single letter z will be freely used to represent the complex number

$$(x, y) \equiv xI + yi \equiv x + iy.$$

Since to each ordered pair of reals (x, y) there corresponds one and only one point in the xy plane—namely that for which x and y are, respectively, the abscissa and the ordinate—as well as one and only one complex number $z \equiv x + iy$, it follows that to each point in the xy plane there corresponds one and only one complex number, namely that whose real part is the abscissa and whose imaginary part is the ordinate. Thus, for purposes of visualizing the complex number $z \equiv x + iy$, one labels the x axis the *axis of reals* or *real axis* and the y axis the *axis of imaginaries* or *imaginary axis* and refers to the xy plane as the *complex plane*. One speaks interchangeably of the *number* z and the *point* z. It will be noted that, in the complex plane, addition of $z \equiv x + iy$ and $w \equiv u + iv$ can be interpreted as addition of the *vectors* from the origin to the points (x, y) and (u, v) (Fig. 1-1).

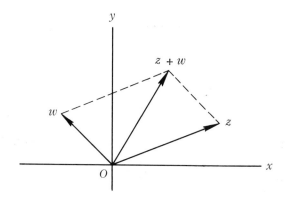

Figure 1-1

It is customary to mention at this point the *complex sphere S*, which is often defined as the sphere whose "south pole" is located at the origin O in the complex plane and whose "north pole" N lies one unit along an s axis introduced perpendicular to the complex plane so that the x, y, and s axes, in that order, set up a right-handed coordinate system (Fig. 1-2). Given any point z in the complex plane, the line through N and z pierces S in a unique point P, which is then regarded as the representation of z on the complex sphere. Conversely, it is clear that, given any point P on the complex sphere—except only N itself—the line through N and P pierces the complex plane in a unique point z. Points on the "equator" of S correspond in this way to points on the unit circle with center at the origin in the complex plane, points above the equator (except N) to points outside this circle in the plane, and points below the equator to points inside the circle. There are many remarkable facts about this *stereographic projection* of the sphere on the plane; for example, the "projections" of the points on two curves on S, which intersect at angle φ at a point P_0, constitute, respectively, two curves in the complex plane, which intersect also at angle φ at the point z_0, which is the projection of P_0. Analysis of such matters is largely geometric and is for the most part irrelevant to the purposes of this book.

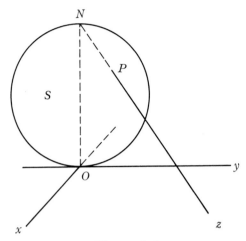

Figure 1-2

One often denotes the real and imaginary parts of a complex number z by $R(z)$ and $I(z)$, respectively. Thus $x = R(z)$, $y = I(z)$, and $z = R(z) + iI(z)$.

Having identified z with the point (x, y) in the complex plane, one considers polar coordinates (r, θ) of that point, agreeing to take r always non-negative (Fig. 1-3). One calls r the *modulus, magnitude, numerical value* (used in such phrases as "z is numerically greater than w"), or *absolute value* of z and writes $|z| = r$; and one calls θ an *argument* or *amplitude* of z and writes arg $z = \theta$. In particular, one calls that value of θ for which $-\pi < \theta \leq \pi$ the *principal value* of the argument and, using the capital letter to single out this value, writes Arg $z = \theta$. Since $x = r \cos \theta$ and $y = r \sin \theta$ for any value of the argument,

$$z = r(\cos \theta + i \sin \theta).$$

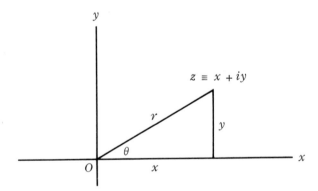

Figure 1-3

This is the *trigonometric form* of the complex number. It is to be noted that, while the modulus of the complex zero is defined (as zero), its argument is *not* defined.

Multiplication of two complex numbers is now capable of a simple geometric interpretation. If the trigonometric forms of the complex numbers z and w are, respectively, $r(\cos\theta + i\sin\theta)$ and $\rho(\cos\varphi + i\sin\varphi)$, then (problem 9a of §1-7)

$$zw = r\rho[\cos(\theta+\varphi) + i\sin(\theta+\varphi)].$$

But $r = |z|$, $\rho = |w|$, and

$$zw = |zw|[\cos(\text{Arg } zw) + i\sin(\text{Arg } zw)].$$

Hence $|zw| = |z|\,|w|$ and $\text{Arg } zw = \theta + \varphi + 2k\pi$ for some integer k. (Indeed,

$$\text{Arg } zw = \text{Arg } z + \text{Arg } w + 2j\pi,$$

where $j = 0, 1,$ or -1, and in any case *an* argument of zw is $\text{Arg } z + \text{Arg } w$.) That is to say, the product of two complex numbers can be located by *multiplying moduli and adding arguments.*

Clearly, $|z| = \sqrt{x^2 + y^2}$ and either $\tan(\arg z) = y/x$ (if $x \neq 0$) or $\cot(\arg z) = x/y$ (if $y \neq 0$). Also, by using the familiar formula for the distance between two points (x, y) and (u, v), one sees that the distance between two points z and w in the complex plane is equal to $|z - w|$.

1-9. Problems.

1. To what loci on the complex sphere S do the points on a given line in the complex plane correspond?

2. A "complex sphere" T, different from the sphere S described above, is of unit radius and has its center at the point $z = 0$. The correspondence between points on T and points in the complex plane is made by lines through the "north pole," as before.
   (a) To what points on T do the points z in the complex plane correspond if $|z| < 1$? $|z| > 1$?
   (b) To what loci on T do the points on a given line in the complex plane correspond?

3. (a) By writing the complex number -1 in trigonometric form, explain the geometric effect on any complex number z of multiplication by -1.
   (b) Repeat (a) above, with reference to multiplication by i.

4. Write $\omega \equiv (-1 + \sqrt{3}i)/2$ in trigonometric form and, from the result, find ω^2 in trigonometric form by squaring the

magnitude and doubling the amplitude. Then square ω in Cartesian form and, from the result, find the magnitude and amplitude of ω^2. Compute ω^3 in any fashion.

5. Write the complex numbers $2(\cos \pi/4 + i \sin \pi/4)$ and $3(\cos \pi/3 + i \sin \pi/3)$ in Cartesian form, find their sum, and write it in trigonometric form (using tables).

6. Develop a geometric rule for
   (a) subtracting $w \equiv u + iv$ from $z \equiv x + iy$,
   (b) dividing $z \equiv r(\cos \theta + i \sin \theta)$ by $w \equiv \rho(\cos \varphi + i \sin \varphi)$ $\neq 0$.

7. Write the following in trigonometric form.
   (a) $-2i$,
   (b) $1 - i$,
   (c) $\sqrt{3} + i$,
   (d) $2 - 3i$ (using tables),
   (e) $2(\cos \pi/4 + i \sin 3\pi/4)$,
   (f) $3(\cos 3\pi/4 - i \sin \pi/4)$,
   (g) $-(\cos \pi + i \sin \pi/2)$,
   (h) $2(\cos \pi/4 + i \sin \pi/3)$ (using tables).

8. Write in trigonometric form and use the geometric rules for multiplication and division to carry out the operations indicated below.
   (a) $(1 - \sqrt{3}i)(\sqrt{3} + i)$,

   (b) $\dfrac{2i}{1 - i}$,

   (c) $\dfrac{1 + \sqrt{3}i}{\sqrt{3} + i}$,

   (d) $\dfrac{(1 + i)(1 + \sqrt{3}i)}{(-1 + \sqrt{3}i)(1 - i)}$.

9. Prove *De Moivre's Theorem*: If $z = r(\cos \theta + i \sin \theta)$ and n is any integer, then $z^n = r^n(\cos n\theta + i \sin n\theta)$. Compare problem 10 of §1-7.

*10. If $z \neq 0$, we can write $z = r[\cos (\theta + 2k\pi) + i \sin (\theta + 2k\pi)]$ for $k = 0, \pm 1, \pm 2, \ldots$, where $r = |z|$ and $\theta = \text{Arg } z$. If we then put $z^{1/n} = \rho(\cos \varphi + i \sin \varphi)$, where n is a positive integer, and use De Moivre's theorem (problem 9 above), we can find the nth roots of z. Do so, showing that there are exactly n *different* such roots.

11. What relationship between arguments of two non-zero complex numbers z and w is equivalent to the condition that the quotient z/w is
   (a) positive real?
   (b) negative real?
   (c) pure imaginary?

1-10. The Conjugate.

By the *conjugate* $\bar{z}$ of $z \equiv x + iy$ is meant the complex number $x - iy$. Geometrically speaking, $\bar{z}$ is the reflection of z in the real axis. It follows that $z\bar{z} = x^2 + y^2 \equiv |z|^2$, $z + \bar{z} = 2x \equiv 2R(z)$, and $z - \bar{z} = 2iI(z)$. Since, if $w = u + iv$, then

$$\overline{z + w} = \overline{(x + u) + i(y + v)} = (x + u) - i(y + v)$$
$$= (x - iy) + (u - iv) \equiv \bar{z} + \bar{w},$$

it follows that *the conjugate of a sum is the sum of the conjugates.* Similarly,

$$\overline{zw} = \overline{(xu - yv) + i(xv + yu)} = (xu - yv) - i(xv + yu)$$
$$= (x - iy)(u - iv) \equiv \bar{z}\bar{w},$$

so that *the conjugate of a product is the product of the conjugates.* Also, as will be established in the problems of §1-13, *the conjugate of a difference is the difference between the conjugates* and *the conjugate of a quotient is the quotient of the conjugates.*

1-11. Descriptions of Certain Loci.

Certain loci can be described very succinctly in terms of the symbols introduced in preceding sections. Thus the equation $|z| = 1$ represents the "unit circle," with radius 1 and center at the origin, in the complex plane; and the inequality $|z| \leq 1$ represents the "closed unit disk," consisting of the unit circle and its interior. Also, the inequality $I(z) > 0$ represents the "open upper half-plane," which is to say the points above the real axis. (What inequality represents the "*open* unit disk"—that is, the interior alone of the unit circle? Try to define the "*closed* upper half-plane" and write down an inequality that represents it.)

1-12. The Triangle Inequality.

THEOREM 1-3. (Triangle Inequality) *Given any two complex numbers z and w,*

$$|z + w| \leq |z| + |w|,$$

equality holding if and only if either (a) *z or w is zero or* (b) Arg *z* = Arg *w*.

Proof. (See also problem 10 of §1-13.) Taking $z = x + iy$ and $w = u + iv$, and observing that the squares of real numbers are non-negative, let us start with

$$(xv - yu)^2 \geq 0 \tag{1-9}$$

and deduce, in succession, the following inequalities:

$$x^2v^2 + y^2u^2 \geq 2xyuv,$$

$$x^2u^2 + x^2v^2 + y^2u^2 + y^2v^2 \geq x^2u^2 + 2xyuv + y^2v^2,$$

$$(x^2 + y^2)(u^2 + v^2) \geq (xu + yv)^2,$$

$$\sqrt{x^2 + y^2}\sqrt{u^2 + v^2} \geq xu + yv, \tag{1-10}$$

$$x^2 + y^2 + 2\sqrt{x^2 + y^2}\sqrt{u^2 + v^2} + u^2 + v^2$$

$$\geq x^2 + y^2 + 2xu + 2yv + u^2 + v^2,$$

$$(\sqrt{x^2 + y^2} + \sqrt{u^2 + v^2})^2 \geq (x + u)^2 + (y + v)^2,$$

$$\sqrt{x^2 + y^2} + \sqrt{u^2 + v^2} \geq \sqrt{(x + u)^2 + (y + v)^2},$$

$$|z| + |w| \geq |z + w|. \tag{1-11}$$

This establishes the inequality.

[It would be a fraud to pretend that, in *discovering* such a proof as the above, one starts with an inequality like (1-9). Instead, one starts with the *last* inequality in the succession and works, step by step, to the first—taking all inequalities along the way as tentative until an indisputable one is reached—in our case (1-9)—and being sure that each inequality is a consequence of the one that *follows* it. The logical development is then obtained by turning the page upside down!]

Next, if we have equality in (1-11), each of the steps from (1-9) to (1-11) is reversible, so that we have both

$$xv - yu = 0 \quad \text{and} \quad xu + yv \geq 0, \tag{1-12}$$

the first relationship following from (1-9) and the second from (1-10). (Which step from (1-9) to (1-11) is not necessarily reversible in the case of inequality?) If (a) either $z = 0$ or $w = 0$, then equality clearly holds in (1-11). If (b) neither $z = 0$ nor $w = 0$, then we can write

$$z = r(\cos \theta + i \sin \theta)$$

and

$$w = \rho(\cos \varphi + i \sin \varphi),$$

where θ and φ are the principal arguments, deduce from (1-12) that $\sin(\varphi - \theta) = 0$ and $\cos(\varphi - \theta) \geq 0$, and hence conclude that $\theta = \varphi$. [What can be said about the quotient z/w in case (b)? See problem 11 of §1-9.]

The inequality of Theorem 1-3 is called the triangle inequality for the reason that z, w, and $z + w$, when regarded as vectors, form the sides of a triangle in the complex plane (Fig. 1-1); the theorem merely states that the length of the side represented by $z + w$ is not greater than the sum of the lengths of the other two, and that it is equal to that sum if and only if either (a) one of the sides represented by z and w is of zero length or (b) these last two sides lie along the same line and have the same direction. (More or less lengthy algebraic derivations—like the above proof—of geometrically obvious facts are often in order because they point the way to derivations of analogous facts which do *not* have clear geometric interpretations.)

The next theorem, like the triangle inequality, is an immediate consequence of a geometric interpretation.

THEOREM 1-4. *Given any two complex numbers z and w, we have*

$$|z + w| \geq |\,|z| - |w|\,|, \tag{1-13}$$

for any side of a triangle is at least as long as the difference between the lengths of the other sides. The inequality (1-13) is derived in a different way in the problems of §1-13.

EXAMPLE 1. $|z| \equiv |x + iy| \leq |x| + |y|$.

EXAMPLE 2. $|z_1 + z_2 + z_3| \leq |z_1 + z_2| + |z_3|$

$$\leq |z_1| + |z_2| + |z_3|.$$

1-13. Problems.

1. Given a point z, let its reflection in the y axis be z_1, the reflection of z_1 in the x axis be z_2, and the reflection of z_2 in the y axis be z_3. Express z_1, z_2, and z_3 in terms of z and $\bar{z}$.

*2. Show that
   (a) $|\bar{z}| = |z|$,
   (b) $|z/w| = |z|/|w|$ $(w \neq 0)$,
   (c) $1/z = \bar{z}/|z|^2$ $(z \neq 0)$,
   (d) $\overline{z - w} = \bar{z} - \bar{w}$,
   (e) $\overline{(z/w)} = \bar{z}/\bar{w}$. $(w \neq 0)$.

3. Given two complex numbers z and w, the sum $z\bar{w} + \bar{z}w$ must be real. Why?

4. If $P(z_0) = 0$, where $P(z)$ is a polynomial in z with real coefficients, then $P(\bar{z}_0) = 0$.
    (a) Why?
    (b) Use this fact to find all of the roots of the equation $z^4 + 2z^3 - 4z - 4 = 0$, given that one root is $-1 - i$.
    (c) Is the statement $\overline{P(z)} = P(\bar{z})$ true for all polynomials $P(z)$?

5. What locus is represented by the equation $|z - z_0| = a$, where z_0 is a fixed point and a is a non-negative number? Verify by first writing the equation in terms of the real and imaginary parts of $z - z_0$.

6. What is the locus represented by the equation $|z| = 2|z - 1|$? Verify as in problem 5.

7. The locus represented by the equation $z = z_0 + tz_1$, where z_0 and z_1 are fixed $(z_1 \neq 0)$ and t is a real parameter $(-\infty < t < \infty)$ is the line passing through the point z_0 and parallel to the line from the origin to z_1.
    (a) Why?
    (b) Write in this form an equation for the line passing through the points $2 - 3i$ and $4 + 5i$.

8. The equation $\text{Arg}\,(z - z_0) = \varphi$, where z_0 is a fixed point and $\varphi\,(-\pi < \varphi \leq \pi)$ is a fixed angle, represents what locus? Verify by setting up an equivalent relationship in terms of the real and imaginary parts of $z - z_0$.

9. In geometric terms, what set of points in the complex plane is characterized by the inequality $aR(z) + bI(z) \leq c\,(a, b, c$ real)?

10. Prove the triangle inequality by expanding the quantity $|z + w|^2 \equiv (z + w)\overline{(z + w)}$. (Problem 3 may help here.)

11. Derive (1-13) from (1-11) by writing, first,
$$|z| = |(z + w) + (-w)|$$
and then
$$|w| = |(z + w) + (-z)|.$$

12. How would one prove that, for any positive integer n,
$$|z_1 + z_2 + \cdots + z_n| \leq |z_1| + |z_2| + \cdots + |z_n|?$$

13. How would one prove that $|z| + |w| \geq |z - w| \geq ||z| - |w||$?

14. By the technique suggested in the proof of Theorem 1-3, prove that $|z| \equiv |x + iy| \geq (|x| + |y|)/\sqrt{2}$ and determine under what conditions there is equality.

Differentiability.
The Elementary Functions

2

2-1. Variables. Constants. Functions.

Let us suppose given a set D of complex numbers or points in the plane which contains at least one member. By a *complex variable* with *domain D* is meant the general point in D or the general point in D subject to such restrictions as may be imposed. The letters z, w, and ζ are those most often used to represent complex variables.

If each number z_0 in a given domain D is made by some rule or formula to determine a unique number w_0, and one denotes by R the set of all numbers w, each so determined by a number z in D, then the variable w is said to be a *function* of z on (or *in* or *over*) D—the rule or formula *being* the function—and one writes $w = f(z)$ [or $g(z)$ or ...]. (An alternative definition which is in current vogue identifies the function with the set of ordered pairs of (complex) numbers (z, w), where z is in D, and w is that number in R which is determined by application of the rule or formula to z. In fact, any set of ordered pairs (z, w) *defines* such a rule or formula if the set of all values of the first element z is D and no two of the ordered pairs have the same first element and different second elements: each z_0 in D then determines that (unique) number w_0 which is the second element in the order pair whose first element is z_0.) The set R is called the *range* of the function $f(z)$. In such a relationship, z is called the *independent variable* and w the *dependent variable*. A complex function whose range consists of a single point is called a *constant*.

If each number z_0 in a given domain D is made by a rule or formula to determine a *set* of numbers w_0, one again writes $w = f(z)$ (or ...), though now with w representing collectively the several values determined by z; in such a case w is called a *multi-valued* function of z. Thus if $w^2 = z$, then for each z except zero two values of w are determined; w is multi-valued on the domain D consisting of all non-zero numbers. One customarily terms a multi-valued function *n-valued* (or *infinitely many-valued*) on a domain D if each z_0 in D determines n different numbers w_0 (or infinitely many different numbers w_0). The function $w = f(z) \equiv \arg z$, where D is the set of all points in the plane except the origin, is infinitely many-valued; its range is the set of all real numbers. Henceforth the functions in this book will be assumed to be single-valued unless the contrary is clearly stated or implied. Now to say that $z_0 \equiv x_0 + iy_0$ determines w_0 is to say that the *pair* of real numbers x_0 and y_0 determines w_0. And to say that $w_0 \equiv u_0 + iv_0$ is determined is to say that the *pair* of real numbers u_0 and v_0 is determined. (It is convenient, in case w is real, to suppose it to be the corresponding complex real. No separate analysis is then needed; one simply has $v \equiv 0$.) Hence to say that $w \equiv u + iv$ is a function of $z \equiv x + iy$ is to say neither more nor less than that u and v are real functions $u(x, y)$ and $v(x, y)$, respectively, of the two real variables x and y for those pairs of values (x, y) for which $z \equiv x + iy$ is in D.

EXAMPLES. For the function

$$w = z^2 \equiv x^2 + 2ixy - y^2$$

we have $u = x^2 - y^2$ and $v = 2xy$. For the function

$$w = \bar{z} \equiv x - iy$$

we have $u = x$ and $v = -y$. For the function

$$w = |z| \equiv \sqrt{x^2 + y^2}$$

we have $u = \sqrt{x^2 + y^2}$ and $v = 0$. For the function

$$w = e^{-y}(\cos x + i \sin x)$$

we have $u = e^{-y} \cos x$ and $v = e^{-y} \sin x$.

2-2. Limits of Variables.

Let w be a complex function $f(z)$ of the complex variable z which is defined for all z within some circle about a point z_0 though not necessarily at z_0 itself. One writes

$$\lim_{z \to z_0} w = w_0 \qquad (2\text{-}1)$$

to signify that $w \equiv f(z)$ is arbitrarily close to w_0 whenever z is sufficiently close to z_0, with $z \neq z_0$. Precisely, this means that, given arbitrary $\epsilon > 0$, there is a $\delta > 0$ such that $|w - w_0| < \epsilon$ whenever $0 < |z - z_0| < \delta$. The verbalizations used to describe this situation are in no essential different from those used to describe the corresponding real limit situation,

$$\lim_{x \to x_0} f(x) = y_0.$$

And, as in the real case, (2-1) is occasionally expressed thus:

$$w \to w_0 \text{ as } z \to z_0.$$

For example, $z + 2 \to i + 2$ as $z \to i$.

Similarly, either of the symbols

$$\lim_{z \to z_0} |f(z)| = \infty,$$

$$|f(z)| \to \infty \quad \text{as} \quad z \to z_0 \tag{2-2}$$

means that [$f(z)$ being defined for all z within some circle about z_0, though not necessarily at z_0 itself] the magnitude of $f(z)$ is arbitrarily large whenever z is sufficiently close to z_0, with $z \neq z_0$. That is, given arbitrary $N > 0$, there is a $\delta > 0$ such that $|f(z)| > N$ whenever $0 < |z - z_0| < \delta$. Thus, $\lim_{z \to 0} 1/|z| = \infty$.

One is also often concerned with "limits as z becomes numerically infinite ($|z| \to \infty$)," as in the examples

$$\lim_{|z| \to \infty} \frac{1}{z} = 0, \qquad |z^2| \to \infty \quad \text{as} \quad |z| \to \infty.$$

These and the other limit situations which may arise parallel so closely real limit situations with which the student is familiar that he need have little fear of misinterpreting them. Indeed, all of them may be reduced to the standard real form

$$\lim_{p \to 0} q = 0, \qquad p > 0, \qquad q \geq 0. \tag{2-3}$$

EXAMPLE 1.   The form (2-3) is taken on by (2-1) if in (2-1) we put

$$p = |z - z_0| \quad \text{and} \quad q = |w - w_0| \equiv |f(z) - w_0|.$$

EXAMPLE 2.   The situation in (2-2) can be expressed in the form (2-3) if we put $p = |z - z_0|$ and $q = 1/|f(z)|$.

EXAMPLE 3.   In whatever way the three complex variables z, ζ, and w are related, the situation symbolized by $\lim_{z, \zeta \to z_0} w = w_0$ means (2-3) with

$$p = \sqrt{|z - z_0|^2 + |\zeta - z_0|^2} \quad \text{and} \quad q = |w - w_0|.$$

The student need not be disturbed by the fact that in (2-3) q is generally not a *function* of p; what (2-3) says is that p and q are *so related that* q is defined for at least certain positive values of p however small *and that* q is small when it is defined and when p is small and positive. Already, in the definition of the integral as the limit of a sum, the student has been confronted with such a situation as (2-3) describes; in this situation the value of the variable $p \equiv \max \varDelta x_j$ by no means determines the value of

$$q \equiv \left| \sum f(x_j') \varDelta x_j - \int_a^b f(x)\, dx \right|,$$

although (2-3) holds true here if $f(x)$ is continuous for $a \le x \le b$ and the $\varDelta x_j$ and the x_j' are determined in the familiar way.

The pains taken in this section to emphasize the generality of (2-3) in describing limit situations have been calculated to lay the groundwork for a general proof that a complex variable w tends to a limit w_0 if and only if its real and imaginary parts u and v, respectively, tend to the real and imaginary parts u_0 and v_0 of w_0—a fact now formally expressed.

THEOREM 2-1. *A necessary and sufficient condition that* $\lim_{p \to 0} w = w_0$ *is that* $\lim_{p \to 0} u = u_0$ *and* $\lim_{p \to 0} v = v_0$; *however* $p\, (> 0)$ *and* w *may be related.*

Proof. The conclusion is an immediate consequence of the inequality

$$|u - u_0|, |v - v_0| \le |w - w_0|$$
$$\equiv \sqrt{|u - u_0|^2 + |v - v_0|^2} \le |u - u_0| + |v - v_0|$$

(Technically, if $\lim_{p \to 0} w = w_0$, then, given arbitrary $\epsilon > 0$, there is a $\delta > 0$ such that $|w - w_0| < \epsilon$ whenever $0 < p < \delta$, so that $|u - u_0|, |v - v_0| < \epsilon$ whenever $0 < p < \delta$, and hence

$$\lim_{p \to 0} u = u_0 \quad \text{and} \quad \lim_{p \to 0} v = v_0.$$

And if $\lim_{p \to 0} u = u_0$ and $\lim_{p \to 0} v = v_0$, then, given arbitrary $\epsilon > 0$, there is a $\delta > 0$ such that $|u - u_0|, |v - v_0| < \epsilon/2$ whenever $0 < p < \delta$, so that $|w - w_0| < \epsilon/2 + \epsilon/2 \equiv \epsilon$ whenever $0 < p < \delta$, and hence $\lim_{p \to 0} w = w_0$.)

In conjunction with the limit theorems of real calculus, Theorem 2-1 facilitates proof that the familiar theorems on sums, products, and quotients in real calculus carry over to complex calculus.

EXAMPLE 4. (The notation used is self-explanatory.) If $w \to w_0 \ne 0$ and $w^* \to w_0^*$, we have $u \to u_0$, $v \to v_0$, $u^* \to u_0^*$, and $v^* \to v_0^*$, so that

$$\frac{u^*u + v^*v}{u^2 + v^2} \to \frac{u_0^*u_0 + v_0^*v_0}{u_0^2 + v_0^2} \quad \text{and} \quad \frac{uv^* - u^*v}{u^2 + v^2} \to \frac{u_0v_0^* - u_0^*v_0}{u_0^2 + v_0^2}.$$

Whence

$$\frac{w^*}{w} \equiv \frac{u^*u + v^*v}{u^2 + v^2} + i\frac{uv^* - u^*v}{u^2 + v^2} \to \frac{u_0^*u_0 + v_0^*v_0}{u_0^2 + v_0^2}$$

$$+ i\frac{u_0v_0^* - u_0^*v_0}{u_0^2 + v_0^2} \equiv \frac{w_0^*}{w_0}.$$

(Here and in most of the remainder of this section the symbol $p \to 0$ and its verbalizations are omitted, since these are always the same.)

Whether one needs to use "ϵ-δ" and related techniques of analysis in any given limit problem depends largely on the complexity of the problem. Examples will be considered in Chapter 9 in which such an approach is hardly avoidable, and the student will probably profit by using these approaches several times, where the text does not do so, before the point is reached where they become indispensable.

EXAMPLE 5.   Several times it will be necessary to use the fact that, given a *polynomial*

$$P(z) \equiv a_0 + a_1z + \cdots + a_nz^n, \quad a_n \neq 0, \quad n \geq 0,$$

there is a positive number R such that $|P(z)| > |a_n|\,|z^n|/2$ for all z numerically greater than $R(|z| > R)$. How one comes to know this depends on his personal mathematical sophistication, and how one demonstrates it depends on the mathematical sophistication of his audience. For some, one need only remark that it follows from the fact that, "by comparison with the term of highest degree, all other terms in a polynomial in z are negligible for large values of $|z|$." For others, one may need to expatiate on this remark, writing first

$$|P(z)| = |a_nz^n|\left|1 + \frac{a_{n-1}/a_n}{z} + \cdots + \frac{a_0/a_n}{z^n}\right|, \tag{2-4}$$

and then calling attention to the fact that the sum of all terms beyond the first in the second factor on the right-hand side of (2-4) is numerically less than 1/2 for all z of sufficiently large magnitude. And if further justification seems to be needed, one may be forced to continue from (2-4), concluding that

$$|P(z)| \geq |a_nz^n|\left[1 - \left(\left|\frac{a_{n-1}/a_n}{z}\right| + \cdots + \left|\frac{a_0/a_n}{z^n}\right|\right)\right],$$

which is greater than $|a_n z^n|(1 - 1/2) \equiv |a_n|\,|z^n|/2$ whenever

$$\left| \frac{a_{n-k}/a_n}{z^k} \right| < \frac{1}{2n} \quad \text{for} \quad k = 1, 2, \ldots, n;$$

that is, whenever

$$|z| > \max_k \sqrt[k]{2n\,|a_{n-k}/a_n|}.$$

EXAMPLE 6. To show that, if $\lim z$ exists, then $\lim |z|$ exists and $\lim |z| = |\lim z|$, it suffices to put $z_0 = \lim z$ and observe that $|z| \to |z_0|$ as $z \to z_0$. (For $|\,|z| - |z_0|\,| < \epsilon$ whenever $|z - z_0| < \epsilon$.)

EXAMPLE 7. If $\lim z$ exists and always $|z| \leq B$, then $|\lim z| \leq B$. To show this, put $z_0 = \lim z$ and suppose that $|z_0| > B$, which is to say that $|z_0| = B + d$ for some positive number d. But then for all z it follows that

$$B \geq |z| = |z_0 + z - z_0| \geq |z_0| - |z - z_0| = B + d - |z - z_0|,$$

so that $|z - z_0| \geq d$, which contradicts the fact that $z \to z_0$. (Indeed, if we take $\epsilon = d$ in the ϵ-δ pattern, we know that there is a $\delta > 0$ such that $|z - z_0| < d$ whenever $0 < p < \delta$.)

2-3. Problems.

1. By making appropriate definitions of p and q, express the following situations in the form (2-3):
   (a) $\lim\limits_{|z| \to \infty} f(z) = w_0$,
   (b) $\lim\limits_{|z| \to \infty} |f(z)| = \infty$,
   (c) $\lim\limits_{z \to z_0,\, \zeta \to \zeta_0} |w| = \infty$.

2. By making appropriate definitions of p and q, express the situation $\lim_{n \to \infty} 1/n! = 0$ in the form (2-3). Note that p need not tend to zero continuously. Is q a function of p here?

3. Evaluate the following limits, where $z = x + iy$:
   (a) $\lim\limits_{z \to 2 - i} (x^2 + iy^2)$,

   (b) $\lim\limits_{z \to 1 + 2i} \dfrac{x}{3 + iy}$,

   (c) $\lim\limits_{|z| \to \infty} \dfrac{1}{1 + |x| + |y|}$,

   (d) $\lim\limits_{|z| \to \infty} \dfrac{ix + y}{x^2 + y^4}$,

4. Show that the following limits do not exist, where $z = x + iy$:

(a) $\lim\limits_{z \to 0} \dfrac{2x}{3y}$,

(b) $\lim\limits_{|z| \to \infty} \dfrac{ix - y}{|z|}$.

5. If $\lim_{p \to 0} |w| = \infty$, where $w = u + iv$, does it follow that $\lim_{p \to 0} |u| = \infty$ and $\lim_{p \to 0} |v| = \infty$?

6. Using Theorem 2-1, prove that, if $w \to w_0$ and $w^* \to w_0{}^*$, then

(a) $w \pm w^* \to w_0 \pm w_0{}^*$,

(b) $ww^* \to w_0 w_0{}^*$.

7. Prove the assertion of Example 6 of §2-2 by means of Theorem 2-1.

8. Prove that, if $\lim z$ exists, then $\lim \bar{z}$ exists and equals $\overline{\lim z}$.

*9. Show that, if $\lim z$ and $\lim w$ exist (both as $p \to 0$), and always $|z| \leq |w|$, then $|\lim z| \leq |\lim w|$.

10. Let $f(z) = a_k z^k + a_{k+1} z^{k+1} + \cdots + a_n z^n$, where k is a positive integer and $a_k \neq 0$. Show that $|f(z)| > |a_k| \, |z^k|/2$ for all z of sufficiently small positive magnitude. Does the result remain valid if k is a negative integer or zero?

11. One says that a *equals* b *modulo* c and writes $a = b \bmod c$ to signify that there is an integer k such that $a = b + kc$. Similarly, one says that s *approaches* b *modulo* c and writes $s \to b \bmod c$ to signify that for each s there is an integer k_s such that $s - b - k_s c \to 0$. Now, given the conditions (a) $|z| \to |z_0|$ and (b) Arg $z \to$ Arg $z_0 \bmod 2\pi$ (both as $p \to 0$), prove the theorem: *Necessary and sufficient conditions that $z \to z_0$ are* (a) *alone in case $z_0 = 0$ and* (a) *and* (b) *together in case $z_0 \neq 0$.*

12. Let $z = x + iy$.

(a)   Show that $\lim \dfrac{x^2 y}{x^4 + y^2}$ is zero if z tends to zero along any line through the origin.

(b)   Show that this limit is not zero as z tends to zero along any parabola with equation of the form $y = ax^2$, $a \neq 0$.

(c)   Letting n be an arbitrary, fixed integer greater than 1, construct a function $f(z)$ for which $\lim f(z)$ is zero as z tends to zero along any curve with equation of the form

$y = ax^m$, $m = 1, 2, \ldots, n - 1$, but for which this limit is not zero as z tends to zero along any curve with equation of the form $y = ax^n$, $a \neq 0$.

2-4. Continuity and Differentiability.

The function $w = f(z)$ is said to be *continuous* at the point z_0 if it is defined for all z sufficiently close to z_0 and if $\lim_{z \to z_0} f(z)$ exists and equals $f(z_0)$. By Theorem 2-1, this is equivalent to the conditions $u \to u_0$ and $v \to v_0$ as $(x, y) \to (x_0, y_0)$, where $z = x + iy$, $z_0 = x_0 + iy_0$,

$$f(z) = u + iv \equiv u(x, y) + iv(x, y),$$

and

$$f(z_0) = u_0 + iv_0 \equiv u(x_0, y_0) + iv(x_0, y_0);$$

and these in turn are equivalent to the conditions that u and v are continuous functions of x and y at the point (x_0, y_0). If $f(z)$ is continuous at each point of a set S it is said to be continuous *on* S.

EXAMPLE 1. The function

$$w = z^2 \equiv x^2 + 2ixy - y^2$$

is continuous at all points z_0 since $u \equiv x^2 - y^2$ and $v \equiv 2xy$ are everywhere continuous functions of x and y.

EXAMPLE 2. The function

$$w = \left| \frac{1}{z} \right| \equiv \frac{1}{\sqrt{x^2 + y^2}}$$

is continuous at all points z_0 except the origin since $u \equiv 1/\sqrt{x^2 + y^2}$ is continuous everywhere except the origin and $v \equiv 0$ is continuous everywhere.

Consideration must be given later to functions which are defined at all points of a curve and vary continuously *along* the curve, yet which may be continuous at no point of the curve. Such situations are covered by the following further definition: Given a set S of points, a function $f(z)$ defined for each z in S, and a point z_0 in S, if $f(z) \to f(z_0)$ as $z \to z_0$ with z always on S, $f(z)$ is said to be continuous at z_0 *with respect to S*.

EXAMPLE 3. The function $f(z)$, defined as 1 for all points z on the x axis and as 0 for all other points z, is continuous at no point on the x axis, but it is continuous *with respect to* the x axis at each point on it.

EXAMPLE 4.   If a function $f(z)$ is continuous at a point z_0, then it is continuous with respect to any set S on which it is defined and which contains z_0.

By Example 4 of §2-2 and problem 6 of §2-3, if two functions w and w^* are continuous at a point z_0 with respect to a set S, then so are their sum, difference, product, and (if the denominator does not vanish at z_0) quotient.

The concept of differentiation in complex calculus parallels that in real calculus, as do the associated symbols and verbalizations.   If $w = f(z)$ is defined at z_0, and if

$$\left[\frac{dw}{dz}\right]_{z_0} \equiv \lim_{\Delta z \to 0} \frac{\Delta w}{\Delta z}$$

exists, where

$$\Delta w = f(z_0 + \Delta z) - f(z_0),$$

one says that $f(z)$ is *differentiable* at z_0 and refers to the process of obtaining the value $[dw/dz]_{z_0}$ as *differentiation* of $f(z)$ at z_0.   If $f(z)$ is differentiable at each point z of a set S, the variable $[dw/dz]_z$ for z in S is a function of z on S; one denotes this function by $f'(z)$, or merely dw/dz or w', and calls it the *derivative* of $f(z)$, or of w, with respect to z.

EXAMPLE 5.   The function $w = z^2$ is differentiable at every point z in the plane, for

$$\lim_{\Delta z \to 0} \frac{\Delta w}{\Delta z} = \frac{\lim (z + \Delta z)^2 - z^2}{\Delta z} = \lim \frac{2z\Delta z + \Delta z^2}{\Delta z}$$
$$= \lim (2z + \Delta z) = 2z.$$

By use of Example 4 of §2-2 and problem 6 of §2-3, it will be shown in the problems of §2-5 that the theorems on derivatives of sums, products, and quotients of differentiable functions are, word for word, the same for complex as for real variables.   Extensions of other familiar theorems from real calculus will also be found in the problems of §2-5.

2-5.   Problems.

1.   By examining the real and imaginary parts, determine for which values of z the following functions are continuous:
   (a) $w = z^3$,
   (b) $w = \bar{z}^2$,
   (c) $w = 1/\bar{z}$,
   (d) $w = (xy + ix)/(1 + iy)$,
   (e) $w = |x| - i|y|$,
   (f) $w = \operatorname{Arg} z$.

2. Show that the functions $R(z)$, $I(z)$, $|z|$, and $\bar{z}$ are everywhere continuous functions of z.

*3. By applying the binomial theorem to expand $(z + \Delta z)^n$, derive the formula for dw/dz when $w = z^n$ and n is a positive integer.

4. Find the derivative with respect to z of $w = 1/z$ by the "delta process."

*5. Using the suggestion in the text, derive the formulas for the derivatives of the sum, product, and quotient of two differentiable functions w and w^*.

6. Using the formulas for derivatives established in problems 3 and 5, differentiate the following functions:

(a) $w = \dfrac{2z - 3}{4z + 5}$,

(b) $w = \dfrac{z^2 + 2}{z^2 - 2}$,

(c) $w = (2x - y) + i(2y + x)$.

*7. Show that if $f(z)$ is differentiable at a point z_0, then $f(z)$ is continuous at z_0.

*8. Show that if $f(z)$ is continuous at a point z_0, then so is $|f(z)|$.

9. Let $p_{n1}, p_{n2}, \ldots, p_{nk(n)}$ be the prime factors of the positive integer n (repeated factors being counted as many times as they occur). Is there a function $f(z)$ which is continuous at the origin and for which $f(1/n) = 1/p_{n1} + 1/p_{n2} + \cdots + 1/p_{nk(n)}$ for $n = 2, 3, \ldots$?

10. Let $p_{n1}, p_{n2}, \ldots, p_{nl(n)}$ be the *distinct* prime factors of the positive integer n. Is there a function $f(z)$ which is continuous at the origin and for which $f(1/n) = 1/p_{n1}p_{n2}\cdots p_{nl(n)}$ for $n = 2, 3, \ldots$?

*11. Prove the *Chain Rule*: If $w = f(z)$ and $z = \varphi(\zeta)$, where f and φ are differentiable, then $dw/d\zeta$ exists and is given by $dw/d\zeta = f'(z)\varphi'(\zeta)$. Assume $\varphi(\zeta)$ differentiable at $\zeta = \zeta_0$ and $f(z)$ differentiable at $z = z_0 \equiv \varphi(\zeta_0)$. Note that

$$\Delta z = [\varphi'(\zeta_0) + \epsilon]\Delta\zeta,$$

where $\epsilon \to 0$ as $\Delta\zeta \to 0$, and

$$\Delta w = [f'(z_0) + \eta]\Delta z,$$

where $\eta \to 0$ as $\Delta z \to 0$, and we may define η as 0 if $\Delta z = 0$.

12. Using the Chain Rule (problem 11 above) and the other differentiation formulas, find dw/dz if
    (a) $w = (z^2 + 3)^7$,
    (b) $w = 1/(2z - 1)$,
    (c) $w = (z + z^2)^5/(z - z^2)^4$.

13. Let $f(z)$ be continuous at $z = z_0$ with respect to a set S, and let $F(w)$ be continuous at $w = f(z_0)$. Show that $G(z) \equiv F[f(z)]$ is continuous at $z = z_0$ with respect to S.

14. Using problem 11 of §2-3, derive a criterion in terms of the modulus and amplitude of the ratio $\Delta w/\Delta z$ for differentiability of a function $w = f(z)$ at a point z_0.

2-6. Conditions for Differentiability.   The Cauchy-Riemann Equations.

Evidently the formal techniques of real calculus are adequate for the differentiation of all rational functions of z. (As in real algebra, a *rational function* is defined to be the quotient of two polynomials.) But what of such functions of

$$z \equiv x + iy \equiv r(\cos \theta + i \sin \theta)$$

as $|z|$, $\bar{z}$, $\sqrt{z}$, $R(z)$, xy, $e^x(\cos y + i \sin y)$, $\ln r + i\theta$?

The function $w = \bar{z}$ fails everywhere to have a derivative. For

$$\frac{\Delta w}{\Delta z} = \frac{\Delta \bar{z}}{\Delta z} = \frac{\overline{\Delta z}}{\Delta z} = \frac{\Delta x - i\Delta y}{\Delta x + i\Delta y},$$

so that if $\Delta z \to 0$ "horizontally" (Δy held equal to zero, whence $\Delta z = \Delta x$), then

$$\lim \frac{\Delta w}{\Delta z} = \lim \frac{\Delta x}{\Delta x} = 1,$$

whereas if $\Delta z \to 0$ "vertically" (Δx held equal to zero, whence $\Delta z = i\Delta y$), then

$$\lim \frac{\Delta w}{\Delta z} = \lim \frac{-i\Delta y}{i\Delta y} = -1;$$

that is, $\lim_{\Delta z \to 0} (\Delta w/\Delta z)$ (unqualified as to "how" Δz is to tend to zero) cannot exist.

A general criterion for differentiability will now be developed, the method of attack having been suggested by the above proof that the function $w = \bar{z}$ is *not* differentiable. It is assumed that the function

$$w = u(x, y) + iv(x, y)$$

of $z \equiv x + iy$ is defined within some circle about a point $z_0 \equiv x_0 + iy_0$. Now, existence of dw/dz at z_0 implies that the limits of

$$\frac{\Delta w}{\Delta z} \equiv \frac{\Delta u + i\Delta v}{\Delta x + i\Delta y}$$

as $\Delta z \to 0$ horizontally and as $\Delta z \to 0$ vertically exist and are equal. That is,

$$\lim_{\Delta x \to 0} \frac{\Delta u + i\Delta v}{\Delta x} \equiv \frac{\partial u}{\partial x} + i\frac{\partial v}{\partial x}$$

and

$$\lim_{\Delta y \to 0} \frac{\Delta u + i\Delta v}{i\Delta y} \equiv -i\frac{\partial u}{\partial y} + \frac{\partial v}{\partial y}$$

exist and are equal, the partials of course being taken at (x_0, y_0). Equality between the corresponding components in these two expressions provides the following result.

   THEOREM 2-2.   *If $w \equiv u + iv$ is a differentiable function of $z \equiv x + iy$ at a given point, then the four first partials of u and v with respect to x and y must there exist and satisfy the equations*

$$\frac{\partial u}{\partial x} = \frac{\partial v}{\partial y}$$

$$\frac{\partial v}{\partial x} = -\frac{\partial u}{\partial y}. \tag{2-5}$$

The derivative of w with respect to z is given by

$$\frac{dw}{dz} = \frac{\partial u}{\partial x} + i\frac{\partial v}{\partial x} = \frac{\partial v}{\partial y} - i\frac{\partial u}{\partial y}.$$

The equations (2-5) are called the *Cauchy-Riemann equations*.
   For the function $w = \bar{z}$ considered above, $u = x$ and $v = -y$, whence $\partial u/\partial x = 1$ and $\partial v/\partial y = -1$, in violation of the first of the Cauchy-Riemann equations. Again $\bar{z}$ proves to be everywhere non-differentiable.
   In order to derive necessary and sufficient conditions that $w = f(z)$ be differentiable at a point, it must be recalled that a real function $\varphi(x, y)$ of the two real variables x and y is said to be *differentiable* at a point (x_0, y_0) if the surface $s = \varphi(x, y)$ in Cartesian xys space has a non-vertical tangent plane at the point (x_0, y_0, s_0), $s_0 \equiv \varphi(x_0, y_0)$. This means, first, that $(\partial \varphi/\partial x)_0$ and $(\partial \varphi/\partial y)_0$—the values of $\partial \varphi/\partial x$ and $\partial \varphi/\partial y$, respectively, at (x_0, y_0)—exist. But it means further that the difference ϵ between the s-values on the surface and on the plane

$$s - s_0 = \left(\frac{\partial \varphi}{\partial x}\right)_0 (x - x_0) + \left(\frac{\partial \varphi}{\partial y}\right)_0 (y - y_0)$$

at the point $(x_0 + \Delta x, y_0 + \Delta y)$ tends to zero "faster" than $\sqrt{\Delta x^2 + \Delta y^2}$. More precisely, differentiability of $\varphi(x, y)$ at the point (x_0, y_0) means that

$$\frac{\epsilon}{\sqrt{\Delta x^2 + \Delta y^2}} \to 0 \quad \text{as} \quad \sqrt{\Delta x^2 + \Delta y^2} \to 0,$$

where

$$\epsilon = \Delta\varphi - \left(\frac{\partial\varphi}{\partial x}\right)_0 \Delta x - \left(\frac{\partial\varphi}{\partial y}\right)_0 \Delta y$$

and

$$\Delta\varphi = \varphi(x_0 + \Delta x, y_0 + \Delta y) - \varphi(x_0, y_0).$$

THEOREM 2-3.   *Conditions necessary and sufficient that* $w = f(z)$ *be differentiable at the point* $z_0 \equiv x_0 + iy_0$ *are that u and v be differentiable functions of the real variables x and y at the point* (x_0, y_0) *and satisfy the Cauchy-Riemann equations there.*

Proof.   By Theorem 2-2, it is necessary that the first partials of u and v exist and satisfy the Cauchy-Riemann equations at the point (x_0, y_0) and that

$$\frac{\Delta w}{\Delta z} \to \frac{\partial u}{\partial x} + i\frac{\partial v}{\partial x}$$

as $\Delta z \to 0$.   Hence we need only prove, *the Cauchy-Riemann equations assumed*, that

$$\frac{\Delta w}{\Delta z} \to \frac{\partial u}{\partial x} + i\frac{\partial v}{\partial x}, \tag{2-6}$$

if and only if u and v are differentiable functions of x and y at the point (x_0, y_0).   But (2-6) is equivalent to each statement in the following succession.

$$\frac{\Delta u + i\Delta v}{\Delta x + i\Delta y} - \frac{\partial u}{\partial x} - i\frac{\partial v}{\partial x} \to 0,$$

$$\frac{\Delta u + i\Delta v - (\partial u/\partial x)\Delta x + (\partial v/\partial x)\Delta y - i(\partial v/\partial x)\Delta x - i(\partial u/\partial x)\Delta y}{\Delta x + i\Delta y} \to 0,$$

$$\frac{[\Delta u - (\partial u/\partial x)\Delta x - (\partial u/\partial y)\Delta y] + i[\Delta v - (\partial v/\partial x)\Delta x - (\partial v/\partial y)\Delta y]}{\Delta x + i\Delta y} \to 0,$$

$$\frac{\epsilon_u}{\sqrt{\Delta x^2 + \Delta y^2}} \to 0 \quad \text{and} \quad \frac{\epsilon_v}{\sqrt{\Delta x^2 + \Delta y^2}} \to 0,$$

where ϵ_u and ϵ_v represent, in that order, the bracketed expressions in the preceding line.   But this is precisely to say that u and v are differentiable functions of x and y at the point (x_0, y_0), and so the theorem is proved.

A useful corollary follows from the fact that a real function $\varphi(x, y)$ of the two real variables x and y is differentiable at a point (x_0, y_0) if $\partial\varphi/\partial x$ and

$\partial\varphi/\partial y$ exist at all points sufficiently close to (x_0, y_0) and are continuous at (x_0, y_0).

THEOREM 2-4. *Conditions sufficient that $w = f(z)$ be differentiable at the point $z_0 \equiv x_0 + iy_0$ are that the first partials of u and v exist at all points sufficiently close to the point (x_0, y_0) and be continuous and satisfy the Cauchy-Riemann equations at (x_0, y_0).*

If a function $f(z)$ is differentiable at a point z_0 and *also is differentiable at each point on the interior of some circle about z_0,* then $f(z)$ is said to be *regular* (or *analytic* or *holomorphic*) at z_0. It follows that a function which is regular at a point is also regular throughout the interior of some circle about that point.

Henceforth free use will be made of the remarkable fact that *regularity of a function $f(z) \equiv u + iv$ at a point implies the continuity of the first partials of u and v there.* There is no analog of this important circumstance in the theory of functions of a single real variable. Its proof is subtle and is deferred to Chapter 9.

EXAMPLE 1. We can check the differentiability of $w = z^2$ for all z by observing that here $u \equiv x^2 - y^2$ and $v \equiv 2xy$ have everywhere continuous first partials which satisfy the Cauchy-Riemann equations.

EXAMPLE 2. The function $w = e^x(\cos y + i \sin y)$ is everywhere differentiable, since $u \equiv e^x \cos y$ and $v \equiv e^x \sin y$ have everywhere continuous first partials which satisfy the Cauchy-Riemann equations. Here

$$\frac{dw}{dz} \equiv \frac{\partial u}{\partial x} + i \frac{\partial v}{\partial x} = e^x \cos y + ie^x \sin y \equiv e^x(\cos y + i \sin y) \equiv w.$$

2-7. Problems.

1. Using the direct method by which it was first shown that the function $w = \bar{z}$ is not differentiable, show that
   (a) the function $w = R(z)$ is nowhere differentiable,
   (b) the function $w = |z|$ is not differentiable at the origin.

2. Use the Cauchy-Riemann equations to establish that the following functions are nowhere differentiable:
   (a) $w = |z|$,
   (b) $w = I(z)$,
   (c) $w = y + ix$.

3. Find constants a and b such that the function $w = (x + y) + i(ax + by)$ is everywhere differentiable.   Substitute these values in the formula for w and express the result, if possible, as a polynomial in z.

4. Let w be a real function of z, $w = u(x, y)$.   What can be said of this function if it is everywhere differentiable?

5. By using the Cauchy-Riemann equations, obtain two further expression for dw/dz in terms of the first partials of u and v.

6. Use Theorem 2-4 to show that the following functions of z are differentiable for the values of $z \equiv x + iy$ indicated, and write down the derivatives:
    (a) $w = z^3$ for all z,
    (b) $w = 1/z$ for all $z \neq 0$,
    *(c) $w = e^y(\cos x - i \sin x)$ for all z,
    (d) $w = |x| + i|y|$ for all z in the first and third quadrants, excluding points on the axes.

*7. Show that, if $w = f(z)$ is regular at a point, then *Laplace's equation*, $\partial^2 \varphi / \partial x^2 + \partial^2 \varphi / \partial y^2 = 0$, is satisfied by $\varphi = u$ and by $\varphi = v$.   Assume that all second-order partials exist and that $\partial^2 \varphi / \partial x \partial y = \partial^2 \varphi / \partial y \partial x$, both for $\varphi = u$ and for $\varphi = v$— an assumption that will be justified in Chapter 9.   [Functions $\varphi(x, y)$ which have continuous second partials and satisfy Laplace's equation are called *harmonic functions* of x and y.]

8. Show that the function $w = |z|^2$ is differentiable at $z = 0$ and nowhere else.

9. Using the preceding problem as a clue, construct a function $f(z)$ which is defined for all z, is differentiable at the n distinct points $z_1, z_2, \ldots, z_n$, and is differentiable nowhere else.

10. Where, if anywhere, is the function $w = \bar{z}^2$
    (a)   differentiable?
    (b)   regular?

11. Let $w \equiv u + iv = f(z)$ and $z \equiv x + iy = \varphi(\zeta)$, where $\zeta = \xi + i\eta$ and $f(z)$ and $\varphi(\zeta)$ are differentiable functions of z and of ζ, respectively, (whence w is a differentiable function of ζ).   Then the Cauchy-Riemann equations are satisfied by u and v (as functions of x and y) and by x and y (as functions of ξ and η).

   (a)   Using these facts and the chain rule for real functions of several real variables, show that the Cauchy-Riemann equations are satisfied by u and v as functions of ξ and η.

   (b)   Establish the chain rule for complex calculus (problem 11 of §2-5) by multiplying $f'(z) \equiv \partial u/\partial x + i\partial v/\partial x$ by $\varphi'(\zeta) \equiv \partial x/\partial \xi + i\partial y/\partial \xi$ and identifying the result with $\partial u/\partial \xi + i\partial v/\partial \xi$.

*12.   Prove that, if $f(z)$ is regular throughout the interior of a circle and $|f(z)|$ is constant there, then $f(z)$ is itself constant there.

13.   Construct a function $f(z)$ which is defined for all z, which satisfies the Cauchy-Riemann equations at the origin, yet which is not differentiable at the origin.

2-8. Identical Vanishing of the Derivative.

The next two theorems correspond to familiar theorems from real calculus.

THEOREM 2-5. *If $w = f(z)$ is a function for which $f'(z) = 0$ throughout the interior R of a circle, then $f(z)$ is constant throughout R.*

Proof. Throughout R we have

$$0 = \frac{\partial u}{\partial x} + i\frac{\partial v}{\partial x} = \frac{\partial v}{\partial y} - i\frac{\partial u}{\partial y},$$

so that all four first partials of u and v vanish identically, u and v are constants, say a and b, respectively, and $w = a + ib$, throughout R.

THEOREM 2-6. *If $g(z)$ and $h(z)$ are functions for which $g'(z) = h'(z)$ throughout the interior R of a circle, then $g(z)$ and $h(z)$ differ by a constant throughout R.*

Proof. Put $f(z) = g(z) - h(z)$ and apply Theorem 2-5.

2-9. The Functions e^z and ln z.

The function examined in Example 2 of §2-6, namely

$$f(z) = e^x(\cos y + i\sin y),$$

satisfies the two conditions (i) $f'(z) = f(z)$ for all z and (ii) $f(0) = 1$.   Now the unique real function $f(x)$ of the real variable x that satisfies the real analogs of (i) and (ii) is e^x. One is therefore led to define the *exponential function* thus: $e^z \equiv e^x(\cos y + i \sin y)$. (It will be shown in the problems of §2-10 that this particular function is the *only* function that satisfies (i) and (ii). Note that there is no inconsistency in this definition when z reduces to a "pure real.")

The *logarithmic function*

$$w \equiv u + iv = \ln z \quad \text{of} \quad z \equiv r(\cos \theta + i \sin \theta),$$

where $\theta = \text{Arg } z$, is defined by the relationship $e^w = z$ for all values of z for which this is possible. Thus

$$e^u(\cos v + i \sin v) = r(\cos \theta + i \sin \theta),$$

so that

$$e^u \cos v = r \cos \theta,$$

$$e^u \sin v = r \sin \theta,$$

from which is found, first (by squaring and adding), that $e^u = r$ and then that $v = \theta + 2k\pi$ for $k = 0, \pm 1, \pm 2, \ldots$, so that $\ln z = \text{Ln } r + i(\theta + 2k\pi)$, where the symbol Ln r represents the real natural logarithm of the non-negative quantity $r \equiv |z|$. Evidently $\ln z$ is defined for, and only for, non-zero values of z and is infinitely many-valued where defined. That value for which $k = 0$ is called the *principal value* and is denoted by Ln z. Thus

$$\ln z = \text{Ln } |z| + i(\text{Arg } z + 2k\pi) \quad \text{and} \quad \text{Ln } z = \text{Ln } |z| + i \text{ Arg } z.$$

EXAMPLE 1. $\ln 1 = \text{Ln } 1 + i(\text{Arg } 1 + 2k\pi) = 2k\pi i$, $k = 0, \pm 1, \pm 2, \ldots$.

EXAMPLE 2. $\ln (-1) = \text{Ln } 1 + i(\pi + 2k\pi) = (2k + 1)\pi i$, $k = 0, \pm 1, \pm 2, \ldots$.

EXAMPLE 3. $\text{Ln } (-1 - i) = \text{Ln } \sqrt{2} - 3\pi i/4$.

To differentiate the logarithmic function, observe first that the functions u and v in the equation $w \equiv u + iv = \text{Ln } z$ are $u = \text{Ln } r \equiv \text{Ln } |z|$ and $v = \theta \equiv \text{Arg } z$. For every z which is not zero (where the logarithm is not defined) nor on the negative x axis (where θ changes abruptly†) the first

---

† This circumstance is due to the definition of the principal value of $\ln z$ and is therefore, in a sense, artificial. If the principal value of arg z had been defined as that value of θ for which $0 \le \theta < 2\pi$ and the definition of Ln z had been correspondingly modified, the analysis about to be made would be valid except for z on the *non-negative* x axis.

four partials of u and v are continuous and satisfy the Cauchy-Riemann equations. It follows that†

$$\frac{dw}{dz} \equiv \frac{\partial u}{\partial x} + i\frac{\partial v}{\partial x} = \frac{1}{r}\frac{\partial r}{\partial x} + i\frac{\partial \theta}{\partial x} = \frac{1}{r}\cos\theta + i\left(-\frac{\sin\theta}{r}\right)$$

$$= \frac{r\cos\theta - ir\sin\theta}{r^2} = \frac{x - iy}{x^2 + y^2} = \frac{1}{x + iy} \equiv \frac{1}{z},$$

a result which is perhaps not surprising! Except again for the points on the non-positive x axis, the derivative of $\ln z$ for each fixed value of k is, of course, the same.

The *power* z^w means, in general, $e^{w \ln z}$, the definition being made for every pair of complex numbers, with the sole restriction that $z \neq 0$. One calls z the *base* and w the *exponent* in this expression. Because of the many-valuedness of the logarithm, z^w is, in general, multi-valued (though by convention the particular power function e^z is taken to mean the single-valued function defined at the beginning of this section); the particular value $e^{w \ln z}$ is called the *principal value*. It is to be noted that if z and w are reals and $z > 0$, the principal value of z^w coincides with the real power of a positive number as defined in calculus.

EXAMPLE 4. $i^i = e^{i(\pi/2 + 2k\pi)i} = e^{-(4k+1)\pi/2}$ for all integral values of k. Curiously, all of these values are real.

EXAMPLE 5. $(-1)^{1/2} = e^{(2k+1)\pi i/2} = e^{k\pi i}e^{\pi i/2}$, as will be shown in problem 2 of §2-10, and this equals $(-1)^k i$ for all integral values of k. Note that there are only two distinct values, a fact which is in agreement with problem 10 of §1-9.

2-10. Problems.

1. Find the values of
   (a) $e^{\pi i/4}$,
   (b) $e^{\ln 2 + \pi i/2}$,
   (c) e^{1+i}.

*2. Show that $e^z e^w = e^{z+w}$. [Take $z = x + iy$ and $w = u + iv$ and use problem 9a of §1-7.]

† From the relation $r = \sqrt{x^2 + y^2}$ it follows that

$$\frac{\partial r}{\partial x} = \frac{x}{\sqrt{x^2 + y^2}} = \cos\theta.$$

Somewhat similarly, one finds that $\partial\theta/\partial x = -\sin\theta/r$.

3. Show that $e^{\pi i} + 1 = 0$. This has been called one of the most remarkable relationships in mathematics, drawing together as it does the five basic quantities e, π, i, 1, and 0.

4. Show that the function $w = e^z$ is periodic of period $2\pi i$.

5. Express the function w of problem 6(c) of §2-7 as a power with e as base.

6. Find

   (a) $\operatorname{Ln} i$,
   (b) $\ln(-1 + i)$,
   (c) $\operatorname{Ln}(\sqrt{2} + \sqrt{2}i)$,
   (d) $\ln(-i)$,
   (e) $\ln(3 - 4i)$ (using tables).

7. Show that $\operatorname{Ln}(1 - i) + \operatorname{Ln}(1 + i) = \operatorname{Ln}(1 - i)(1 + i)$, by computing each member of the equation separately.

8. Find z if $\operatorname{Ln} z = \operatorname{Ln} 2 + 5\pi i/6$.

*9. Prove directly that $\ln(zw) = \ln z + \ln w$, in the sense that all of the infinitely many values of either side of this equation are included in the infinitely many values of the other side.

10. Is it always true that $\operatorname{Ln}(1/z) = -\operatorname{Ln} z$?

11. Assuming that the derivative of $w = \ln z$ exists, obtain the formula for dw/dz by differentiating implicitly the equation $e^w = z$.

12. Evaluate

   (a) $(-1)^i$,
   (b) $i^{\sqrt{2}}$,
   (c) $(1 + i)^{1+i}$,
   (d) i^{2+i},
   (e) $(-1)^{i-2}$,
   (f) $(2 - i)^{1+2i}$.

13. Show that the moduli of the several values of a^i are independent of the modulus of a so long as $a \neq 0$.

14. Show that z^n is single-valued if n is an integer and $z \neq 0$. Is the definition $e^{n \ln z}$ equivalent to the earlier definition (as a product of n z's if $n > 0$, and so on)?

15. Show that z^r ($z \neq 0$) has only a finite number of distinct values if r is a rational number p/q, where p and q are integers without common factors, and determine how many there

are. Show that $(z^r)^q = z^p$ for each of these values. (Compare problem 10 of §1-9.)

*16. Find $\ln a^z$.

17. Show that, among the (generally, doubly infinite) set of values of $(a^z)^w$ and also among the (generally, doubly infinite) set of values of $(a^w)^z$ occur the (at most, singly infinite) set of values of a^{zw} but that, in general, there is no coincidence between the values of $(a^z)^w$ which are not among those of a^{zw} and any of those of $(a^w)^z$ which are not among those of a^{zw}. [Problem 16 will be useful here.]

*18. Discuss possible ambiguities arising out of applying the general definition of z^w in case $z = e$. (These ambiguities are often avoided by denoting the single-valued function $e^x(\cos y + i \sin y)$ by some symbol other than e^z in the first place.)

*19. Show that, in the notation of §1-8, the general complex number different from 0 can be written as $z = re^{i\theta}$. This is the *exponential form* of z.

*20. Prove that, if for all z a function $f(z)$ is regular and satisfies the condition $f'(z) = f(z)$, and if $f(0) = 1$, $f(z) = e^z$ for all z. [Put $g(z) = e^z$ and show that $g(z)f'(z) - f(z)g'(z) = 0$ for all z and that $g(z)$ never vanishes. Then note that $[g(z)f'(z) - f(z)g'(z)]/[g(z)]^2 = 0$ for all z.]

21. Show that, for every (complex) number n and every value of z that is not zero or real and negative, $d(z^n)/dz = nz^{n-1}$, where the powers signify principal values.

22. (a) Why is the symbol z^w assigned no value by the definition in §2-9 when $z = 0$?
    (b) In what sense is the supplementary definition $0^w = 0$ "reasonable" when w is real and positive?
    (c) Would the definition $0^w = 0$ be in the same sense reasonable for any other values of w?

23. Students of real calculus are often curious about the nature of the function $y = x^n$ when x is negative and n is real but not rational. Let x be a real variable, $-\infty < x < \infty$, and n a real constant, and put $f(x) = x^n$.
    (a) Discuss $f(x)$ when $x < 0$ if by the symbol x^n is meant the principal value (as is the case in real calculus when $x > 0$).

(b)   Discuss $f(x)$ when $-\infty < x < \infty$ if by the symbol x^n is meant the multi-valued function and 0^n is defined as 0 if $n > 0$.

2-11.   The Elementary Functions.

The *hyperbolic functions* are defined in the obvious way:

$$\sinh z \equiv \frac{e^z - e^{-z}}{2}, \quad \cosh z \equiv \frac{e^z + e^{-z}}{2}, \quad \tanh z \equiv \frac{\sinh z}{\cosh z} \equiv \frac{e^z - e^{-z}}{e^z + e^{-z}},$$

and so on.   But how shall the *circular* ("trigonometric") *functions* of a complex variable be defined?   Note first that, for real x,

$$e^{ix} = \cos x + i \sin x, \tag{2-7}$$

$$e^{-ix} = \cos x - i \sin x. \tag{2-8}$$

Addition of (2-7) and (2-8) gives $\cos x = (e^{ix} + e^{-ix})/2$, and subtraction of (2-8) from (2-7) gives $\sin x = (e^{ix} - e^{-ix})/2i$.   The definitions to which one is led are, then,

$$\sin z \equiv \frac{e^{iz} - e^{-iz}}{2i}, \quad \cos z \equiv \frac{e^{iz} + e^{-iz}}{2}, \quad \tan z \equiv \frac{\sin z}{\cos z} \equiv \frac{e^{iz} - e^{-iz}}{i(e^{iz} + e^{-iz})},$$

and so on.   Evidently the circular and the hyperbolic functions are intimately related; for example, $\cosh iz = \cos z$ and $\sin iz = i \sinh z$.

Curiously, such "absurd" equations as $\cos z = 3$ can now be solved— although it must, of course, be recognized that "z" here could not represent a geometric angle and, in fact, that the symbol "3" itself represents a *complex* real.   The general equation $\cos w = z$ can be solved for w by writing a succession of equivalent equations (to understand the equation $\ln(z \pm \sqrt{z^2 - 1}) = \pm \ln(z + \sqrt{z^2 - 1})$, observe that in case the sign is negative the two parenthesized expressions are reciprocals and use problem 9 of §2-10):

$$\frac{e^{iw} + e^{-iw}}{2} = z, \quad e^{2iw} - 2ze^{iw} + 1 = 0, \quad e^{iw} = z \pm \sqrt{z^2 - 1},$$

$$iw = \ln(z \pm \sqrt{z^2 - 1}) = \pm \ln(z + \sqrt{z^2 - 1}),$$

$$w = \mp i \operatorname{Ln}(z + \sqrt{z^2 - 1}) + 2k\pi, \quad k = 0, \pm 1, \pm 2, \ldots.$$

What has just been done is to derive an explicit expression for the (multi-valued) inverse of the cosine function, $w = \cos^{-1} z$.   In similar fashion one can derive explicit expressions for the inverses of the other circular functions and of the hyperbolic functions.

If to the circular functions and their inverses, and the hyperbolic functions and their inverses, and the exponential function e^z and its inverse ln z one adjoins the *algebraic functions* (such functions w of z as are defined by equations of the form $P(z, w) = 0$ where P is a polynomial)†, one collects what may be called the *basic elementary functions*. Starting with z and permitting oneself to operate functionally with any of the basic elementary functions and to add, subtract, multiply, and divide—and to perform these operations as many times as one wishes (though only a "finite number of times")—one obtains what are called the *elementary functions*. (The restriction to "a finite number of times" means that such *additional* functions as might be defined in terms of limits of successions of such operations are not classified as elementary.)

EXAMPLE. The function $1/\sin(z + \ln z)$ is elementary: to the *logarithm* of z is *added* z; then the *sine* is taken; finally, the *reciprocal* is taken (that function which w is of z in the relationship $wz - 1 = 0$).

2-12. Problems.

1. Find z if $\sin z = 2$.

2. Express cosh z in terms of circular functions.

3. Express sin z in terms of hyperbolic functions.

4. Show that sin z and cos z are periodic of period 2π.

5. Find a period (not "real") of sinh z and cosh z.

*6. For which values of z does cos z vanish? cosh z?

*7. Working with their exponential definitions, show that the derivatives of sin z, cos z, tan z, sinh z, cosh z, and tanh z are what one would expect by analogy with the derivatives of the corresponding real functions of the real variable x.

8. Show that equations (2-7) and (2-8) remain valid if in them the real "x" is replaced by the complex "z."

9. Show that $e^z = \cosh z + \sinh z$ and $e^{-z} = \cosh z - \sinh z$.

10. Using the exponential definitions, derive formulas for $\sin(z + w)$ and $\cos(z + w)$. [Problem 8 may be useful here.]

† The student should define a *polynomial in several complex variables*, using the definition for real variables as a pattern.

11. Use problems 2, 3, and 10 to show that $\sin z \equiv \sin (x + iy) = \sin x \cosh y + i \cos x \sinh y$.

12. Find an explicit expression for $\sinh^{-1} z$.

13. Derive an explicit expression for $\tan^{-1} z$.   Can you determine a period for the tangent function from your result?

14. Prove that $\tan^2 z + 1 = \sec^2 z$.

15. In defining the elementary functions we could have taken as basic only the algebraic, exponential, and logarithmic functions.   Why?

16. The algebraic functions include such of their own inverses as exist.   Why?

17. Show that

    (a) $\overline{e^z} = e^{\bar{z}}$

    (b) $\overline{\cosh z} = \cosh \bar{z}$,

    (c) $\overline{\sinh z} = \sinh \bar{z}$,

    (d) $\overline{f(z)} = f(\bar{z})$ if $f(z)$ is any of the six hyperbolic functions,

    (e) $\overline{g(z)} = g(\bar{z})$ if $g(z)$ is any of the six circular functions.

Infinite Series

3

Much, if not most, of the material in this chapter will have a familiar ring to the student. Here are extended in rather obvious ways many ideas and facts which are familiar from the calculus courses.

3-1. Sequences.

An *infinite sequence* is a succession of elements W in one-to-one correspondence with the non-negative integers—which is therefore representable as $W_0, W_1, W_2, \ldots, W_n, \ldots$. A brief notation is $\{W_n\}$. In the cases with which this book is concerned the elements W_n will generally be complex numbers, or complex functions of a complex variable z, all defined on a common set S of values of z. As just described, a sequence of constants (one often assumes the adjective "infinite" implied) is called *convergent* if $\lim_{n\to\infty} W_n$ exists. If the value of this limit is W, then the sequence is said to *converge to* W, and W is said to be the *limit* of the sequence. A sequence of constants that is not convergent is called *divergent*. If the W_n are functions $W_n(z)$ of z, the sequence of numbers $\{W_n(z)\}$ for a particular value of z in S may or may not converge. If S' is that subset of S for values of z in which the sequence of numbers $\{W_n(z)\}$ converges, and one writes $W(z) = \lim_{n\to\infty} W_n(z)$ for these values of z, then one says that the sequence of functions converges to the limit $W(z)$ on S' and diverges elsewhere in S.

EXAMPLE 1. The sequence $\{i^{n+1}\}$, or $i, -1, -i, 1, i, \ldots,$ $i^{n+1}, \ldots$ is divergent, since $\lim_{n\to\infty} W_n$ fails to exist.

EXAMPLE 2.   Consider the sequence $\{W_n\}$ in which $W_n = (a - az^{n+1})/(1 - z)$ for all n, a being a non-zero constant and z a variable not equal to 1.   For each z which is numerically less than 1 (that is, $|z| < 1$) this sequence of functions converges to $a/(1 - z)$, since $|W_n - a/(1 - z)| \equiv |a/(1 - z)| \, |z|^{n+1}$ tends to zero as n becomes infinite for such values of z.

3-2.   Series.

An *infinite series* or, simply, a *series*, of complex numbers or of complex functions of a complex variable z, all defined on a common set of values of z, is denoted by $w_0 + w_1 + w_2 + \cdots + w_n + \cdots$, where the w_k represents such numbers or functions, and is to be identified with the sequence of *partial sums* $\{W_n\}$ given by $W_n = w_0 + w_1 + \cdots + w_n$.   The symbol $\sum_{n=0}^{\infty} w_n$ is used alternatively to represent the series, or, when there can be no ambiguity, $\sum_0^{\infty} w_n$, or even merely $\sum w_n$.   [Various modifications of these symbols are self-explanatory; thus $\sum_{n=2}^{\infty} 1/(n^2 - 1)$ means $\frac{1}{3} + \frac{1}{8} + \cdots + 1/(n^2 - 1) + \cdots$.]   A series is said to be *convergent* if the above-mentioned sequence $\{W_n\}$ is convergent.   If this sequence converges to W, one says that the series *converges to* W, calls W the *sum* of the series, and writes $\sum w_n = W$.   A series that is not convergent is called *divergent*.

EXAMPLE 1.   The series $1 + i - 1 - i + 1 + \cdots + i^n + \cdots$, or $\sum_0^{\infty} i^n$, diverges, since for $k = 0, 1, \ldots$ we have $W_{4k} = 1$, $W_{4k+1} = 1 + i$, $W_{4k+2} = i$, and $W_{4k+3} = 0$, so that $\lim_{n \to \infty} W_n$ fails to exist.

EXAMPLE 2.   Consider the series $\sum w_n$ in which $w_n = az^n$ for all n, a being a non-zero constant and z a variable.   For this series of functions we have (since it is a geometric series)

$$W_n = \frac{a - az^{n+1}}{1 - z}$$

for all $z \neq 1$.   But this is the general element of the sequence of Example 2, §3-1, so that we may write

$$\sum_{n=0}^{\infty} az^n = \frac{a}{1 - z} \quad \text{if} \quad |z| < 1.$$

The next theorem is the analog of a well-known result for real series and is proved in the same way.

THEOREM 3-1. *A necessary condition for $\sum w_n$ to converge is that* $\lim_{n \to \infty} w_n = 0$.

Another rather obvious fact concerning the algebra of series carries over from the real calculus:

THEOREM 3-2. *If $\sum w_n$ and $\sum z_n$ converge, then so does the series $\sum (aw_n + bz_n)$, where a and b are constants; indeed*

$$\sum (aw_n + bz_n) = a \sum w_n + b \sum z_n.$$

Proof. $\displaystyle\sum_{k=0}^{n} (aw_k + bz_k) = a \sum_{k=0}^{n} w_k + b \sum_{k=0}^{n} z_k$

$$\to a \sum_{k=0}^{\infty} w_k + b \sum_{k=0}^{\infty} z_k \quad \text{as} \quad n \to \infty.$$

3-3. Absolute Convergence. Product Series.

If $\sum |w_n|$ converges, then the series $\sum w_n$ is said to be *absolutely convergent*. If $\sum w_n$ is convergent but not absolutely convergent, then it is said to be *conditionally convergent*.

THEOREM 3-3. *If $\sum w_n$ is absolutely convergent, then it is convergent.*

Proof. Let the real and imaginary parts of w_n be u_n and v_n, respectively, and the nth partial sums of these parts be U_n and V_n, also respectively. Now for each n we have

$$\sum_{k=0}^{n} |u_k| \le \sum_{k=0}^{n} |w_k| \le \sum_{k=0}^{\infty} |w_k|,$$

so that $\sum u_k$ is absolutely convergent and therefore convergent, which means that U_n tends to a limit, say U, as n becomes infinite. Similarly, V_n tends to a limit, say V. Thus

$$\sum_{k=0}^{n} w_k \equiv U_n + iV_n \to U + iV;$$

that is, $\sum w_n$ converges, as asserted.

If two series $\sum w_n$ and $\sum z_n$ are so related that $|w_n| \le |z_n|$ for all n greater than some integer N, one says that the first is *dominated* by the second and writes $\sum w_n \ll \sum z_n$. *If a series is dominated by an absolutely convergent* series, *then it itself is absolutely convergent.* This is a consequence of the "comparison test" of elementary calculus.

A formula for the representation of the product of two absolutely convergent series is now derived. (A related theorem is proved in problem 8 of §10-3.)

THEOREM 3-4. *If both $\sum w_k$ and $\sum z_k$ are absolutely convergent, then*

$$\left(\sum_0^\infty w_k\right)\left(\sum_0^\infty z_k\right) = \sum_0^\infty (w_0 z_k + w_1 z_{k-1} + \cdots + w_k z_0).$$

Moreover, this Product Series *is absolutely convergent.*

Proof. For $n = 0, 1, \ldots$ we have†

$$
\begin{aligned}
\left(\sum_0^n w_k\right)\left(\sum_0^n z_k\right) =\ & w_0 z_0 + w_0 z_1 + \cdots + w_0 z_n \\
& + w_1 z_0 + w_1 z_1 + \cdots + w_1 z_n \\
& + \quad \cdot \quad \cdot \quad \cdot \quad \cdot \quad \cdot \\
& + w_n z_0 + w_n z_1 + \cdots + w_n z_n \\
=\ & w_0 z_0 \\
& + w_0 z_1 + w_1 z_0 \\
& + w_0 z_2 + w_1 z_1 + w_2 z_0 \\
& + \cdot \quad \cdot \quad \cdot \quad \cdot \quad \cdot \\
& + w_0 z_n + w_1 z_{n-1} + \cdots + w_n z_0 \\
& + R_n \\
\equiv\ & \sum_0^n (w_0 z_k + w_1 z_{k-1} + \cdots + w_k z_0) + R_n,
\end{aligned}
$$

(3-1)

where

$$
\begin{aligned}
R_n =\ & w_1 z_n + w_2 z_{n-1} + \cdots + w_{n-1} z_2 + w_n z_1 \\
& + w_2 z_n + w_3 z_{n-1} + \cdots + w_n z_2 \\
& + \quad \cdot \quad \cdot \quad \cdot \quad \cdot \quad \cdot \\
& + w_n z_n \\
\equiv\ & \sum_1^n z_k(w_{n-k+1} + w_{n-k+2} + \cdots + w_n).
\end{aligned}
$$

(3-2)

† The terms parenthesized just below the array (3-1) are collected along lines parallel to the northeast-southwest diagonal in that array, from the northwest corner down to, and including, that diagonal. The horizontally grouped terms in the array (3-2) are collected according to the same pattern below the northeast-southwest diagonal, down to the southeast corner. The terms in the sum just below the array (3-2) are column sums from that array, from right to left.

Let us now put $p = \begin{Bmatrix} n/2 \text{ if } n \text{ is even} \\ (n-1)/2 \text{ if } n \text{ is odd} \end{Bmatrix}$ and deduce a succession of inequalities:

$$|R_n| \le \sum_1^n |z_k|(|w_{n-k+1}| + |w_{n-k+2}| + \cdots + |w_n|)$$

$$\le \sum_1^p |z_k|(|w_{n-p+1}| + |w_{n-p+2}| + \cdots + |w_n|)$$

$$+ \sum_{p+1}^n |z_k|(|w_1| + |w_2| + \cdots + |w_n|)$$

$$\le \sum_{k=0}^\infty |z_k| \left(\sum_{j=0}^\infty |w_j| - \sum_{j=0}^{n-p} |w_j| \right)$$

$$+ \left(\sum_{k=0}^\infty |z_k| - \sum_{k=0}^p |z_k| \right) \sum_{j=0}^\infty |w_j|.$$

Since both p and $n - p$ become infinite as n does, the two parenthesized quantities tend to zero, so R_n tends to zero and we have

$$\sum_0^n (w_0 z_k + w_1 z_{k-1} + \cdots + w_k z_0)$$

$$\equiv \sum_0^n w_k \sum_0^n z_k - R_n \to \sum_0^\infty w_k \sum_0^\infty z_k,$$

as was to be proved.

To see that the product series converges absolutely, we note that

$$\sum_0^\infty |w_0 z_k + w_1 z_{k-1} + \cdots + w_k z_0|$$

$$\ll \sum_0^\infty (|w_0|\,|z_k| + |w_1|\,|z_{k-1}| + \cdots + |w_k|\,|z_0|)$$

and that the dominating series is convergent by the argument of the preceding part of the proof [by which argument it is indeed equal to $(\sum |w_k|)(\sum |z_k|)$].

EXAMPLE. For $|z| < 1$ we have

$$\frac{1}{1-z} = 1 + z + z^2 + \cdots + z^n + \cdots$$

and

$$\frac{1}{1+z} = 1 - z + z^2 - \cdots + (-1)^n z^n + \cdots.$$

Both of these geometric series being absolutely convergent, we have

$$\frac{1}{1-z}\frac{1}{1+z} = 1 + (-z + z) + (z^2 - z^2 + z^2)$$
$$+ (-z^3 + z^3 - z^3 + z^3)$$
$$+ \cdots + (-1)^n[z^n - z^n + \cdots + (-1)^n z^n] + \cdots$$
$$\equiv 1 + z^2 + \cdots + z^{2k} + \cdots.$$

This was of course to be expected. (Why?)

3-4. Power Series.

A series of the form $\sum_{n=0}^{\infty} a_n(z - z_0)^n$, in which z_0 and the a's are constants, is called a *power series in* $(z - z_0)$. Such are the series with which this book will be primarily concerned. Of particular concern will be power series in z, $\sum_0^{\infty} a_n z^n$ [to which form the general power series in $(z - z_0)$ can be brought by putting $w = z - z_0$].

THEOREM 3-5. *If a power series in z, $\sum a_n z^n$, converges for $z = z_1 \neq 0$, then it is absolutely convergent for all z such that $|z| < |z_1|$; if it diverges for $z = z_2$, then it diverges for all z such that $|z| > |z_2|$.*

Proof. Since the series converges for $z = z_1$, Theorem 3-1 tells us that $a_n z_1^n \to 0$ as $n \to \infty$, so that there is a positive number M such that $|a_n z_1^n| < M$ for all n. If now $|z| < |z_1|$ we have

$$\sum |a_n z^n| \equiv \sum |a_n z_1^n| \left|\frac{z}{z_1}\right|^n \ll \sum M \left|\frac{z}{z_1}\right|^n.$$

But $\sum M|z/z_1|^n$ is a geometric series with common ratio $|z/z_1| < 1$ and hence converges. The first conclusion of the theorem follows.

Suppose next that $\sum a_n z^n$ converged for some z such that $|z| > |z_2|$. By the part of the theorem just proved, then, $\sum a_n z_2^n$ would converge (in fact, absolutely), and this is contrary to assumption. This completes the proof.

3-5. Circle and Radius of Convergence.

By means of Theorem 3-5 and certain facts about the interval of convergence of a real power series, a sharpening of that theorem will now be proved. (A direct proof is given in Chapter 10.)

THEOREM 3-6. *A power series $\sum a_n z^n$ in z either converges absolutely for all z, converges only for $z = 0$, or has associated with it a positive number ρ with the property that the series diverges for all z numerically greater than ρ and converges absolutely for all z numerically less then ρ. (Fig. 3-1.)*

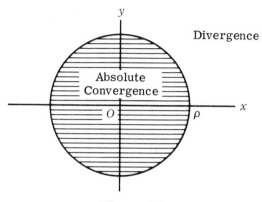

Figure 3-1

This number ρ is called the *radius of convergence* of the series $\sum a_n z^n$. One uses the same symbols and terminology in case the series converges only for $z = 0$ (writing, in this case, $\rho = 0$) or converges for all z (now writing $\rho = \infty$).

Proof. Assume that the *real* series $\sum |a_n| x^n$, where x is a real variable, either converges absolutely for all x, converges only for $x = 0$, or has associated with it a positive number σ with the property that the series diverges for all x numerically greater than σ and converges absolutely for all x numerically less than σ. Also assume known that one writes $\sigma = 0$ if this real series converges only for $x = 0$ and $\sigma = \infty$ if it converges for all x. We are going to identify the number ρ above with the number σ here (including the "infinite values").

First, if $\sum |a_n| x^n$ converges for all x, then $\sum |a_n z^n| \equiv \sum |a_n| |z|^n$ converges for all z, since $|z|$ is a particular value for x. Next, if $\sum |a_n| x^n$ converges only for $x = 0$, then $\sum a_n z^n$ converges only for $z = 0$. For if $\sum a_n z_1{}^n$ converges for some $z_1 \neq 0$, then, by Theorem 3-5, $\sum |a_n| x^n$ converges for all x numerically less than $|z_1|$. Finally, if there is a positive number σ with the property described in the preceding paragraph, then we see that (i) $\sum |a_n z^n| \equiv \sum |a_n| |z|^n$ converges for all z numerically less than σ and that (ii) $\sum a_n z^n$ diverges for all z numerically greater than σ. (For if $\sum a_n z_1{}^n$ converged for some z_1 numerically greater than σ, then, by

Theorem 3-5, $\sum |a_n| x^n$ would converge—in particular—for all x strictly between σ and $|z_1|$, which is impossible.)

The circle $|z| = \rho$ [interpreted to be the single point $(0, 0)$ in case $\rho = 0$, and to be the entire plane if $\rho = \infty$] is called the *circle of convergence* of the series $\sum a_n z^n$. Thus, except when $\rho = 0$ or ∞, the series converges absolutely inside and diverges outside its circle of convergence.

If in the more general power series $\sum a_n(z - z_0)^n$ one puts $w = z - z_0$, it is seen that there are associated with this series a radius of convergence ρ and a circle of convergence (with center at z_0) within which (unless $\rho = 0$) the series converges absolutely and outside of which (unless $\rho = \infty$) it diverges.

EXAMPLE 1.   The radius of convergence of the series $\sum_1^\infty z^n/n^2$, being the same as the semi-interval of convergence of the real series $\sum_1^\infty x^n/n^2$, is 1.   By direct substitution, we have $\sum |z^n/n^2| = \sum 1/n^2$ for all z on the circumference of the circle of convergence, so that the series converges absolutely within *and* on its circle of convergence.

EXAMPLE 2.   The circle $|z - 2| = 1$ is the circle of convergence of the series $\sum_0^\infty (z - 2)^n$, but the series converges at no point on the circumference.

3-6. Problems.

1. State which of the following sequences are convergent, naming the limits:

    (a) $\{ni^n\}$,

    (b) $\{i^n/n\}$,

    (c) $\left\{ \dfrac{n + i^n}{n} \right\}$,

    (d) $\left\{ \left(\dfrac{1 + i}{2} \right)^n \right\}$,

    (e) $\left\{ \left(\dfrac{1 + i}{\sqrt{2}} \right)^n \right\}$.

2. Suppose that $\sum a_n z_1{}^n$ converges, but only conditionally. Show that the radius of convergence of the series $\sum a_n z^n$ is $|z_1|$.

*3. Let the radius of convergence of the series $\sum a_n z^n$ be ρ and that of $\sum b_n z^n$ be $\sigma \neq \rho$. Argue carefully that the radius of convergence of the series $\sum (a_n + b_n) z^n$ is min (ρ, σ), that is, the smaller of ρ and σ. Give an example to show the necessity of the restriction $\sigma \neq \rho$.

4. Show that the series $\sum c w_n$ and $\sum w_n$ either both converge or both diverge if $c \neq 0$.

5. Consider two series,

$$z_0 + z_1 + \cdots + z_n + \cdots, \tag{i}$$

$$w_0 + w_1 + \cdots + w_n + \cdots, \tag{ii}$$

where

$$w_0 = z_0 + z_1, w_1 = z_2 + z_3, \ldots, w_n = z_{2n} + z_{2n+1}, \ldots.$$

(a) Show that if the series (i) converges absolutely, then so does the series (ii).

(b) Construct an example in which the series (ii) converges absolutely while the series (i) converges only conditionally.

*6. Show that the radius of convergence of the series $\sum z^n/n!$ is infinite.

7. Exhibit a power series in z for which the radius of convergence is zero.

8. Find the circle of convergence of the series $\sum (2z)^n$ and determine the behavior of the series on the circumference.

9. Show that the radius of convergence of the series $\sum_1^\infty z^n/n$ is 1 and examine the behavior of the series for $z = 1, -1, i$.

10. Find the circle of convergence of the series $\sum n(z - i)^n$ and determine the behavior of the series on the circumference.

11. What sort of behavior, as regards convergence and divergence, will a series of the form $\sum a_n/z^n$ exhibit?

12. Interpreting n^z in the following to mean $e^{z \, \mathrm{Ln}\, n}$, show that $\sum_1^\infty 1/n^z$ is absolutely convergent in the "open half-plane" $R(z) > 1$.

*13. Show that, if either of the series $\sum_0^\infty w_n$ and $\sum_k^\infty w_n$, where k is any positive integer, is absolutely convergent, conditionally convergent, or divergent, then so is the other, respectively.

*14. Let k be a fixed positive integer and ρ the radius of convergence of the series $\sum a_n z^n$. Show that (a) ρ is also the radius of convergence of the series $\sum a_n z^{n+k}$ and (b) if $\rho > 0$, the series $\sum a_n z^{n-k}$ is absolutely convergent for $0 < |z| < \rho$ and divergent for $|z| > \rho$.

*15. Prove that

$$\left(\sum a_n z^n\right)\left(\sum b_n z^n\right) = \sum (a_0 b_n + a_1 b_{n-1} + \cdots + a_n b_0)z^n$$

within the smaller of the circles of convergence of the series $\sum a_n z^n$ and $\sum b_n z^n$.

16. Find a power series in z for the function $1/(1 - z)^2$ by squaring the power series in z for the function $1/(1 - z)$ as given in the text.

17. In problem 6 above it was shown that the series

$$f(z) \equiv 1 + z + \frac{z^2}{2!} + \frac{z^3}{3!} + \cdots + \frac{z^n}{n!} + \cdots$$

is absolutely convergent for all z. Now show by multiplication of series that $f(z) \cdot f(-z) = 1$ for all z, being sure to prove that the coefficient of z^k for *general* $k > 0$ in the product series is zero.

18. The terms of the form $w_k z_j$ in the sum defining R_n in the proof of Theorem 3-4 are included among those in the difference

$$\left(\sum_0^n w_k\right)\left(\sum_0^n z_k\right) - \left(\sum_0^p w_k\right)\left(\sum_0^p z_k\right).$$

Using this fact as a clue, show briefly that $R_n \to 0$ as $n \to \infty$.

19. Denoting by $f(z)$ the value of the power series $\sum a_n z^n$ where this series converges, discuss the existence of $f(\bar{z})$ and the relationship between $f(\bar{z})$ and $\overline{f(z)}$

    (a)   in case the a_n are all real,
    (b)   in the alternative case.

3-7. Termwise Differentiation of Power Series. A Uniqueness Theorem.

A theorem preliminary to the main result of this section follows.

THEOREM 3-7. *The radii of convergence of the series $\sum a_n z^n$ and $\sum b_n z^n$ are the same if $b_n = R(n)a_n$ for $n = 0, 1, 2, \ldots$, where*

$R(n)$ is any rational function of n which is defined for these values of n and does not vanish identically.

Proof. Let ρ be the radius of convergence of $\sum a_n z^n$ and σ that of $\sum b_n z^n$. We may assume that not both ρ and σ are zero, and we will suppose that $\rho > 0$, the "value" ∞ not excluded. (Examination of the remainder of the proof, especially the last paragraph, will show that to consider the case $\sigma > 0$ separately would be superfluous.) Let z be any complex number numerically less than ρ. Finally, let x_1 be any real number between $|z|$ and ρ. Then

$$\sum |b_n z^n| = \sum |R(n)|\, |a_n x_1{}^n| \left(\frac{|z|}{x_1}\right)^n.$$

As in the proof of Theorem 3-5, we may conclude that there is a positive number M such that $|a_n x_1{}^n| < M$ for all n. Hence $\sum |b_n z^n| \ll \sum M|R(n)|t^n$, where $0 < t \equiv |z|/x_1 < 1$. But application of the ratio test to the real series $\sum M|R(n)|t^n$ gives us

$$\lim_{n \to \infty} \frac{M|R(n+1)|t^{n+1}}{[M|R(n)|t^n]} \equiv t \lim_{n \to \infty} \left|\frac{R(n+1)}{R(n)}\right| = t.$$

Thus $\sum b_n z^n$ converges for all z numerically less than ρ, so that $\rho \leq \sigma$.

On the other hand, for all values of n larger than any real zero of $R(n)$, we have $a_n = S(n)b_n$, where $S(n) \equiv 1/R(n)$ is a defined rational function of n. The argument just completed, along with problem 13 of §3-6, therefore shows (when the roles of the a_n and the b_n are reversed) that $\sigma \leq \rho$. The conclusion is immediate.

The main theorem follows.

THEOREM 3-8. *The function* $f(z) = \sum_0^\infty a_n z^n$ *is regular within the circle of convergence* $|z| = \rho$ *of the series (ρ assumed positive or infinite), and* $f'(z) = \sum_1^\infty n a_n z^{n-1}$ *there.*

Proof. Let z be any point within the circle of convergence of the series, and let R be a positive number for which $|z| < R < \rho$. It will obviously suffice to show that

$$\left| \frac{f(z + \Delta z) - f(z)}{\Delta z} - \sum_1^\infty n a_n z^{n-1} \right| \to 0$$

as $\Delta z \to 0$, where at all times $|z| + |\Delta z| < R$ (whence of necessity $|z + \Delta z| < \rho$). (The crucial fact here is that the circle of convergence of the *derived series* $\sum_1^\infty n a_n z^{n-1}$ is the same as that of the original series $\sum_0^\infty a_n z^n$, which follows from Theorem 3-7 and problems 13 and 14 of §3-6.)   But

$$\left| \frac{f(z + \Delta z) - f(z)}{\Delta z} - \sum_1^\infty n a_n z^{n-1} \right|$$

$$= \left| \frac{\sum_0^\infty a_n (z + \Delta z)^n - \sum_0^\infty a_n z^n}{\Delta z} - \sum_1^\infty n a_n z^{n-1} \right|$$

$$= \left| \frac{\sum_1^\infty a_n [(z + \Delta z)^n - z^n]}{\Delta z} - \sum_1^\infty n a_n z^{n-1} \right|$$

$$= \left| \sum_1^\infty a_n \left[\frac{(z + \Delta z)^n - z^n}{\Delta z} - n z^{n-1} \right] \right|$$

$$= \left| \Delta z \sum_2^\infty a_n \left[\frac{n(n-1)}{2!} z^{n-2} + \frac{n(n-1)(n-2)}{3!} z^{n-3} \Delta z \right. \right.$$

$$\left. \left. + \cdots + \Delta z^{n-2} \right] \right|$$

$$= \left| \Delta z \right| \left| \sum_2^\infty a_n n(n-1) \left[\frac{1}{2 \cdot 1} z^{n-2} + \frac{1}{3 \cdot 2}(n-2) z^{n-3} \Delta z \right. \right.$$

$$+ \frac{1}{4 \cdot 3} \frac{(n-2)(n-3)}{2!} z^{n-4} \Delta z^2$$

$$+ \frac{1}{5 \cdot 4} \frac{(n-2)(n-3)(n-4)}{3!} z^{n-5} \Delta z^3$$

$$\left. \left. + \cdots + \frac{1}{n(n-1)} \Delta z^{n-2} \right] \right|$$

$$\leq \left| \Delta z \right| \sum_2^\infty n(n-1) \left| a_n \right| (|z| + |\Delta z|)^{n-2}$$

$$\leq \left| \Delta z \right| \sum_2^\infty n(n-1) |a_n| R^{n-2},$$

provided that the last series here converges.   But indeed it does, by Theorem 3-7 and problems 13 and 14 of §3-6.   The conclusion follows at once.

Theorem 3-8 implies that a power series in z may be differentiated termwise within its circle of convergence as many times as desired.   If in the more general power series $f(z) \equiv \sum_0^\infty a_n (z - z_0)^n$, one puts $w = z - z_0$ and notes that, by the chain rule, $f^{(k)}(z) = f^{(k)}(w)$ for $k = 0, 1, 2, \ldots$, it is seen that this power series too may be differentiated termwise within its circle of convergence as many times as desired.

If z is put equal to z_0 in each of the succession of equations

$$f(z) = \sum_0^\infty a_n(z - z_0)^n,$$

$$f'(z) = \sum_1^\infty na_n(z - z_0)^{n-1},$$

$$f''(z) = \sum_2^\infty n(n - 1)a_n(z - z_0)^{n-2},$$

$$\cdots,$$

$$f^{(k)}(z) = \sum_k^\infty n(n - 1)(n - 2)\ldots(n - k + 1)a_n(z - z_0)^{n-k},$$

$$\cdots,$$

it follows that

$$a_0 = f(z_0), \ a_1 = f'(z_0), \ a_2 = f''(z_0)/2!, \ldots, \ a_k = f^{(k)}(z_0)/k!,\ldots.$$

Hence

$$f(z) = f(z_0) + f'(z_0)(z - z_0) + f''(z_0)\frac{(z - z_0)^2}{2!}$$

$$+ \cdots + f^{(k)}(z_0)\frac{(z - z_0)^k}{k!} + \cdots \equiv \sum_0^\infty f^{(k)}(z_0)\frac{(z - z_0)^k}{k!}$$

for $|z - z_0| < \rho$, where ρ is the radius of convergence of the series $\sum a_n(z - z_0)^n$. In particular, if $f(z) = \sum a_n z^n$ for $|z| < \rho$, then $f(z) = \sum f^{(n)}(0)z^n/n!$ for $|z| < \rho$.

A simple but highly important corollary follows.

THEOREM 3-9. (Uniqueness Theorem) *If* $\sum a_n(z - z_0)^n = \sum b_n(z - z_0)^n$ *for all* z *within a circle* $C: |z - z_0| = R > 0$, *then* $a_n = b_n$ *for* $n = 0, 1, 2,\ldots.$

Proof. Both a_n and b_n are given by the same formula, $f^{(n)}(z_0)/n!$, for $n = 0, 1, 2, \ldots$, where $f(z)$ is the common value of the two series within C.

Another useful corollary follows from the fact that a differentiable function is continuous.

THEOREM 3-10. *The function* $f(z) \equiv \sum_0^\infty a_n(z - z_0)^n$ *is continuous within the circle of convergence of the series.*

EXAMPLE. Let $f(z) = \sum_0^\infty z^n/n!$. Here $\rho = \infty$. Also,

$$f'(z) = \sum_1^\infty \frac{z^{(n-1)}}{(n - 1)!} = \sum_0^\infty \frac{z^n}{n!} \equiv f(z) \quad \text{for all } z.$$

Since $f(0) = 1$, problem 20 of §2-10 enables us to conclude that

$$e^z \equiv e^x(\cos y + i \sin y) = \sum_0^\infty \frac{z^n}{n!} \quad \text{for all } z. \tag{3-3}$$

3-8. Problems.

1. We know that $1/(1 - z) = 1 + z + z^2 + \cdots + z^n + \cdots$
   for $|z| < 1$. By differentiating both sides of this equation,
   derive a series formula for $1/(1 - z)^2$ which is valid for
   $|z| < 1$.

*2. Using the definitions which were made in Chapter 2 for $\sin z$
   and $\cos z$, and the series expansion for e^z derived in the
   example of §3-7, find the series expressions in powers of z
   for these circular functions.

3. Proceed with the hyperbolic functions $\sinh z$ and $\cosh z$ as we
   did with the circular functions in the preceding problem.

4. If the function Ln z has a series representation of the form
   $\sum_0^\infty a_n(z - 1)^n$ for z sufficiently near the point $z = 1$, find
   what it must be.

*5. If the *indefinite integral* of $f(z)$—symbolized by $\int f(z)dz$—
   is defined as the general function $F(z)$ (if such exists) for
   which $F'(z) = f(z)$, find a power series expansion of $\int f(z)\, dz$
   in case $f(z) = \sum_0^\infty a_n(z - z_0)^n$ for values of z near z_0.

6. Let the radius of convergence of the series $\sum_0^\infty a_n z^n$ be $\rho > 0$.
   If we put $f(z) = \sum_0^\infty a_n/z^n$, determine the part of the plane in
   which we can be sure that $f'(z)$ exists and find a series representation for $f'(z)$ there. (Put $w = 1/z$ and use the chain
   rule.)

7. By use of the series representations in powers of z of the
   functions $1/(1 - z)$, $1/(1 + z)$, and $1/(1 - z^2)$—all of them
   geometric series—verify the "partial fractions decomposition"

   $$\frac{1}{1 - z^2} = \frac{1}{2}\left(\frac{1}{1 - z} + \frac{1}{1 + z}\right).$$

8. Using the series representation in powers of z for the
   function $f(z) = 1/(1 - z^2)$ and the definition of $\int f(z)dz$
   given in problem 5 above, find a series representation for

the indefinite integral of $1/(1 - z^2)$ and state where it is certain that this representation is valid.

9. Assuming that the function $\tan z$ has a power series representation of the form $a_0 + a_1 z + a_2 z^2 + \cdots + a_n z^n + \cdots$ with positive radius of convergence, find $a_0, a_1, a_2,$ and a_3.

*10. Prove Theorem 3-9 by use of problems 13 and 14 of §3-6 as follows. Put $z = z_0$ to show that $a_0 = b_0$; deduce that

$$\sum_{1}^{\infty} a_n(z - z_0)^{n-1} = \sum_{1}^{\infty} b_n(z - z_0)^{n-1}$$

for all z within C; put $z = z_0$ in this last equation to show that $a_1 = b_1$; and so on. Explain carefully by what right we may, after dividing by $z - z_0$, put $z = z_0$ in the resulting equation.

11. Put $z = i\varphi$, where φ is real, in (3-3) and thereby recapture the familiar Maclaurin series for $\sin \varphi$ and $\cos \varphi$.

12. Put $z = x$, where x is real, in (3-3) and thereby recapture the familiar Maclaurin series for e^x.

13. Put $z = re^{i\theta}$ in (3-3) and thereby evaluate these two particular *trigonometric series*

$$\sum_{0}^{\infty} \frac{(r^n \cos n\theta)}{n!} \quad \text{and} \quad \sum_{0}^{\infty} \frac{(r^n \sin n\theta)}{n!}.$$

14. Prove directly, by the method used in proving Theorem 3-8, that a power series is continuous within its circle of convergence.

15. The series $\sum kz^k$ may be expressed in "closed form" for $|z| < 1$ as follows:

$$\sum kz^k = z \sum kz^{k-1} = z \frac{d}{dz} \sum z^k = z \frac{d}{dz} \frac{1}{1 - z} = \frac{z}{(1 - z)^2}.$$

Use similar devices to express the series $\sum k^2 z^k$ in closed form.

Integration

4

4-1. Simple Curves of Class C_1.

By a *continuous curve* in the xy plane is meant a set c of points (x, y) which can be represented by parametric equations $x = x(t)$, $y = y(t)$ for t in an interval $I: t_0 \le t \le T$, where $x(t)$ and $y(t)$ are continuous in I (one-sidedly at the ends) and there is no subinterval of I throughout which both $x(t)$ and $y(t)$ are constant. Such plane curves are the only type considered in this book. Denoting the point $x(t_0) + iy(t_0)$ by $x_0 + iy_0$ or z_0 and the point $x(T) + iy(T)$ by $X + iY$ or Z, one says that c *joins* z_0 and Z. Further, mutually independent definitions follow. If z_0 and Z coincide, then c is a *closed* curve. If the parametrization can be so effected that no point on c is given by more than one value of t for $t_0 \le t < T$, then c is a *simple* curve. (This restriction avoids "multiple points," so that c does not cross or touch itself and so that under the parametrization there is no "back-tracking" along any portion of c.) If the parametrization can be so effected that $x'(t)$ and $y'(t)$ exist and are continuous on I (one-sidedly at the ends, with the derivatives interpreted as one-sided there) and do not vanish simultaneously for any value of t on the interior of I, then c is *of class C_1*. Definitions similar to those above are made for curves in three dimensions. Each curve of any of the types here defined will be assumed in the theoretical developments in this book to have been parametrized in the manner required in the relevant definition.

As shown in calculus, a simple curve of class C_1 has length, and it is possible to speak of a subdivision of c into n *arcs* by points $z_0 \equiv x_0 + iy_0$, $z_1 \equiv x_1 + iy_1, \ldots, z_n \equiv x_n + iy_n \equiv Z$ that correspond to a set of increasing values $t_0, t_1, \ldots, t_n \equiv T$ of t, the points of the kth arc being those which correspond to the values of t for which $t_{k-1} \le t \le t_k$. In fact, the length of c, being the limit of the lengths of inscribed polygons, is precisely

$$\lim_{\max|\Delta z_k| \to 0} \sum_1^n |\Delta z_k|,$$

where $\Delta z_k = z_k - z_{k-1}$ for $k = 1, 2, \ldots, n$.

4-2. Definite Integral of a Continuous Function. Line Integrals.

Letting $f(z) \equiv u(x, y) + iv(x, y)$ be any function that is continuous with respect to a simple curve c of class C_1 that joins two points z_0 and Z, suppose c is divided into n arcs as described above and an arbitrary point $\zeta_k \equiv \xi_k + i\eta_k$ picked on the kth of these arcs for each k. Consider the sum

$$\sum_1^n f(\zeta_k)\Delta z_k \equiv \sum_1^n u(\xi_k, \eta_k)\Delta x_k + i \sum_1^n u(\xi_k, \eta_k)\Delta y_k$$

$$+ i \sum_1^n v(\xi_k, \eta_k)\Delta x_k - \sum_1^n v(\xi_k, \eta_k)\Delta y_k, \quad (4\text{-}1)$$

where $\Delta x_k = x_k - x_{k-1}$ and $\Delta y_k = y_k - y_{k-1}$, for $k = 1, 2, \ldots, n$. The first of the four sums on the right-hand side of (4-1), namely

$$\sum_1^n u(\xi_k, \eta_k)\Delta x_k, \quad (4\text{-}2)$$

has a simple geometric interpretation. Imagine an s axis erected perpendicular to the xy plane so that the x, y, and s axes, in that order, set up a right-handed coordinate system, as in the construction of the complex sphere, §1-6, and consider the skew curve with parametric equations $x = x(t)$, $y = y(t)$, and $s = u[x(t), y(t)]$ in xys space. The projection of this skew curve on the xs plane is the curve with parametric representation $x = x(t)$, $s = u[x(t), y(t)]$ in that plane, and the sum (4-2) is an approximation to the "area under it" from $x = x_0$ to $x = X$, this area being obtained exactly by letting $\max |\Delta x_k| \to 0$ and being equal to

$$\int_{t_0}^T u[x(t), y(t)]x'(t)dt.$$

This integral is called the *line integral* from z_0 to Z along c of $u(x, y)dx$ and is written alternatively in either of the forms

$$\int_{z_0(c)}^Z u(x, y)dx, \qquad \int_{(x_0, y_0)(c)}^{(X,Y)} u(x, y)dx.$$

(Here z_0 and Z are to be regarded as names for points in the plane; they are not, in general, the limits of integration for the variable x.)

The other sums on the right-hand side of (4-1) tend to similar line integrals as max $|\Delta x_k|$ and max $|\Delta y_k|$ tend to zero—in short, as max $|\Delta z_k|$ tends to zero.

The limit of the left-hand side of (4-1) as max $|\Delta z_k|$ tends to zero is called the *definite integral from* z_0 *to* Z *along* c *of* $f(z)\, dz$, or simply *of* $f(z)$, and is written as $\int_{z_0(c)}^{Z} f(z)dz$. What has been shown is that this limit exists and is given by

$$\int_{z_0(c)}^{Z} f(z)dz \equiv \lim_{\max |\Delta z_k| \to 0} \sum_{1}^{n} f(\zeta_k)\Delta z_k$$

$$= \int_{z_0(c)}^{Z} u(x, y)dx + i \int_{z_0(c)}^{Z} u(x, y)dy$$

$$+ i \int_{z_0(c)}^{Z} v(x, y)dx - \int_{z_0(c)}^{Z} v(x, y)dy,$$

or, more compactly,

$$\int_{z_0(c)}^{Z} f(z)dz = \int_{z_0(c)}^{Z} (u + iv)(dx + idy),$$

which is precisely what one obtains by purely formal manipulation of the integrand on the left-hand side.

4-3. Evaluation of the Integral.

Since

$$\int_{z_0(c)}^{Z} u(x, y)dx = \int_{t_0}^{T} u[x(t), y(t)]x'(t)dt$$

and the other line integrals can be expressed similarly, formal manipulation of the symbol $\int_{z_0(c)}^{Z} f(z)dz$ may be carried a step further, thus:

$$\int_{z_0(c)}^{Z} f(z)dz = \int_{t_0}^{T} \{u[x(t), y(t)] + iv[x(t), y(t)]\}[x'(t) + iy'(t)]dt. \quad (4\text{-}3)$$

EXAMPLE 1. If c is the curve $x = t$, $y = t^2$, $0 \le t \le 1$, then

$$\int_{0(c)}^{1+i} \bar{z}dz = \int_{0(c)}^{1+i} (x - iy)(dx + idy)$$

$$= \int_{0(c)}^{1+i} xdx + i \int_{0(c)}^{1+i} xdy + i \int_{0(c)}^{1+i} (-y)dx - \int_{0(c)}^{1+i} (-y)dy$$

$$= \int_0^1 tdt + i \int_0^1 t \cdot 2tdt + i \int_0^1 (-t^2)dt - \int_0^1 (-t^2)2tdt$$

$$= \tfrac{1}{2} + \tfrac{2}{3}i - \tfrac{1}{3}i + \tfrac{1}{2} = 1 + \tfrac{1}{3}i.$$

Evidently the integral (4-3) need not be separated into the several individual integrals. The integral in the next example is computed without doing so.

EXAMPLE 2. If c is the line segment $y = 2x$, $1 \le x \le 2$, then (taking x itself as the parameter) we have

$$\int_{1+2i(c)}^{2+4i} (4x + iy)dz = \int_1^2 (4x + 2ix)(1 + 2i)dx = \int_1^2 10ixdx = 15i.$$

4-4. Some General Properties of the Integral. A Bounding Theorem.

It is clear that, if c is a simple curve of class C_1 which joins the points z_0 and Z and with respect to which a function $f(z)$ is continuous, then for every point Z' between z_0 and Z,

$$\int_{z_0(c)}^{Z} f(z)dz = \int_{z_0(c_1)}^{Z'} f(z)dz + \int_{Z'(c_2)}^{Z} f(z)dz,$$

where c_1 is the portion of c which joins z_0 and Z' and c_2 is the portion which joins Z' and Z. In case c consists of m abutting simple curves of class C_1, one *defines* (without inconsistency) $\int_{z_0(c)}^{Z} f(z)dz$ as the sum of the m separate integrals along the individual curves, the initial subdivisions being in each case, of course, in the "direction from z_0 to Z" along the individual curve involved.

A curve c which consists of a finite number of abutting simple curves of class C_1 will be called in this book a *path*; the individual simple curves themselves may be called *segments* of c. The adjectives *simple* and *closed*, introduced in §4-1, are applicable to paths, since paths are continuous curves. For a path c it is clear that

$$\int_{z_0(c)}^{Z} [kf(z) + lg(z)]dz = k\int_{z_0(c)}^{Z} f(z)dz + l\int_{z_0(c)}^{Z} g(z)dz$$

for every pair of functions $f(z)$ and $g(z)$ that are continuous with respect to c and for every pair of constants k and l, and that

$$\int_{z_0(c)}^{Z} f(z)dz = -\int_{Z(c)}^{z_0} f(z)dz$$

for every function $f(z)$ that is continuous with respect to c.

[In the integral from Z to z_0 the orientation of c is of course reversed. For example, if $x = x(t)$, $y = y(t)$ is a parametrization of the sort described in §4-1, then a possible parametrization for the integral from Z to z_0 is given by $x = x(T - t)$, $y = y(T - t)$ for $0 \le t \le T - t_0$.]

An important *bounding theorem* for integrals follows.

THEOREM 4-1. *If $f(z)$ is continuous with respect to a path c of length s that joins the points z_0 and Z, and if $|f(z)| \le M$ for all z on c, then $\left|\int_{z_0(c)}^{Z} f(z)dz\right| \le Ms$.*

Proof. It suffices to suppose that c consists of a single segment of class C_1. Using the notation of §4-2, we have, for every subdivision of c,

$$\left|\sum f(\zeta_k)\Delta z_k\right| \le \sum |f(\zeta_k)| |\Delta z_k| \le M\sum |\Delta z_k|$$

and, since the length of an arc is not less than that of any inscribed polygon, $M \sum |\Delta z_k| \leq Ms$. The conclusion now follows from Example 7 of § 2-2.

4-5. Problems.

1. The set c of points (x, y) for which $x = \sin^2 t$ and $y = \sin t \cos t$ with $0 \leq t \leq 2\pi$ is a simple curve, although the point $(1, 0)$ is given by both $t = \pi/2$ and $t = 3\pi/2$. Explain.

2. Let c be the semicircle $x^2 + y^2 = 1$, $x \geq 0$. Appealing to the definition of the line integral as the limit of a sum, find the values of the integrals

   (a) $\int_{-i(c)}^{i} 2dy$,

   (b) $\int_{-i(c)}^{i} 2dx$.

3. Let c be the curve $x = t^2$, $y = t$, $0 \leq t \leq 1$ and let $u(x, y) = x + y$. Draw the curve in the ys plane, the area under which is equal to the line integral $\int_{(0,0)\,(c)}^{(1,1)} udy$ and—by calculating that area directly—evaluate the integral.

4. Let c be the curve $x = \sin t$, $y = 1 - \cos t$, $0 \leq t \leq \pi$ and let $u(x, y) = y$. Draw the curve in the xs plane, the area under which is equal to the line integral $\int_{(0,0)\,(c)}^{(0,2)} udx$ and—by calculating that area directly (with the concept of "negative area" taken into account)—evaluate the integral.

5. Let c be the curve $x = t$, $y = t^2$, $0 \leq t \leq 1$. Find by integration the values of

   (a) $\int_{0(c)}^{1+i} (x + y)dx$,

   (b) $\int_{(0,0)(c)}^{(1,1)} (x + y)dy$.

6. Let c be the curve $x = \cos \theta$, $y = \sin \theta$, $0 \leq \theta \leq \pi$ and z_0 and Z be the points $(1, 0)$ and $(-1, 0)$, respectively. Find the values of the line integrals

   (a) $\int_{z_0(c)}^{Z} (x + y)dx$,

   (b) $\int_{z_0(c)}^{Z} (x + y)dy$.

7. If we write $z(t) = x(t) + iy(t)$, where $x = x(t)$, $y = y(t)$ are appropriate parametric representations of a curve of class C_1, in what sense that is *not* purely formal may we write $dz = [x'(t) + iy'(t)]dt$?

8. Evaluate $\int_{0(c)}^{1+i} |z|^2 dz$ when c is an appropriate portion of the curve

(a) $x = t^2, y = t^3$;
(b) $y = x$;
(c) $x = y^2$.

9. Evaluate $\int_{0(c)}^{1+i} z^2 dz$ when c is, in succession, each of the curves of integration of problem 8.

10. Evaluate $\int_{(1,0)(c)}^{(0,1)} z dz$ when c is an appropriate portion of the curve

(a) $x = t, y = 1 - t$;
(b) $x = \cos \theta, y = \sin \theta$.

11. Verify Theorem 4-1 for parts (a) and (b) of problems 8, 9, and 10.

*12. In problem 8 of §2-5 we showed that continuity of $f(z)$ at a point implies continuity of $|f(z)|$ there. Is it true that, if $f(z)$ is continuous with respect to a curve of class C_1, so is $|f(z)|$? Using problem 9 of §2-3, deduce the inequality $\left| \int_{z_0(c)}^{Z} f(z) dz \right| \le \int_{z_0(c)}^{Z} |f(z)| ds$, where c is a simple curve of class C_1 joining z_0 and Z with respect to which $f(z)$ is continuous and ds is the element of arc on c. (The real integral on the right-hand side of the inequality is of the sort that one deals with in finding the mass of a filament or the centroid of an arc. Only the notation is new.)

13. Let c be the path consisting of the portion of the x axis from 0 to 1, followed by the portion of the line $x = 1$ from 1 to $1 + i\pi/2$. Evaluate the integrals

(a) $\int_{0(c)}^{1+i\pi/2} e^z dz$,

(b) $\int_{0(c)}^{1+i\pi/2} e^{\bar{z}} dz$,

(c) $\int_{0(c)}^{1+i\pi/2} |e^z| dz$.

4-6. Open Region. Connected and Simply Connected Open Regions.

Frequent reference has been made so far in this book to sets of points which constitute interiors of circles. It is now desirable to generalize this type of point set. Given a set R of points in the plane, a point z of R that is the center of some circle whose interior consists entirely of points of R is called an *interior point* of R. A set R of points *each* of which is an interior point of R is called an *open set* or *open region*. (The definition of *region* without the qualifying adjective will be given in Chapter 9.)

EXAMPLE 1. (a) The interior of a square. (b) The entire plane. (c) The *annulus*, or ring-shaped portion of the plane between two concentric, non-congruent circles. (d) The points interior to the circle $|z| = 1$ together with those interior to the circle $|z - 3| = 1$. (e) The interior of a simple closed curve c. [It is easy to see that (e) is an open region in most of the cases that the student will meet. The proof, in general, is too complicated to present here, hinging as it does on the *Jordan curve theorem*—a theorem that establishes with great ingenuity the mere existence of an "interior" of c, which is to say, of a non-null set of points in the plane none of which can be joined to points of arbitrarily great remoteness by continuous curves that have no points in common with c.]

By a "staircase path" from a point z_0 to a point Z in the plane is meant any broken line whose initial and terminal points are z_0 and Z, respectively, and each of whose line segments—assumed finite in number—is perpendicular to each line segment on which it abuts. The "orientation" of a staircase path will be taken to mean the angle φ obtained by reducing or augmenting the inclination of any of its segments by that integral multiple of $\pi/2$ that causes φ to satisfy the inequality $0 \leq \varphi < \pi/2$.

A plane point set R is said to be a *connected open region* if it is an open region such that, given any two points z_0 and Z in R, there exist in R staircase paths with all orientations joining z_0 and Z. (It will be shown in Chapter 11 that one need only require the existence of such a staircase path with a *single* orientation; the existence of the others follows from this.)

EXAMPLE 2. (a), (b), and (c) of Example 1 above. The set (d) of Example 1 is clearly not connected.

A plane point set R is called a *simply connected open region* if it is a connected open region such that all of the points on the interior of any simple closed path in R are points of R.

EXAMPLE 3. (a) and (b) of Example 1 above. The set (c) of Example 1 is not simply connected.

4-7. Problems.

1. Consider this definition: An interior point of a plane set R of points is a point z of R that is the center of some square with

sides parallel to the axes, all points interior to and on the square being points of R. Is this equivalent to the definition given in §4-6?

In problems 2 through 14, is the point set described open? If open, is it connected? Simply connected?

2. The points interior to the circle $|z| = 2$ together with those interior to the circle $|z - 1| = 2$.

3. The points z for which either $|z| < 1$ or $|z - 2| < 1$.

4. All points in the plane except those on the x axis.

5. All points in the plane except those on the positive x axis.

6. All points in the plane except those on the non-negative x axis.

7. All points in the plane except the origin.

8. All points in the plane except the origin and the points on the spiral $r = e^\theta$.

9. All points in the plane except the points on the spiral $r = e^\theta$.

10. All points in the plane except the points on the curve $y = \sin(1/x)$ for $x > 0$ and the segment of the y axis for which $-1 \le y \le 1$.

11. All points in the plane except those on the line segments $x = 1/n$, $0 < y < 1/n$ for $n = 1, 2, \ldots$.

12. All points in the plane except those on the line segments $x = 1/n$, $0 \le y \le 1/n$ for $n = 1, 2, \ldots$.

13. All points in the plane except the origin and the points on the line segments $x = 1/n$, $0 \le y \le 1/n$ for $n = 1, 2, \ldots$.

14. All points in the plane except those on the non-negative y axis and those on the line segments $x = 1/n$, $0 \le y \le n$ for $n = 1, 2, \ldots$.

15. Let the point set S consist of all points z for which either (or both) $|z| < 2$ or $1 \le |z - z_0| < 2$. For which values of z_0 is S open?

4-8. Line Integrals Independent of the Path.

Perhaps the most important of all the theorems in complex variable theory is that which bears the name of Cauchy. It is presented as Theorem 4-14 in this book. Since proof of Cauchy's theorem as presented here is based on expression of the complex integral in terms of four real line integrals as in §4-2, it is now necessary to embark on a succession of theorems about such integrals. (If c is a simple closed path, the symbol $\oint_{(c)}$ indicates integration around it in the counterclockwise direction.)

THEOREM 4-2. *If $P(x, y)$ and $Q(x, y)$ are continuously differentiable functions within and on a rectangle whose sides are parallel to the axes, then*

$$\oint_{(c)} (P dx + Q dy) = \iint_A \left(\frac{\partial Q}{\partial x} - \frac{\partial P}{\partial y}\right) dA,$$

where c is the perimeter of the rectangle and A is its interior.

This is a special case of *Green's theorem*, in which c is any simple closed path and A is its interior.

Proof. Letting the corners of the rectangle be (x_0, y_0), (X, y_0), (X, Y), (x_0, Y)—named in order as we proceed counterclockwise around c from the southwest corner—we have

$$\oint_{(c)} (P dx + Q dy) = \int_{x_0}^{X} P(x, y_0) dx + \int_{y_0}^{Y} Q(X, y) dy$$
$$+ \int_{X}^{x_0} P(x, Y) dx + \int_{Y}^{y_0} Q(x_0, y) dy$$
$$= \int_{x_0}^{X} [P(x, y_0) - P(x, Y)] dx$$
$$+ \int_{y_0}^{Y} [Q(X, y) - Q(x_0, y)] dy$$
$$= \int_{x_0}^{X} \int_{Y}^{y_0} \frac{\partial P(x, y)}{\partial y} dy dx + \int_{y_0}^{Y} \int_{x_0}^{X} \frac{\partial Q(x, y)}{\partial x} dx dy$$
$$= \int_{x_0}^{X} \int_{y_0}^{Y} \left(\frac{\partial Q}{\partial x} - \frac{\partial P}{\partial y}\right) dy dx \equiv \iint_A \left(\frac{\partial Q}{\partial x} - \frac{\partial P}{\partial y}\right) dA.$$

(To understand the interchange in order of integration, regard the iterated integral as representing a volume.)

The next theorem is an obvious corollary to Theorem 4-2.

THEOREM 4-3. *If $P(x, y)$ and $Q(x, y)$ are continuously differentiable and satisfy the condition*

$$\frac{\partial P}{\partial y} = \frac{\partial Q}{\partial x} \tag{4-4}$$

within and on a rectangle whose sides are parallel to the axes, then $\oint_{(c)} (P dx + Q dy) = 0$, where c is the perimeter of the rectangle.

THEOREM 4-4. *Let R be a simply connected open region within which $P(x, y)$ and $Q(x, y)$ are continuously differentiable and satisfy*

(4-4). *Then* $\oint_{(c)} (Pdx + Qdy) = 0$ *for every simple closed staircase path c in R whose segments are parallel to one or the other of the axes.*

Proof. If each segment of c is extended indefinitely, a finite number of rectangles are formed (Fig. 4-1). Letting $R_1, R_2, \ldots,$

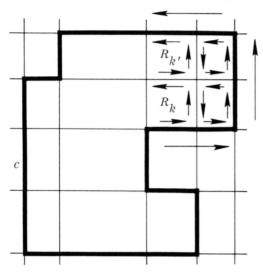

Figure 4-1

R_n denote the perimeters of those among these rectangles whose interiors are on the interior of c, we see by Theorem 4-3 that

$$\oint_{(R_k)} (Pdx + Qdy) = 0 \quad \text{for } k = 1, 2, \ldots, n,$$

so that

$$\sum \oint_{(R_k)} (Pdx + Qdy) = 0.$$

Taking the symbol $\int_{(s_{kj})}$ to mean integration along side s_{kj} of rectangle R_k in the proper direction, $j = 1, 2, 3, 4$, we see that this means that $\sum_k \sum_j \int_{(s_{kj})} (Pdx + Qdy) = 0$. Now every s_{kj} which is not a segment of c is matched by an $s_{k'j'}$ (we may say that $s_{k'j'}$ is "s_{kj} in the opposite direction") such that

$$\int_{(s_{k'j'})} (Pdx + Qdy) = - \int_{(s_{kj})} (Pdx + Qdy),$$

so that the only terms in our double sum which do not cancel one another out are those which represent integrals along the several segments of c. And since the latter occur in such directions that their sum constitutes the counterclockwise integral around c, the conclusion follows.

THEOREM 4-5. *Let R be a simply connected open region within which $P(x, y)$ and $Q(x, y)$ are continuously differentiable and satisfy* (4-4). *Then, if (x_0, y_0) and (X, Y) are any two points in R,*

$$\int_{(x_0, y_0)(c_1)}^{(X, Y)} (Pdx + Qdy) = \int_{(x_0, y_0)(c_2)}^{(X, Y)} (Pdx + Qdy),$$

for every two staircase paths c_1 and c_2 in R whose segments are parallel to one or the other of the axes and which join (x_0, y_0) and (X, Y).

Proof. Since it is possible to assume that (x_0, y_0) and (X, Y) are the only points that c_1 and c_2 have in common, we may invoke Theorem 4-4 by taking as the path c of that theorem the path c_1 followed by the path c_2 in reverse direction, or the path c_2 followed by the path c_1 in reverse direction—whichever combination provides c with the counterclockwise direction. The result is that

$$\int_{(x_0, y_0)(c_1)}^{(X, Y)} (Pdx + Qdy) - \int_{(x_0, y_0)(c_2)}^{(X, Y)} (Pdx + Qdy) = 0,$$

which is what was to be proved.

THEOREM 4-6. *If R is a simply connected open region within which $P(x, y)$ and $Q(x, y)$ are continuously differentiable and satisfy* (4-4), *then there is a function $F(x, y)$ for which $\partial F/\partial x = P$ and $\partial F/\partial y = Q$ throughout R.*

Proof. For each point (X, Y) in R, let us define

$$F(X, Y) \equiv \int_{(x_0, y_0)(c)}^{(X, Y)} [P(x, y)dx + Q(x, y)dy], \tag{4-5}$$

where (x_0, y_0) is an arbitrary but fixed point in R, and c is any staircase path in R whose segments are parallel to one or the other of the axes and that joins (x_0, y_0) and (X, Y)—the possibility of this definition following from Theorem 4-5. Let us now take ΔX ($\neq 0$) numerically so small that $(X + \Delta X, Y)$ lies within a circle about (X, Y) whose interior is contained in R. By Theorem 4-5, we can write

$$F(X + \Delta X, Y) - F(X, Y) = \left[\int_{(x_0, y_0)(c)}^{(X, Y)} + \int_{(X, Y)(c')}^{(X + \Delta X, Y)} \right.$$
$$\left. - \int_{(x_0, y_0)(c)}^{(X, Y)} \right] (Pdx + Qdy)$$
$$= \int_{X(c')}^{X + \Delta X} P(x, Y)dx,$$

where c' is the line segment for which $y = Y$ and $X \leq x \leq X + \Delta X$. Hence, by the mean-value theorem,

$$F(X + \Delta X, Y) - F(X, Y) = P(\bar{x}, Y)\Delta X$$

for some $\bar{x}$ such that $X \gtrless \bar{x} \gtrless X + \Delta X$, and we may conclude at once that $\partial F(X, Y)/\partial X = P(X, Y)$.   Similarly, we can show that $\partial F(X, Y)/\partial Y = Q(X, Y)$, thus completing the proof.

There are clearly an infinite number of functions $F(x, y)$ of the sort specified in this theorem; they can be obtained by adding arbitrary constants to the particular function described above.

EXAMPLE 1.   The functions $P \equiv 2x$ and $Q \equiv 2y$ satisfy the conditions of Theorem 4-6 if R is the entire plane.   Taking (x_0, y_0) as the origin and integrating first horizontally and then vertically, we obtain

$$F(X, Y) = \int_0^X 2x\,dx + \int_0^Y 2y\,dy = X^2 + Y^2,$$

which is to say that $F(x, y) = r^2$, where r is the polar radius.

EXAMPLE 2.   The functions $P \equiv -y/(x^2 + y^2)$ and $Q \equiv x/(x^2 + y^2)$ satisfy the conditions of Theorem 4-6 if R is the entire plane except the non-positive x axis.   Taking (x_0, y_0) as the point $(1, 0)$ and integrating first vertically and then horizontally, we have

$$F(X, Y) = \int_0^Y \frac{dy}{1 + y^2} - \int_1^X \frac{Y\,dx}{x^2 + Y^2},$$

which equals zero if $Y = 0$ and otherwise equals

$$\text{Arctan } Y - \text{Arctan } \frac{X}{Y} + \text{Arctan } \frac{1}{Y},$$

which equals

$$\frac{\pi}{2} - \text{Arctan } \frac{X}{Y} \qquad \text{if } Y > 0$$

and

$$-\frac{\pi}{2} - \text{Arctan } \frac{X}{Y} \qquad \text{if } Y < 0.$$

Thus $F(x, y) = \theta$, the principal value of the polar angle.

THEOREM 4-7.   *If R is a simply connected open region within which $P(x, y)$ and $Q(x, y)$ are continuously differentiable and satisfy (4-4), then for every pair of points (x_1, y_1) and (x_2, y_2) in R the value of $\int_{(x_1, y_1)(c)}^{(x_2, y_2)} (P\,dx + Q\,dy)$ is the same for each path c in R that joins (x_1, y_1) and (x_2, y_2).   In fact, this value is $F(x_2, y_2) - F(x_1, y_1)$, where F is the function of Theorem 4-6.   Moreover, $F(X, Y)$ can be taken to be*

$$F(X, Y) = \int_{(x_0, y_0)(c)}^{(X, Y)} (P\,dx + Q\,dy), \qquad (4\text{-}6)$$

where (x_0, y_0) is any fixed point in R, and c is any path in R that joins (x_0, y_0) and (X, Y).

Proof. We may assume that c consists of a single element of class C_1; the general case follows by addition of integrals over the several segments. By Theorem 4-6, we have

$$\int_{(x_1, y_1)(c)}^{(x_2, y_2)} (P dx + Q dy) = \int_{t_1}^{t_2} \frac{dF}{dt} \, dt,$$

where c has been appropriately parametrized, and t_1 and t_2 are the values of t corresponding to (x_1, y_1) and (x_2, y_2), respectively, and this equals

$$F[x(t_2), y(t_2)] - F[x(t_1), y(t_1)] \equiv F(x_2, y_2) - F(x_1, y_1),$$

as asserted. The equality (4-6) is a consequence of applying what we have just proved to the integral in (4-5).

An immediate corollary to Theorem 4-7 follows.

THEOREM 4-8. *If R is a simply connected open region within which $P(x, y)$ and $Q(x, y)$ are continuously differentiable and satisfy (4-4), then $\oint_{(c)} (P dx + Q dy) = 0$ for every closed path c in R.*

THEOREM 4-9. *If R is a simply connected open region within which $P(x, y)$ and $Q(x, y)$ are continuously differentiable, then a necessary and sufficient condition that $\oint_{(c)} (P dx + Q dy) = 0$ for every closed path c in R is that P and Q satisfy (4-4) in R.*

Proof. The sufficiency is expressed by Theorem 4-8. To prove the necessity we need only deduce a contradiction from the supposition that (4-4) fails to hold at some point P_1 in R. So supposing, we may assume for definiteness that $\partial P/\partial y - \partial Q/\partial x > 0$ at P_1. Since the partials are continuous, we will also have† $\partial P/\partial y - \partial Q/\partial x > 0$ throughout the interior A of some square in R with center at P_1 and sides parallel to the axes, so that

$$\iint_A \left(\frac{\partial P}{\partial y} - \frac{\partial Q}{\partial x} \right) dA > 0.$$

But we are now assuming that $\oint_{(c)} (P dx + Q dy) = 0$ for every

† Such intuitively obvious facts are examined critically in Chapter 9.

closed path c in R and, in particular, the path c which is the perimeter of the square. The equality

$$\oint_{(c)} (Pdx + Qdy) = \iint_A \left(\frac{\partial Q}{\partial x} - \frac{\partial P}{\partial y} \right) dA,$$

provided by Theorem 4-2, thus constitutes the contradiction we needed.

Theorem 4-9 is sometimes stated in the following alternative form.

THEOREM 4-10. *If R is a simply connected open region within which $P(x, y)$ and $Q(x, y)$ are continuously differentiable, then a necessary and sufficient condition that, for every pair of points (x_1, y_1) and (x_2, y_2) in R, the value of $\int_{(x_1, y_1)(c)}^{(x_2, y_2)} (Pdx + Qdy)$ is the same for each path c in R which joins (x_1, y_1) and (x_2, y_2) is that P and Q satisfy (4-4) in R.*

4-9. Problems.

1. Find the function $F(X, Y)$ of Example 2, §4-8, by integrating from $(1, 0)$ along the x axis to the circle $x = R \cos \theta$, $y = R \sin \theta$ on which (X, Y) lies and then along the shorter arc of that circle to (X, Y).

2. Evaluate $\oint_{(c)}(Pdx + Qdy)$, where P and Q are as in Example 2, §4-8, and c is

    (a)   the circle $x = a \cos t$, $y = a \sin t$, $0 \le t \le 2\pi$,
    (b)   the square with vertices at (b, b), $(-b, b)$, $(-b, -b)$, and $(b, -b)$.

3. Show that the functions

$$P \equiv \frac{2xy}{(x^2 + y^2)^2}$$

    and

$$Q \equiv \frac{y^2 - x^2}{(x^2 + y^2)^2}$$

    are continuously differentiable and satisfy (4-4) everywhere except the origin. Name a region R for which the conclusion of Theorem 4-8 will hold for these functions. Then evaluate $\oint_{(c)} (Pdx + Qdy)$ if c is the circle $x = a \cos t$, $y = a \sin t$, $0 \le t \le 2\pi$.

*4. Let $F(x, y)$ be a function of two independent variables x and y, with differential $dF = Pdx + Qdy$, where $P \equiv \partial F/\partial x$ and $Q \equiv \partial F/\partial y$ are continuously differentiable. The theorem on reversal of order of differentiation tells us that P and Q satisfy (4-4). Making use of this fact and Theorem 4-6, state a "necessity and sufficiency theorem" (with suitably restrictive hypotheses) that an expression $P(x, y)dx + Q(x, y)dy$, where x and y are independent, is the differential of some function for all points in a certain type of point set.

5. Using problem 4 above and (4-5), find a function $F(x, y)$ for which

$$dF = [\cos (x + y) + e^y + xy]dx$$
$$+ [\cos (x + y) + xe^y + \varphi(x)]dy.$$

[First find $\varphi(x)$; then find $F(X, Y)$ by integrating from a convenient point (x_0, y_0) along a convenient path.]

6. Given any two functions $P(x, y)$ and $Q(x, y)$ that are continuously differentiable in the entire plane and any point (X, Y) in the plane, let us define

$$F(X, Y) \equiv \int_{(0, 0)(c)}^{(X, Y)} (Pdx + Qdy),$$

where c is the portion of the y axis from the origin to the point $(0, Y)$ followed by the portion of the line $y = Y$ from the point $(0, Y)$ to the point (X, Y). Show first, as in the proof of Theorem 4-6, that $\partial F(X, Y)/\partial X$ exists and equals $P(X, Y)$. What happens when we attempt to show that $\partial F(X, Y)/\partial Y$ exists and equals $Q(X, Y)$?

7. The functions P and Q of Example 2, §4-8, satisfy the conditions of Theorem 4-6 if R is the entire plane except the origin and *any* half-line terminating at the origin. Let R be the entire plane except the non-positive y axis. Let $F^*(X, Y)$ be the function obtained by integrating $Pdx + Qdy$ from the point $(1, 0)$ to the point (X, Y) along a path c that lies entirely in R. Taking c to be a segment of the x axis followed by an arc of the circle about the origin on which (X, Y) lies, deduce that $F^*(x, y)$ coincides with the function $F(x, y)$ of Example 2 throughout the first, second, and fourth quadrants but differs from it by 2π in the third. Explain.

8. Show that the conditions of Theorem 4-6 are met by the functions $P \equiv -y/(a^2x^2 + y^2)$, $Q \equiv x/(a^2x^2 + y^2)$, where

$a \neq 0$ is a constant, if R is the entire plane except the non-positive x axis, and find a function $F(x, y)$ for which $\partial F/\partial x = P$ and $\partial F/\partial y = Q$.

9. Show that the functions $P(x, y)$ and $Q(x, y)$ below satisfy the conditions of Theorem 4-6 in a simply connected open region R (which name) and find a corresponding function $F(x, y)$.

(a) $P(x, y) = e^x(x \sin y + y \cos y)$,
$Q(x, y) = e^x(x \cos y - y \sin y)$;

(b) $P(x, y) = \cos x \sinh y$,
$Q(x, y) = \sin x \cosh y$;

(c) $P(x, y) = x/(x^2 + y^2)$,
$Q(x, y) = y/(x^2 + y^2)$;

(d) $P(x, y) = \operatorname{Ln} y + y/x$,
$Q(x, y) = \operatorname{Ln} x + x/y$.

4-10. Integrals of Regular Functions.
Cauchy's and Morera's Theorems.

The theorems of this section are built on the groundwork laid in §4-8.

THEOREM 4-11. *If R is a simply connected open region within which $u(x, y)$ and $v(x, y)$ are continuously differentiable, then a necessary and sufficient condition that $f(z) \equiv u + iv$ be regular throughout R is that throughout R the ordered pairs of functions $(u, -v)$ and (v, u) satisfy (4-4) in the role of the ordered pair (P, Q).*

Proof. Equation (4-4) becomes one of the Cauchy-Riemann equations in each case.

It is necessary in the next theorem to use the (as yet unproved) fact that regularity of a function $f(z) \equiv u + iv$ implies the continuous differentiability of u and v, as mentioned in §2-6.

THEOREM 4-12. *If the function $f(z)$ is regular throughout a simply connected open region R, then for every pair of points $z_1 \equiv x_1 + iy_1$ and $z_2 \equiv x_2 + iy_2$ in R the value of $\int_{z_1(c)}^{z_2} f(z)dz$ is the same for each path c in R which joins z_1 and z_2.*

Proof. The conclusion follows upon application of Theorem 4-7 to the real and imaginary parts of

$$\int_{z_1(c)}^{z_2} f(z)dz \equiv \int_{(x_1, y_1)(c)}^{(x_2, y_2)} (udx - vdy) + i \int_{(x_1, y_1)(c)}^{(x_2, y_2)} (vdx + udy). \qquad (4\text{-}7)$$

It follows that, if $z_0 \equiv x_0 + iy_0$ is an arbitrary point in R, the function

$$F(Z) \equiv \int_{z_0(c)}^{Z} f(z)dz \tag{4-8}$$

is defined for each $Z \equiv X + iY$ in R independently of the path c so long as c joins z_0 and Z and lies entirely in R. Indeed,

$$F(Z) = U(X, Y) + iV(X, Y), \tag{4-9}$$

where

$$U(X, Y) = \int_{(x_0, y_0)(c)}^{(X, Y)} (udx - vdy),$$
$$V(X, Y) = \int_{(x_0, y_0)(c)}^{(X, Y)} (vdx + udy).$$

Application of Theorem 4-7 to the real and imaginary parts of $\int_{z_1(c)}^{z_2} f(z)dz$, exhibited in (4-7), leads to the next result. (See also problem 13 of §4-12.)

THEOREM 4-13. *If the function $f(z)$ is regular throughout a simply connected open region R, then for every pair of points z_1 and z_2 in R and every path c in R which joins z_1 and z_2,*

$$\int_{z_1(c)}^{z_2} f(z)dz = F(z_2) - F(z_1), \tag{4-10}$$

where $F(z)$ is given by (4-8).

An alternative statement of Theorem 4-13 follows.

THEOREM 4-14. (Cauchy's Theorem) *If the function $f(z)$ is regular throughout a simply connected open region R, then $\oint_{(c)} f(z)dz = 0$ for each closed path c in R.*

Cauchy's theorem is the foundation on which most of what follows in this book is built. Its importance cannot be overemphasized. A partial converse is now stated.

THEOREM 4-15. (Morera's Theorem) *If $f(z)$ is continuous throughout a simply connected open region R and $\oint_{(c)} f(z)dz = 0$ for each closed path c in R, then $f(z)$ is regular throughout R.*

Provisional proof. Let us assume at the moment that u and v are continuously differentiable, where $f(z) = u + iv$, deferring a complete proof to Chapter 9. The vanishing of the integral is equivalent to the vanishing of the two real integrals $\oint_{(c)} (udx - vdy)$ and $\oint_{(c)} (vdx + udy)$ and this, by the assumed continuous differentiability of u and v and Theorem 4-9, implies that u and v satisfy the Cauchy-Riemann equations. The provisional proof is complete.

4-11. Evaluation of Definite Integrals of Regular Functions.

In order to evaluate integrals by means of (4-10), it is now appropriate to examine more closely the function $F(Z)$ defined in (4-8) and broken up into its real and imaginary parts in (4-9). It follows from Theorems 4-7 and 4-6 that

$$\frac{\partial U(X, Y)}{\partial X} = u(X, Y) = \frac{\partial V(X, Y)}{\partial Y}$$

and

$$\frac{\partial V(X, Y)}{\partial X} = v(X, Y) = -\frac{\partial U(X, Y)}{\partial Y}.$$

Thus U and V satisfy the Cauchy-Riemann equations. Since u and v are also continuous, it follows that, throughout R, $F(Z)$ is differentiable; moreover,

$$F'(z) \equiv \frac{\partial U(x, y)}{\partial x} + i \frac{\partial V(x, y)}{\partial x} = u(x, y) + iv(x, y) \equiv f(z).$$

Thus $F(z)$ is an indefinite integral of $f(z)$.

THEOREM 4-16. *If the function $f(z)$ is regular throughout a simply connected open region R, then for every pair of points z_1 and z_2 in R and every path c in R which joins z_1 and z_2,*

$$\int_{z_1(c)}^{z_2} f(z)dz = \Phi(z_2) - \Phi(z_1),$$

where $\Phi(z)$ is ANY *indefinite integral of $f(z)$ in R.*

Proof. If $\Phi(z) = U^*(x, y) + iV^*(x, y)$, then $\partial U^*/\partial x = \partial V^*/\partial y$ and $\partial V^*/\partial x = -\partial U^*/\partial y$, so that

$$\int_{z_1(c)}^{z_2} f(z)dz \equiv \int_{z_1(c)}^{z_2} \Phi'(z)dz$$

$$= \int_{(x_1, y_1)(c)}^{(x_2, y_2)} \left(\frac{\partial U^*}{\partial x} + i \frac{\partial V^*}{\partial x}\right)(dx + idy)$$

$$= \int_{(x_1, y_1)(c)}^{(x_2, y_2)} \left(\frac{\partial U^*}{\partial x} dx - \frac{\partial V^*}{\partial x} dy\right)$$

$$+ i \int_{(x_1, y_1)(c)}^{(x_2, y_2)} \left(\frac{\partial V^*}{\partial x} dx + \frac{\partial U^*}{\partial x} dy\right)$$

$$= \int_{(x_1, y_1)(c)}^{(x_2, y_2)} \left(\frac{\partial U^*}{\partial x} dx + \frac{\partial U^*}{\partial y} dy\right)$$

$$+ i \int_{(x_1, y_1)(c)}^{(x_2, y_2)} \left(\frac{\partial V^*}{\partial x} dx + \frac{\partial V^*}{\partial y} dy\right)$$

$$= U^*(x_2, y_2) - U^*(x_1, y_1) + i[V^*(x_2, y_2) - V^*(x_1, y_1)]$$

$$= \Phi(x_2, y_2) - \Phi(x_1, y_1),$$

the integration of the "exact differentials" in the penultimate step being justified as in the proof of Theorem 4-7.

EXAMPLE 1.   Since the function $f(z) = z^2$ is regular through-out the entire plane, and since the function $\Phi(z) = z^3/3$ is an indefinite integral of $f(z)$, we have $\int_{z_1(c)}^{z_2} z^2 dz = z_2{}^3/3 - z_1{}^3/3$ for any two points z_1 and z_2 and any path c which joins them.

EXAMPLE 2.   The function $f(z) = e^y(\sin x + i \cos x)$ is reg-ular throughout the entire plane.   Hence it has an indefinite integral, which we may find by adding an arbitrary constant to the function $F(z)$ obtained by putting, for $Z = X + iY$,

$$F(Z) = \int_{0(c_1)}^{X} f(z)dz + \int_{X(c_2)}^{X+iY} f(z)dz,$$

where c_1 is the segment from $x = 0$ to $x = X$ of the x axis and c_2 is the segment from $y = 0$ to $y = Y$ of the line $x = X$.   The inte-gration gives us

$$\begin{aligned} F(Z) &= \int_0^X (\sin x + i \cos x)dx + i \int_0^Y e^y(\sin X + i \cos X)dy \\ &= [-\cos x + i \sin x]_0^X + [ie^y(\sin X + i \cos X)]_0^Y \\ &= ie^Y(\sin X + i \cos X) + 1. \end{aligned}$$

EXAMPLE 3.   Let R be the entire plane except the non-positive real axis.   If Z is any point in R, and c is any path which joins the points 1 and Z and lies in R, then

$$\int_{1(c)}^{Z} \frac{dz}{z} = \operatorname{Ln} z \Big|_1^Z = \operatorname{Ln} Z.$$

4-12. Problems.

1.   Evaluate as expeditiously as possible, c being any path which joins the lower and upper limits of integration:

(a) $\int_{0(c)}^{1+i} z^3 dz,$

(b) $\int_{-\pi i(c)}^{\pi i} e^z dz,$

(c) $\int_{1(c)}^{i} \cos z dz.$

2.   Let R be the entire plane except the non-positive x axis and c any convenient path that joins the points 1 and i and lies in R.   Evaluate $\int_{1(c)}^{i} z^{1/2} dz$ if

(a) $z^{1/2}$ represents the principal value of the power,

(b) $z^{1/2}$ represents the other value.

3. Let R be the interior of the circle $|z - 1| = 1$. Find the indefinite integral of $1/z$ within R by evaluating $\int_{1(c)}^{Z} dz/z$, where c consists of the segment of the x axis from 1 to X, followed by the segment of the line $x = X$ from X to $Z \equiv X + iY$. Compare your answer to Ln Z as defined in §2-9.

4. Find by integration the indefinite integral of
$$f(z) = e^{-x}(\cos y - i \sin y).$$

5. By using a different region R from that in Example 3, §4-11, evaluate $\int_{1(c)}^{Z} dz/z$, where Z is in the third quadrant and c is the portion of the x axis from 1 to $|Z|$ followed by the smallest *positive* arc in the circle $r = |Z|$. Why is the answer not Ln Z?

*6. Evaluate $\oint_{(c)} dz/z$, where c is the circle $|z| = a$. Use the parametrization $z = ae^{it}$, $0 \le t \le 2\pi$.

*7. Evaluate $\oint_{(c)} z^n dz$, where c is the circle of problem 6 above and n is a negative integer other than -1.

8. Given a function $f(x, y)$ for which $\partial f/\partial x = \partial f/\partial y = 0$ at all points in a connected open region R, show that f must be constant in R. [Let (x_1, y_1) and (x_2, y_2) be any two points in R, and c a staircase path that joins them, with segments parallel to one or the other of the axes. Express the difference $f(x_2, y_2) - f(x_1, y_1)$ as a sum of appropriate integrals over the several segments of c.]

9. Evaluate $\int_{-i(c)}^{i} dz/(1 - z^2)$, where c is the segment of the y axis from $y = -1$ to $y = 1$
   (a) by decomposing the integrand into partial fractions and using Theorem 4-16,
   (b) by calculating the integral directly.

10. Use problem 8 to "improve" the statements of Theorems 2-5 and 2-6.

11. It is possible to "improve" our statement of Morera's theorem by replacing the term "path" by the term "staircase path with segments parallel to the axes." Explain.

12. Theorem 4-10 is a restatement of Theorem 4-9. Make the same sort of restatement of Cauchy's and Morera's theorems as given in the text.

*13. Prove Theorem 4-13 by writing

$$\int_{z_1(c)}^{z_2} f(z)dz = \int_{z_0(c_2)}^{z_2} f(z)dz - \int_{z_0(c_1)}^{z_1} f(z)dz,$$

where c_2 and c_1 are appropriately chosen paths, and by using (4-8).

The Taylor Expansion

5

5-1. Equivalent Paths of Integration.

The theorem of this section is basic to both this and the following chapter.

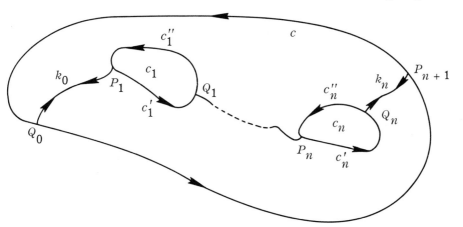

Figure 5-1

THEOREM 5-1. (Fig. 5-1) *Let c be a simple closed path and $c_1, c_2, \ldots, c_n$ simple closed paths on the interior of c no two of which nor their interiors have any points in common. If $f(z)$ is regular on c, on each of the c_j, and at all points on the interior of c that are not on the interior of any of the c_j, then*

$$\oint_{(c)} f(z)dz = \sum \oint_{(c_j)} f(z)dz,$$

where integration is, as usual, counterclockwise in all cases.

In general, the possibility of the construction used in the proof below is not easy to prove.   [See, for example, H. E. Vaughan, "On Two Theorems of Plane Topology," *Am. Math. Monthly* 60 (1953), 462–468.]   However, in all of the applications in this book the constructions can be seen to be quite straightforward.

Proof.   Let Q_0 and P_{n+1} be any two distinct points on c, and P_j, Q_j any two distinct points on c_j for $j = 1, 2, \ldots, n$.   Let k_j be a simple path from Q_j to P_{j+1} for $j = 0, 1, \ldots, n$, all points of the k_j being on the interior of c and none on the interior of any of the c_j, and none of the k_j having any points in common with any other of the k_j.   Let c_j' be the partial arc of c_j that is traversed counterclockwise from P_j to Q_j and c_j'' the remaining arc, also so traversed, for $j = 1, 2, \ldots, n$.

Let c'' be the path consisting of k_0, followed by† $-c_1''$, followed by k_1, followed by $-c_2''$, followed by $\ldots$, followed by k_{n-1}, followed by $-c_n''$, followed by k_n, followed by the partial arc, in the counterclockwise sense, of c from P_{n+1} to Q_0.   And let c' be the path consisting of $-k_n$, followed by $-c_n'$, followed by $-k_{n-1}$, followed by $-c_{n-1}'$, followed by $\ldots$, followed by $-k_1$, followed by $-c_1'$, followed by $-k_0$, followed by the partial arc, in the counterclockwise sense, of c from Q_0 to P_{n+1}.   Then both c' and c'' are closed paths, each of which lies in a simply connected open region of regularity of $f(z)$, so that, by Cauchy's Theorem,

$$\oint_{(c')} f(z)dz = \oint_{(c'')} f(z)dz = 0.$$

Hence, also

$$\oint_{(c')} f(z)dz + \oint_{(c'')} f(z)dz = 0.$$

But the contributions to these integrals along the k_j cancel, whereas those along the $-c_j'$ and the $-c_j''$ combine to give integrals around the $-c_j$, and the remaining contributions combine to give the integral around c.   Finally, then,

$$\oint_{(c)} f(z)dz + \sum \oint_{(-c_j)} f(z)dz = 0,$$

from which the conclusion of the theorem follows immediately.

5-2.   Cauchy's Integral Formula.

No less basic than the preceding theorem to Chapters 5 and 6 is the one which follows.

† Reversal of direction along a path p is denoted by $-p$.   Thus

$$\int_{(-p)} f(z)dz = -\int_{(p)} f(z)dz.$$

THEOREM 5-2.   (Cauchy's Integral Formula)   *If $f(z)$ is regular throughout a simply connected open region R, Z is any point in R, and c is any simple closed path in R with Z on its interior, then*

$$f(Z) = \frac{1}{2\pi i} \oint_{(c)} \frac{f(z)dz}{z - Z}.$$

Proof.   The function $g(z) \equiv f(z)/(z - Z)$ is regular in R except at Z.   Enclosing Z in a sufficiently small circle c_1, we may therefore satisfy the conditions of Theorem 5-1 and write

$$\oint_{(c)} \frac{f(z)dz}{z - Z} = \oint_{(c_1)} \frac{f(z)dz}{z - Z}.$$

Now a possible parametrization of c_1 is given by $z = Z + ae^{i\varphi}$, $0 \le \varphi \le 2\pi$, where a is the radius of c_1, so that we have

$$\oint_{(c)} \frac{f(z)dz}{z - Z} = \int_0^{2\pi} \frac{f(Z + ae^{i\varphi})ae^{i\varphi}id\varphi}{ae^{i\varphi}}$$

$$= i \int_0^{2\pi} [u^*(a, \varphi) + iv^*(a, \varphi)]d\varphi, \tag{5-1}$$

where $u^*(a, \varphi)$ and $v^*(a, \varphi)$ are the real and imaginary parts, respectively, of $f(Z + ae^{i\varphi})$.   [The asterisks are used to avoid confusion with the standard notations $u(x, y)$ and $v(x, y)$.]   Since $u^*(a, \varphi)$ and $v^*(a, \varphi)$ are continuous functions of φ, we can apply the mean-value theorem for integrals to the last member in (5-1), obtaining

$$\oint_{(c)} \frac{f(z)dz}{z - Z} = 2\pi i[u^*(a, \varphi') + iv^*(a, \varphi'')]$$

for certain values φ' and φ'' of φ, or

$$\oint_{(c)} \frac{f(z)dz}{z - Z} = 2\pi i\{R[f(z')] + iI[f(z'')]\}, \tag{5-2}$$

where z' and z'' both lie on c_1.   Since (5-2) is true for all sufficiently small a, we may let a tend to zero to obtain—since $f(z)$ is continuous—

$$\oint_{(c)} \frac{f(z)dz}{z - Z} = 2\pi i\{R[f(Z)] + iI[f(Z)]\} \equiv 2\pi if(Z),$$

as was to be proved.

It is interesting to observe that Cauchy's integral formula implies that the values of $f(z)$ are determined *throughout the interior of c* by the values *on c* alone.

EXAMPLE 1. If $f(z) \equiv 0$ for z on the path c of Cauchy's Integral Formula and $f(z)$ is regular within and on c, then $f(z) \equiv 0$ for z on the interior of c.

EXAMPLE 2. $e^i = \dfrac{1}{2\pi i} \oint_{(c)} \dfrac{e^z dz}{z - i}$ if c is the circle $|z| = 2$.

EXAMPLE 3. If the origin is on the interior of a simple closed path c, then

$$\oint_{(c)} \frac{\sin z}{z} \, dz = 2\pi i \left[\frac{1}{2\pi i} \oint_{(c)} \frac{\sin z}{z - 0} \, dz \right] = 2\pi i \sin 0 = 0.$$

5-3. Taylor's Series.

In Chapter 3 it was seen that a power series in $z - z_0$ converges within its circle of convergence to a function that is regular there. A remarkable fact is the following converse.

THEOREM 5-3. (Taylor's Series) *If $f(z)$ is regular in an open region R, z_0 is any point in R, and K is a circle with center at z_0, which with its interior lies in R, then, for every Z on the interior of K,*

$$f(Z) = \sum_{0}^{\infty} a_n (Z - z_0)^n,$$

where $\qquad\qquad\qquad\qquad\qquad\qquad\qquad\qquad\qquad\qquad$ (5-3)

$$a_n = \frac{1}{2\pi i} \oint_{(K)} \frac{f(z) dz}{(z - z_0)^{n+1}} = \frac{1}{n!} f^{(n)}(z_0) \quad \text{for } n = 0, 1, \ldots.$$

This is the *Taylor series* for $f(Z)$ at the point z_0.

Proof. First, we recall that

$$1 + r + r^2 + \cdots + r^n = \frac{1 - r^{n+1}}{1 - r}$$

if $r \neq 1$, so that

$$\frac{1}{1 - r} = 1 + r + r^2 + \cdots + r^n + \frac{r^{n+1}}{1 - r}$$

for such values of r. Hence the coefficient of $f(z)$ in the integrand of Cauchy's integral formula can be written

$$\frac{1}{z - Z} = \frac{1}{(z - z_0) - (Z - z_0)} = \frac{1}{(z - z_0)\left(1 - \dfrac{Z - z_0}{z - z_0}\right)}$$

$$= \frac{1}{z - z_0}\left[1 + \frac{Z - z_0}{z - z_0} + \left(\frac{Z - z_0}{z - z_0}\right)^2\right.$$

$$\left. + \cdots + \left(\frac{Z - z_0}{z - z_0}\right)^n + \frac{\left(\dfrac{Z - z_0}{z - z_0}\right)^{n+1}}{1 - \dfrac{Z - z_0}{z - z_0}}\right],$$

so that

$$f(Z) \equiv \frac{1}{2\pi i}\oint_{(K)} \frac{f(z)dz}{z - Z}$$

$$= \frac{1}{2\pi i}\oint_{(K)} \frac{f(z)dz}{z - z_0} + \frac{1}{2\pi i}\oint_{(K)} \frac{f(z)dz}{(z - z_0)^2}(Z - z_0)$$

$$+ \cdots + \frac{1}{2\pi i}\oint_{(K)} \frac{f(z)dz}{(z - z_0)^{n+1}}(Z - z_0)^n + R_{n+1}(Z),$$

where

$$R_{n+1}(Z) = \frac{1}{2\pi i}\oint_{(K)} \frac{(Z - z_0)^{n+1}f(z)dz}{(z - z_0)^{n+2}\left(1 - \dfrac{Z - z_0}{z - z_0}\right)}$$

$$= \frac{1}{2\pi i}\oint_{(K)}\left(\frac{Z - z_0}{z - z_0}\right)^{n+1}\frac{f(z)dz}{z - Z}.$$

To determine the behavior of $R_{n+1}(Z)$ as $n \to \infty$, let r_0 be the radius of K and B a *bound* on $|f(z)|$ for z on K—that is, a number such that $|f(z)| \le B$ for all z on K—and put $r_1 = |Z - z_0|$. [The existence of the bound follows from the continuity of $|f(z)|$ on K. A proof is given in Chapter 9.] Then, using Theorem 4-1, we see that

$$|R_{n+1}(Z)| \le \frac{1}{2\pi}2\pi r_0\left(\frac{r_1}{r_0}\right)^{n+1}\frac{B}{r_0 - r_1} = \frac{Br_0}{r_0 - r_1}\left(\frac{r_1}{r_0}\right)^{n+1},$$

and, therefore, since $r_1 < r_0$, that $R_{n+1}(Z) \to 0$ as $n \to \infty$. If we now put

$$S_n(Z) = \sum_0^n \frac{1}{2\pi i}\oint_{(K)} \frac{f(z)dz}{(z - z_0)^{k+1}}(Z - z_0)^k,$$

we have

$$|S_n(Z) - f(Z)| = |R_{n+1}(Z)| \to 0 \quad \text{as } n \to \infty,$$

so that the series of which $S_n(Z)$ is the nth partial sum converges to $f(Z)$. This establishes the first part of (5-3). The remaining part follows from the remarks subsequent to Theorem 3-8.

Two corollaries to the preceding theorem follow.

THEOREM 5-4. *If $f(z)$ is regular at a point Z, then $f^{(n)}(Z)$ exists and is given by the formula*

$$f^{(n)}(Z) = \frac{n!}{2\pi i} \oint_{(c)} \frac{f(z)dz}{(z - Z)^{n+1}} \quad \text{for } n = 0, 1, \ldots,$$

where c is any simple closed path about Z within and on which $f(z)$ is regular.

Proof. With c such a path as is named in the theorem, let K be a circle about Z which with its interior lies on the interior of c. The conclusion follows upon application of Theorem 5-1 and the last equality in (5-3).

The significance of this result—that *regularity implies differentiability to all orders*—cannot be overemphasized.

The next theorem is an immediate consequence of Theorem 5-4.

THEOREM 5-5. *From Cauchy's integral formula the derivatives of $f(Z)$ can be obtained by "differentiation under the integral sign."*

It is to be noted that the proof of Theorem 5-3 implies that the radius of convergence of the series in (5-3) is at least r_0. It may actually be larger—even infinite. The Taylor series given in (5-3) is often called the *expansion of $f(Z)$ about the point z_0* or the *expansion of $f(Z)$ in powers of $Z - z_0$.*

EXAMPLE 1. To find the expansion of $f(z) = e^z$ about the point πi we may compute

$$f^{(n)}(\pi i) = e^{\pi i} = -1 \quad \text{for } n = 0, 1, \ldots$$

and hence obtain

$$e^z = -1 - (z - \pi i) - \frac{(z - \pi i)^2}{2!} - \cdots - \frac{(z - \pi i)^n}{n!} - \cdots.$$

Observe that this expansion is valid for all z, since the radius r_0 of the circle K in the proof of Theorem 5-3 can be taken as large as desired.

EXAMPLE 2. To find the expansion of $f(z) = 1/z$ in powers of $(z - i)$ we may proceed expeditiously thus:

$$\frac{1}{z} = \frac{1}{i + (z - i)} = \frac{1}{i} \frac{1}{1 + \dfrac{z - i}{i}}$$

$$= \frac{1}{i}\left[1 - \frac{z - i}{i} + \frac{(z - i)^2}{-1} - \cdots + (-1)^n \frac{(z - i)^n}{i^n} + \cdots \right]$$

$$= -i + (z - i) + i(z - i)^2 - \cdots + i^{n-1}(z - i)^n + \cdots,$$

the expansion being valid (since the r_0 in the proof of Theorem 5-3 may be taken arbitrarily close to 1 but not greater than 1) for $|z - i| < 1$.

EXAMPLE 3. To evaluate $\oint_{(c)} z^3 dz/(z^3 - 3z + 2)$, where c is any simple closed path which passes through neither of the roots of $z^3 - 3z + 2 \equiv (z - 1)^2(z + 2)$, we may observe that the integrand can be written as

$$1 + \frac{3z - 2}{z^3 - 3z + 2} = 1 + \frac{8/9}{z - 1} + \frac{1/3}{(z - 1)^2} - \frac{8/9}{z + 2}.$$

(The possibility of decomposing the *general* complex rational function into "partial fractions" will be proved in Chapter 6.) Now $\oint_{(c)} 1dz = 0$ for every c, since the function 1 is regular everywhere; $\oint_{(c)} dz/(z - 1)$ equals zero or $2\pi i$ according as the point 1 is not or is on the interior of c; $\oint_{(c)} dz/(z + 2)$ equals zero or $2\pi i$ according as the point -2 is not or is on the interior of c; and $\oint_{(c)} dz/(z - 1)^2 = 0$ if the point 1 is not on the interior of c and equals $2\pi i d(1)/dz = 0$ (again) if the point 1 *is* on the interior of c. Hence the entire integral can be evaluated in the several cases.

5-4. Problems.

*1. As in real calculus, a Taylor series in powers of z is called a *Maclaurin series*. By use of the theory in §5-3, find the Maclaurin series for the functions

(a) e^z;
(b) a^z, $a \neq 0$ (principal value);
(c) $\sin z$;
(d) $\cos z$;
(e) $\text{Ln}\,(1 + z)$;
(f) $(1 + z)^m$ (principal value).

2. Obtain the expansion of Example 1, §5-3, by first writing $e^z = e^{\pi i}e^{(z-\pi i)}$ and then writing the second factor in its known series form.

3. Expand $f(z) = e^z$ about the point $1 + i$.

4. Expand $f(z) = z^3$ about the point i.

5. Expand $f(z) = \sin z$ about the point $-i$.

*6. Expand $f(z) = \text{Ln } z$ in powers of $(z - 1)$.

7. Expand $f(z) = 1/(1 - z)$ in powers of $(z + i)$.

8. About which points does the function $f(z) = \tan z$ not have an expansion? (See problem 6 of §2-12.) Find the first three terms in the expansion of this function in powers of $z - i$.

9. Observing that $f(z) \equiv 3z/(z^2 + z - 2)$ can be written as

$$f(z) = \frac{1}{z - 1} + \frac{2}{z + 2} = -\frac{1}{1 - z} + \frac{1}{1 + z/2},$$

and applying the general formula

$$\frac{1}{1 - w} = 1 + w + w^2 + \cdots + w^n + \cdots \quad \text{for } |w| < 1$$

to both fractions, and collecting terms, find the value of $f^{(n)}(0)$ in terms of n.

10. By first writing the function of problem 9 above in the form

$$f(z) = -\frac{1}{(1 - z_0) - (z - z_0)} + \frac{2}{(2 + z_0) + (z - z_0)},$$

obtain the expansion of $f(z)$ in powers of $z - z_0$ for general $z_0 \neq 1, -2$.

11. By using the series in powers of z for $\sin z$, show how the integral in Example 3, §5-2, can be evaluated directly by means of Cauchy's theorem.

*12. By appealing to the last equality in (5-3), give the values of $\oint_{(c)} \sin z\, dz/z^n$, where n is a positive integer and c is any simple closed path with the origin on its interior.

13. If c is a simple closed path with the point z_0 on its interior, evaluate

(a) $\oint_{(c)} \dfrac{e^z}{z - z_0}\, dz$,

(b) $\oint_{(c)} \dfrac{e^z}{(z - z_0)^n}\, dz$ for positive integral n.

*14. Show that $\oint_{(c)} dz/(z - z_0)^n = 0$ if n is any integer except 1 and that $\oint_{(c)} dz/(z - z_0) = 2\pi i$, where c is a simple closed path with z_0 on its interior. Solve both by the methods of the examples of §5-3 and by replacing c by the circle

$$z = z_0 + \rho e^{i\varphi}$$

for constant ρ and calculating directly. (Compare to problems 6 and 7 of §4-12.)

15. Evaluate $\oint_{(c)} z^k dz/(z - z_0)^n$, where k and n are positive integers and c is any simple closed path with z_0 on its interior.

16. Evaluate $\oint_{(c)} dz/(2 - z)z^n$, where c is the circle $|z| = 1$.

17. Explain (theoretically) how to evaluate $\oint_{(c)} R(z)dz$, where $R(z)$ is any rational function of z, and c is any simple closed path that passes through no points at which $R(z)$ is undefined.

*18. Let $z_1, z_2, \ldots, z_k$ be the distinct roots of a polynomial

$$P(z) \equiv a_0 + a_1 z + a_2 z^2 + \cdots + a_n z^n$$

of degree not less than 2. Then (assuming partial fractions decomposition theory)

$$\frac{1}{P(z)} = \frac{A_1}{z - z_1} + \frac{A_2}{z - z_2} + \cdots + \frac{A_k}{z - z_k}$$

$$+ \text{ terms of the form } \frac{B_{jl}}{(z - z_j)^l} \text{ with } l > 1.$$

Show that $A_1 + A_2 + \cdots + A_k = 0$ by observing that $\oint_{(K)} dz/P(z)$ has the same value on all circles $|z| = R$ for sufficiently large R and that $\lim_{R \to \infty} \oint_{(K)} dz/P(z) = 0$. (Recall Example 5 of §2-2 and use Theorem 4-1.)

*19. Show that, if the Taylor expansion of a function $f(z)$ about a point z_0 has radius of convergence R, $f(z)$ cannot be regular throughout the interior of any circle about z_0 of radius larger than R.

20. State the radius of convergence of the Taylor series for the function $f(z) \equiv \sec z/(z + i)$ in powers of

(a) z,

(b) $z - i$.

21. Let $f(z)$ be regular for $|z - z_0| < r_0$ and suppose that the Taylor expansion of $f(z)$ about z_0 has radius of convergence $R > r_0$. Does it follow that $f(z)$ is regular for $|z - z_0| < R$?

22. Show how to evaluate the integral of Example 3, §5-3, without using the partial fractions decomposition. [Note that the integrand may be written as $\varphi(z)/(z + 2)$ in the neighborhood of $z = -2$, where $\varphi(z) \equiv z^3/(z - 1)^2$ is regular at that point, and that the integrand may be written as $\psi(z)/(z - 1)^2$ in the neighborhood of $z = 1$ for an appropriate function $\psi(z)$ that is regular at *that* point.]

5-5. Identity Theorems.

THEOREM 5-6. *If two functions $f(z)$ and $g(z)$ are regular within a circle $K: |z - z_0| = a$ and coincide on an infinite sequence of distinct points $z_1, z_2, \ldots, z_k, \ldots$ for which $\lim_{k \to \infty} z_k = z_0$, then $f(z) = g(z)$ throughout the interior of K.*

Proof. By Theorem 5-3, $f(z)$ and $g(z)$ have expansions

$$f(z) = a_0 + a_1(z - z_0) + a_2(z - z_0)^2 \\ + \cdots + a_n(z - z_0)^n + \cdots,$$

$$g(z) = b_0 + b_1(z - z_0) + b_2(z - z_0)^2 \\ + \cdots + b_n(z - z_0)^n + \cdots,$$

both of which are valid at least for all z on the interior of K. Assuming (as we may) that the z_k are all on the interior of K, we have

$$a_0 + a_1(z_k - z_0) + a_2(z_k - z_0)^2 + \cdots + a_n(z_k - z_0)^n + \cdots$$
$$= b_0 + b_1(z_k - z_0) + b_2(z_k - z_0)^2 + \cdots + b_n(z_k - z_0)^n + \cdots \qquad (5\text{-}4)$$

for $k = 1, 2, \ldots$. If we now let $k \to \infty$ and invoke the continuity of the two series, we may conclude that

$$a_0 + a_1 0 + a_2 0 + \cdots + a_n 0 + \cdots$$
$$= b_0 + b_1 0 + b_2 0 + \cdots + b_n 0 + \cdots,$$

or that $a_0 = b_0$. Suppressing the common value of a_0 and b_0 from equation (5-4) and dividing the resulting equation by $z_k - z_0$, which we may assume $\neq 0$, we obtain

$$a_1 + a_2(z_k - z_0) + \cdots + a_n(z_k - z_0)^{n-1} + \cdots$$
$$= b_1 + b_2(z_k - z_0) + \cdots + b_n(z_k - z_0)^{n-1} + \cdots$$

for $k = 1, 2, \ldots$. Recalling problem 14 of §3-6, we see that letting $k \to \infty$ now gives us $a_1 = b_1$. Continuing in this way, we find that $a_n = b_n$ for $n = 0, 1, \ldots$, which completes the proof. (Compare problem 10 of §3-8.)

THEOREM 5-7.   *If two functions $f(z)$ and $g(z)$ are regular within a circle K and coincide on an infinite sequence of distinct points z_1, $z_2, \ldots, z_n, \ldots$ for which $\lim_{n \to \infty} z_n = z_0$ and z_0 is on the interior of K, then $f(z) = g(z)$ throughout the interior of K.*

Proof.   Let us assume that z_0 is not the center of K, this case having been disposed of in Theorem 5-6. If K_0 is the circle about z_0 that is internally tangent to K, then $f(z) = g(z)$ throughout the interior of K_0 by Theorem 5-6. Letting z' be any point on the interior of K which is not on the interior of K_0, we may join z_0 to z' by a line segment l and construct a succession of circles with centers on l, starting with K_0, each center on the interior of the preceding circle and the last circle containing z' on its interior. Successive applications of Theorem 5-6 establish the identity of $f(z)$ and $g(z)$ on the interior of each of these circles so that, in particular, $f(z') = g(z')$, which is all that we needed to prove.

5-6.   The Algebra of Power Series.

Given two power series in z, $f(z) \equiv \sum a_n z^n$ and $g(z) \equiv \sum b_n z^n$, with positive radii of convergence R_1 and R_2, respectively, Theorems 3-2 and 3-4 ensure that

$$f(z) \pm g(z) = \sum (a_n \pm b_n)z^n \quad \text{for } |z| < \min (R_1, R_2)$$

(see also problems 3 and 15 of §3-6), and that

$$f(z)g(z) = \sum (a_0 b_n + a_1 b_{n-1} + \cdots + a_n b_0)z^n \quad \text{for } |z| < \min (R_1, R_2).$$

What, finally, of the possibility of expressing the quotient $q(z) \equiv f(z)/g(z)$ as a power series in z?

First, $q(z) = f(z)r(z)$, where $r(z) = 1/g(z)$, so that $q(z)$ will be regular where both $f(z)$ and $r(z)$ are regular. But $r(z)$ will be regular where $g(z)$

is regular *and does not vanish.* And if $g(0) \neq 0$, then there is a positive
number R_3 such that $g(z)$ does not vanish for $|z| < R_3$, so that $r(z)$ is
regular for $|z| < \min (R_2, R_3)$. Hence $q(z)$ has a series expansion

$$\sum c_n z^n = q(z) \equiv \frac{f(z)}{g(z)}$$

if $g(0) \neq 0$, the expansion being valid at least for $|z| < R \equiv \min (R_1, R_2, R_3)$.
From the power series expressions for $f(z)$ and $g(z)$, it follows that

$$\sum a_n z^n = (\sum b_n z^n)(\sum c_n z^n) \equiv \sum (b_0 c_n + b_1 c_{n-1} + \cdots + b_n c_0) z^n$$

for $|z| < R$. Therefore, by Theorem 3-9, the c's must satisfy the equations

$$
\begin{aligned}
a_0 &= b_0 c_0, \\
a_1 &= b_0 c_1 + b_1 c_0, \\
a_2 &= b_0 c_2 + b_1 c_1 + b_2 c_0, \\
&\cdots \\
a_n &= b_0 c_n + b_1 c_{n-1} + \cdots + b_n c_0, \\
&\cdots
\end{aligned}
\tag{5-5}
$$

Since $b_0 \equiv g(0) \neq 0$, (5-5) yields, in succession,

$$
\begin{aligned}
c_0 &= \frac{a_0}{b_0}, \\
c_1 &= \frac{a_1 - b_1 c_0}{b_0}, \\
c_2 &= \frac{a_2 - b_1 c_1 - b_2 c_0}{b_0}, \\
&\cdots \\
c_n &= \frac{a_n - b_1 c_{n-1} - b_2 c_{n-2} - \cdots - b_n c_0}{b_0}, \\
&\cdots
\end{aligned}
\tag{5-6}
$$

It is therefore to be concluded that $f(z)/g(z) = \sum c_n z^n$ for

$$|z| < \min (R_1, R_2, R_3),$$

where the c's are given by (5-6). But, as can be easily verified, these c's are
precisely the numbers d_n obtained in the conventional long division process:

$$\frac{d_0 + d_1 z + \cdots + d_n z^n + \cdots}{b_0 + b_1 z + \cdots + b_n z^n + \cdots \overline{)\, a_0 + a_1 z + \cdots + a_n z^n + \cdots}}.$$

Thus the quotient $f(z)/g(z)$ can be obtained as a power series in z by
elementary long division, the result so obtained being valid within every

circle about the origin within which $f(z)$ and $g(z)$ are regular and $g(z)$ does not vanish.

EXAMPLE. Provided only that $|z| < 1$ the quotient $\sin z/(1 - z)$ is given through the third power of z in the display below:

$$
\begin{array}{l}
z + z^2 + 5z^3/6 + \cdots \\
\hline
z \qquad\quad - \quad z^3/6 + \cdots \,\big|\, 1 - z \\[4pt]
z - z^2 \\
\hline
\quad\ z^2 \\[4pt]
\quad\ z^2 - z^3 \\
\hline
\qquad\quad 5z^3/6 \\[4pt]
\qquad\qquad \cdots
\end{array}
$$

5-7. The Maximum Modulus Principle.

In the proof of Theorem 5-8, the following will be assumed (a proof is given in Chapter 9). *If $f(x)$ is a continuous real function of the real variable x for $a \le x \le b$ and if $F(x) \le M$ there, then $\int_a^b F(x)dx \le M(b - a)$, equality holding if and only if $F(x) = M$ throughout the interval.*

THEOREM 5-8. (Maximum Modulus Theorem) *Let $f(z)$ be regular on the interior of a circle $K_a\colon |z - z_0| = a$ and not constant there. Then there are points z arbitrarily close to z_0 for which $|f(z)| > |f(z_0)|$.*

A sharper form of the maximum modulus theorem will be proved in Chapter 9.

Proof. If the conclusion is false, then $|f(z)| \le |f(z_0)|$ throughout the interior of some circle $K_b\colon |z - z_0| = b\ (\le a)$. But then, if ρ is an otherwise arbitrary number for which $0 < \rho < b$ and K_ρ is the circle $|z - z_0| = \rho$, we have

$$2\pi|f(z_0)| = \left| \oint_{(K\rho)} \frac{f(z)dz}{z - z_0} \right| \le \oint_{(K\rho)} \left| \frac{f(z)}{z - z_0} \right| ds$$

$$= \int_0^{2\pi} \frac{|f(z)|}{\rho}\, \rho d\theta = \int_0^{2\pi} |f(z)| d\theta \le |f(z_0)| 2\pi,$$

so that—since the first and last members of this extended inequality are equal—$|f(z)| = |f(z_0)|$ on the entire circumference of K_ρ. Next, because of the arbitrariness of ρ, we may conclude that $|f(z)|$ is constant throughout the interior of K_b. Problem 12 of §2-7 now assures us that $f(z)$ is itself constant throughout the interior of K_b, and Theorem 5-7 extends this property throughout the interior of K_a, thereby completing the proof.

5-8. Problems.

1. Show that, in the hypotheses of Theorem 5-7, the phrase "a circle K" can be replaced by "a square S." By "an ellipse E." (In Chapter 7 it will be shown that the phrase may be replaced by "a connected open region" in general.)

2. The functions $f(z) = \sin(1/z)$ and $g(z) = 0$ (identically) are regular in the circle $|z - 1| < 1$ and coincide in value at the points $z = 1/n\pi$ for $n = 1, 2, \ldots$. Explain why this situation does not violate Theorem 5-7.

3. Prove Theorem 5-8 by noting that, under the hypotheses, $f(z) = a_0 + a_k(z - z_0)^k + a_{k+1}(z - z_0)^{k+1} + \cdots$, $a_k \neq 0$, for all z on the interior of K_a; putting $z - z_0 = \rho e^{i\varphi}$; and so choosing φ that $|f(z)| > |a_0| \equiv |f(z_0)|$ for sufficiently small $\rho > 0$. What does this analysis prove in addition to the one in the text?

4. Sketch the graph of $M \equiv f(R) \equiv \max_{|z|=R} |z^2 + z|$ for $R \geq 0$.

5. If $f(z)$ is regular for $|z| \leq 1$ and $f(1/p_n) = 1/p_n^2$, where p_n is the nth prime number and $n = 1, 2, \ldots$, find $f(1/10)$.

6. If $f(z)$ is regular for $|z| \leq 1$, $f'(1/n) = 1/n$ for $n = 1, 2, \ldots$, and $f(1) = 1$, find $f(i/2)$.

7. Using the series in powers of z for $\sin z$ and $\cos z$, derive, by multiplication of series, the series in powers of z for the function $f(z) = \sin z \cos z$ and check your answer by writing down at once the series for $\frac{1}{2} \sin 2z$.

8. First stating for which values of z the long division process with power series in z is guaranteed by the theory to be valid, find the terms through the one in z^3 obtained by this process for the following quotients:

    (a) $(1 + z)/(1 - z)$,
    (b) $\cos z/(1 + z)$,
    (c) $\tan z \equiv \sin z/\cos z$,
    (d) $(1 - z)/e^z$,
    (e) $\dfrac{\sin z}{e^z - 1} \equiv \dfrac{\sin z/z}{(e^z - 1)/z}$ for $z \neq 0$.

9. Write down the equations (5-6) in case $q(z)$ is the *reciprocal* of $g(z)$. For which values of z does our theory guarantee the validity of the expansion obtained from these equations?

10. Use the equations derived in problem 9 to find the terms through the one in z^4 in the expansion of sec $z \equiv 1/\cos z$ near the origin.

11. Using the fact that $1/(1 - z) = 1 + z + z^2 + \cdots + z^n + \cdots$ for $|z| < 1$, check the quotient obtained in the Example of §5-6 by *multiplication* of series.

12. Repeat problem 11 with reference to problem 8(a).

13. Repeat problem 11 with reference to problem 8(b).

14. Check the quotient obtained in problem 8(d) by writing $(1 - z)/e^z = (1 - z)e^{-z}$ and using the formula for multiplication of series.

15. If in the hypotheses of Theorem 5-6 the condition "regular" is replaced by "continuous," the conclusion of the theorem does not necessarily follow. Construct an example to illustrate this point.

5-9. Entire Functions. Liouville's Theorem.

If a function $f(z)$ is regular for all z, it is called *entire* or *integral*. Among the special functions already discussed in this book several are entire; examples are e^z, sin z, and all polynonials. It is clear that the Taylor expansion of an entire function about any point $z = z_0$ has infinite radius of convergence. As might be expected, the behavior of entire functions for large values of $|z|$ is generally complicated. The first theorem of this section has to do with *bounded entire* functions. A function $f(z)$ is said to be *bounded* (on a point set S) if there is a number B such that $|f(z)| \leq B$ for all z (in S).

THEOREM 5-9. (Liouville's Theorem) *An entire function which is bounded reduces to a constant.*

Proof. We are given a number B such that $|f(z)| \leq B$ for all z, however large $|z|$ may be. But in the expansion

$$f(z) = a_0 + a_1 z + \cdots + a_k z^k + \cdots,$$

we have, by the first formula for a_n in (5-3),

$$|a_k| \leq \frac{1}{2\pi} \int_0^{2\pi} \frac{B}{r_0^{k+1}} r_0 d\theta \equiv \frac{B}{r_0^k}.$$

for every $r_0 > 0$, so that $a_k = 0$ for $k > 0$, and we have $f(z) = a_0$, a constant.

Before extending Liouville's theorem, it is necessary to introduce a new concept. Let two functions $f(z)$ and $g(z)$ be defined for all z of sufficiently large magnitude and both become numerically infinite as $|z| \to \infty$. If there are two positive numbers A and B such that $0 < A \le |f(z)/g(z)| \le B$ whenever $|z|$ is sufficiently large, one says that $f(z)$ *becomes infinite to the same order (of magnitude) as* $g(z)$ or that $f(z)$ *is of the order of* $g(z)$, as $|z|$ becomes infinite. Since if $f(z)$ is a polynomial,

$$f(z) = a_0 + a_1 z + \cdots + a_n z^n, \qquad a_n \ne 0,$$

the ratio $|f(z)/z^n|$ tends to $|a_n| \ne 0$ as $|z| \to \infty$, it is clear that a polynomial of degree greater than zero becomes infinite to the same order as its term of highest degree, as $|z|$ becomes infinite.

THEOREM 5-10.   *If an entire function $f(z)$ is of the order of z^n as $|z|$ becomes infinite, where n is a positive integer, then $f(z)$ is a polynomial of degree n.*

Proof.   As in the proof of Liouville's theorem, let us write $f(z) = a_0 + a_1 z + \cdots + a_k z^k + \cdots$ and use the first formula for a_n in (5-3).   It follows that

$$|a_k| \le \frac{1}{2\pi} \oint_{(K)} \frac{B|z|^n}{|z|^{k+1}} \, ds$$

for some positive number B and all circles $K: |z| = r_0$ for which r_0 is sufficiently large.   Hence

$$|a_k| \le \frac{1}{2\pi} \int_0^{2\pi} \frac{B r_0^{\,n}}{r_0^{\,k+1}} \, r_0 d\theta \equiv \frac{B}{r_0^{\,k-n}}$$

for such r_0, so that $a_k = 0$ for $k > n$.   Thus $f(z)$ is a polynomial of degree not greater than n.   But if the degree of $f(z)$ is *less* than n, then $\lim_{|z| \to \infty} |f(z)/z^n| = 0$, so that $f(z)$ is not of the order of z^n. This completes the proof.

The behavior of entire functions that are not polynomials is radically different, and such functions are given the special name *transcendental entire functions*.   Thus a transcendental entire function is a function $f(z)$ whose power series expansion $a_0 + a_1 z + \cdots + a_n z^n + \cdots$ has infinite radius of convergence and an infinite number of non-vanishing coefficients.

THEOREM 5-11.   *If $f(z)$ is entire, a necessary and sufficient condition that it be transcendental is that, for each positive number B*

and each non-negative integer n, there be points z of arbitrarily large magnitude such that $|f(z)| > B|z^n|$.

Proof. The sufficiency is obvious, since if $f(z)$ is a polynomial of degree k, then $|f(z)| \leq B|z^k|$ for some B and all z—at least of sufficiently large magnitude. The necessity follows from the fact that, if $|f(z)| \leq B|z^k|$ for some B, some non-negative integer n, and all z of sufficiently large magnitude, then, as in the proof of Theorem 5-10, the a_k in the expansion of $f(z)$ in powers of z vanish for all $k > n$.

5-10. The Fundamental Theorem of Algebra.

THEOREM 5-12. (Fundamental Theorem of Algebra) *Given any polynomial $P(z) \equiv a_0 + a_1 z + \cdots + a_n z^n$, $a_n \neq 0$, of degree $n > 0$, the equation $P(z) = 0$ has a root.*

In some phrasings of "the fundamental theorem" it is stated that the equation $P(z) = 0$ has exactly n roots, multiplicity being taken into account. But, once the existence of a *single* root has been established, this apparently more precise statement is an immediate consequence of the "factor theorem" of elementary algebra. (See also problems 10 and 11 of §6-17.)

Proof. If we suppose the contrary, then $f(z) \equiv 1/P(z)$ is entire and therefore has an expansion $f(z) = \sum b_k z^k$ that is valid for all z. Moreover (Example 5 of §2-2), for $|z| > R$, say, $|f(z)| < 2/|a_n| \, |z^n|$. Hence, by Theorems 5-11 and 5-10, $f(z)$ must be constant, which is impossible.

5-11. Problems.

1. Which of the circular and hyperbolic functions are entire?

2. If $f(z)$ and $g(z)$ are both entire transcendental functions, give reasons why it must, or may not, be true that the following are entire transcendental functions:
   (a) $S(z) \equiv f(z) + g(z)$,
   (b) $P(z) \equiv f(z)g(z)$.

3. Given that both $f(z)$ and $g(z)$ are entire, state a condition under which it is certain that the quotient $f(z)/g(z)$ will be entire. Is the function $F(z) \equiv \sin z/z$ for $z \neq 0$ and $F(0) \equiv 1$ entire?

4. If $f(z)$ and $g(z)$ are entire, why is $f[g(z)]$ entire?

5. Show that a polynomial $P(z)$ is bounded inside of every circle.

6. Show that the function $f(z) \equiv 1/(z^2 - z) \equiv 1/(z - 1) - 1/z$ is bounded on the set S consisting of the entire plane from which have been removed the interiors of the circles $|z| = r_1$ and $|z - 1| = r_2$, where r_1 and r_2 are any two positive numbers.

7. Using problem 5 and what is suggested by problem 6, make a statement about a set of points on which the general rational function $R(z) \equiv P(z)/Q(z)$ [$P(z)$ and $Q(z)$ polynomials having no non-constant factor in common] is bounded.

8. (a) If $f(z)$ becomes infinite to the same order as $g(z)$ as $|z| \to \infty$, show that $g(z)$ becomes infinite to the same order as $f(z)$ as $|z| \to \infty$.

   (b) If $f(z)$ becomes infinite to the same order as $g(z)$ as $|z| \to \infty$ and $g(z)$ becomes infinite to the same order as $h(z)$ as $|z| \to \infty$, show that $f(z)$ becomes infinite to the same order as $h(z)$ as $|z| \to \infty$.

*9. If $\lim_{|z| \to \infty} |f(z)/g(z)|$ exists—call it L—state a necessary and sufficient condition in terms of L that, if $|g(z)| \to \infty$ as $|z| \to \infty$, then $f(z)$ will become infinite to the same order as $g(z)$.

10. On the basis of the analysis in §5-9, what is the most that can be said of an entire function $f(z)$ if there are positive constants a and b such that, for all z of sufficiently large magnitude,

    (a) $|f(z)| \le a|z^b|$?

    (b) $|f(z)| \ge a|z^b|$?

11. Let $f(z)$ be a transcendental entire function that never vanishes. Show that, for each $B > 0$ and each positive integer n, there are points z of arbitrarily large magnitude such that $|f(z)| < B/|z^n|$.

12. If $\lim_{|z| \to \infty} |f(z)|/|z|^n$ exists finite and non-zero for some real number n, where $f(z)$ is entire, then n must be a non-negative integer. Why?

13. If $f(z)$ is entire,

$$\lim_{|z| \to \infty} \frac{f(|z|)}{|z|} = 2, \quad \text{and} \quad \lim_{|z| \to \infty} \frac{f(-|z|)}{|z|} = 3,$$

then $f(z)$ is transcendental. Why?

5-12. The Casorati-Weierstrass Theorem for Transcendental Entire Functions.

The behavior of transcendental entire functions $f(z)$ for z of large magnitude is even more spectacular than Theorem 5-11 seems to suggest. Two preliminary theorems are needed in the present development, however, before the main result can be derived in Theorem 5-15.

THEOREM 5-13. *Let $f(z)$ be regular in an open region R, except possibly at the point z_0 in R. Let K be a circle of radius r_1 and center z_0, which, with its interior, lies in R, and let k be any circle concentric with K and of radius r_0 for which $r_0 < r_1$. Then, if Z is any point in the open annular region A between k and K,*

$$f(Z) = \frac{1}{2\pi i} \oint_{(K)} \frac{f(z)dz}{z - Z} - \frac{1}{2\pi i} \oint_{(k)} \frac{f(z)dz}{z - Z}. \tag{5-7}$$

Proof. The function $f(z)/(z - Z)$ of z is regular at all points of R except Z and, possibly, z_0. Letting k' be a circle with center at Z and of radius so small that k' lies in A, we obtain (applying Theorem 5-1)

$$\frac{1}{2\pi i} \oint_{(K)} \frac{f(z)dz}{z - Z} = \frac{1}{2\pi i} \oint_{(k)} \frac{f(z)dz}{z - Z} + \frac{1}{2\pi i} \oint_{(k')} \frac{f(z)dz}{z - Z}. \tag{5-8}$$

But, by Cauchy's integral formula, the last term in (5-8) is $f(Z)$, and this is all that we needed to show.

THEOREM 5-14. *Let $f(z)$ be regular in an open region R, except possibly at the point z_0 in R. Let K be a circle of radius r_1 and center z_0, which, with its interior, lies in R. Then, if $f(z)$ is bounded within and on K, the series representation (5-3) is valid with the first formula for a_n for every Z on the interior of K, except possibly z_0.*

Proof. The conditions of the proof of Theorem 5-13 are met upon construction of the circle k of that theorem, provided that $r_0 < |Z - z_0|$. Hence (5-7) obtains, so that

$$\left| f(Z) - \frac{1}{2\pi i} \oint_{(K)} \frac{f(z)dz}{z - Z} \right| = \left| \frac{1}{2\pi i} \oint_{(k)} \frac{f(z)dz}{z - Z} \right|. \tag{5-9}$$

Since the left-hand side of (5-9) is independent of r_0, it will suffice to show that the right-hand side tends to zero as $r_0 \to 0$, for the left-hand side will then be known to be zero and we will have the integral representation of $f(Z)$ from which the series in (5-3) was developed. Then let $|f(z)| \leq B$ for z within and on K, parameterize k thus: $z - z_0 = r_0 e^{i\varphi}$, and note that

$$|z - Z| \geq |Z - z_0| - r_0 > 0$$

for all z on k. We now have

$$\left| \frac{1}{2\pi i} \oint_{(k)} \frac{f(z)dz}{z - Z} \right| \leq \frac{1}{2\pi} \int_0^{2\pi} \frac{B}{|Z - z_0| - r_0} r_0 d\varphi$$

$$= \frac{Br_0}{|Z - z_0| - r_0},$$

and the last expression here does indeed tend to zero with r_0.

THEOREM 5-15. (Casorati-Weierstrass Theorem for Transcendental Entire Functions) *A transcendental entire function $f(z)$ takes on values arbitrarily close to every (complex) number outside of every circle.*

Proof. If the conclusion is false, then there is some number w_0 to which $f(z)$ does not come arbitrarily close outside of every circle. Hence there is also a positive number R such that $f(z)$ does not come arbitrarily close to w_0 for $|z| > R$, which means that there is a positive number B such that $1/|f(z) - w_0| \leq B$ for all z numerically greater than R. Putting $g(z) = 1/[f(z) - w_0]$, we may therefore conclude that $g(z)$ is regular, non-constant, and bounded for $|z| > R$. If, further, we put $h(z) = g(1/z)$, then $h(z)$ is regular, non-constant, and bounded for $0 < |z| < 1/R$. According to Theorem 5-14, this implies that there is a non-negative integer k such that

$$h(z) = a_k z^k + a_{k+1} z^{k+1} + \cdots,$$
$$a_k \neq 0, \quad \text{for } 0 < |z| < 1/R,$$

so that $h(z)/z^k \to a_k \neq 0$ as $z \to 0$. Hence $z^k g(z) \to a_k \neq 0$ as $|z| \to \infty$ and therefore

$$\left| \frac{f(z)}{z^k} \right| \equiv \left| \frac{w_0}{z^k} + \frac{1}{z^k g(z)} \right| \to \frac{1}{|a_k|} \quad \text{as } |z| \to \infty.$$

But problem 9 of §5-11 and Theorem 5-10 now assure us that $f(z)$ is a polynomial, contrary to hypothesis.

Picard's theorem states that a transcendental entire function actually *takes on* all (complex) values with, at most, one exception, outside of every circle, but no simple proof seems to be known.

5-13. Problems.

1. Verify Picard's theorem for

    (a) $f(z) = \sin z$. Are any values not taken on?
    (b) $f(z) = e^z$. Are any values not taken on?

2. The function $f(z) = \tanh z$ is, to be sure, not entire. (Why?) However, it does pretty well at taking on arbitrary values. Which ones does it not take on?

3. Show that, under the conditions of Theorem 5-14, $f(z)$ can be defined or "redefined" if necessary at z_0 in such a way that $f(z)$ will be regular throughout the interior of R.

4. Let $f(z)$ be regular in an open region R, except possibly at a point z_0 in R, and let $\lim_{z \to z_0} (z - z_0)^k f(z)$ exist finite and nonzero for some positive integer k. By using Theorem 5-14, show that $f(z)$ can be expressed as a series of the form

$$f(z) = \frac{a_{-k}}{(z - z_0)^k} + \frac{a_{-k+1}}{(z - z_0)^{k-1}} + \cdots + \frac{a_{-1}}{z - z_0}$$
$$+ a_0 + a_1(z - z_0) + \cdots + a_n(z - z_0)^n$$
$$+ \cdots, \ a_{-k} \neq 0$$

   for all z sufficiently near, but not equal to, z_0. Do we have the same result if the integer k is negative?

5. Picard's theorem implies that a transcendental entire function takes on each (complex) value, with at most one exception, *an infinite number of times* outside of every circle. Explain.

6. Assuming the truth of Picard's theorem, prove the Casorati-Weierstrass theorem.

7. Let $f(z)$ be a transcendental entire function. Show that

    (a) there is a sequence of points $\{z_n\}$ such that $|z_n| \to \infty$ and $|f(z_n)| \to \infty$ as $n \to \infty$,
    (b) the function $g(z) \equiv 1/f(z)$, where $f(z) \neq 0$, takes on values arbitrarily close to every (complex) number outside of every circle.

8. If $f(z)$ is a transcendental entire function, $\epsilon > 0$ is arbitrary, and w_0 is an arbitrary (complex) number, the Casorati-Weierstrass theorem assures us that there are points z of arbitrarily large magnitude such that $|f(z) - w_0| < \epsilon$. Show that, if n is an arbitrary positive number, there are also points ζ of arbitrarily large magnitude such that $|f(\zeta) - w_0| < \epsilon/|\zeta|^n$.

9. Show that Picard's theorem is equivalent to the statement that every transcendental entire function that fails to vanish anywhere outside of some circle must take on the value 1 at some point outside of every circle.

The Laurent Expansion

6

6-1. Neighborhoods.

For convenience, the set of points interior to any circle with center at z_0 is called a *neighborhood* of z_0. (An alternative definition that is sometimes used is examined in problem 1 of §6-3.) The usefulness of this simple concept is now illustrated.

EXAMPLE 1. If a function is regular at a point z_0, then it is regular at each point z in some neighborhood of z_0.

EXAMPLE 2. If $f(z)$ is regular at a point z_0 and takes on the value $f(z_0)$ at some point other than z_0 in every neighborhood of z_0, then $f(z)$ is constant in a neighborhood of z_0. (This is a consequence of Theorem 5-6).

The phrase "in the neighborhood of z_0" is sometimes met; it means "in every sufficiently small neighborhood of z_0."

EXAMPLE 3. If $f(z)$ is continuous at z_0, then $|f(z)| < |f(z_0)| + 1$ in the neighborhood of z_0.

6-2. Limit Points of Sets and of Sequences.

Given a point set S, a point z_0 is said to be a *limit point of S* if an infinite number of different points of S lie in every neighborhood of z_0.

EXAMPLE 1. Every point in the plane is a limit point of the set of points $z \equiv x + iy$ for which both x and y are rational numbers.

99

EXAMPLE 2.   Every point of an open set is a limit point of that set.

EXAMPLE 3.   A set consisting of only a finite number of points has no limit points.

EXAMPLE 4.   The set of the points z_n of a convergent sequence $\{z_n\}$ has either no limit points (in case there are only a finite number of distinct values among the z_n) or exactly one limit point.

The idea of a limit point of a *sequence* is rather subtly different from that of a limit point of a *set*.   Given a sequence $\{z_n\}$, a point Z is said to be a *limit point of* $\{z_n\}$ if in every neighborhood of Z lie an infinite number of the z_n with different subscripts—whether these z_n are different from one another or not.   As indicated in Example 4 above, the *set* S of the points represented by the elements of a sequence need have no limit points; yet every convergent *sequence* has a (unique) limit point.

EXAMPLE 5.   The *sequence*

$$\frac{2}{1}, -\frac{3}{2}, \frac{4}{3}, \ldots, \frac{(-1)^n(n+2)}{n+1}, \ldots$$

has two limit points, namely 1 and -1.   The *set* S of the points represented by the elements of this sequence has also two limit points, again 1 and -1.

EXAMPLE 6.   The *sequence* $\{[1 + (-1)^n]n/(n+1)\}$ has two limit points, namely 0 and 2.   The *set* S of the points represented by the elements of this sequence, however, has only one limit point, namely 2.

6-3. Problems.

*1.   A neighborhood of a point z_0 is sometimes defined as *any* open set of which z_0 is a member.   Calling a neighborhood so defined a "general neighborhood" and a neighborhood as defined in the text a "circular neighborhood," show that

(a)   if a property P is true of every point z in some general neighborhood of a point z_0, then it is true of every point z in some circular neighborhood of z_0, and conversely;

(b)   if a property P is true of some point z in every general neighborhood of a point z_0, then it is true of some point z in every circular neighborhood of z_0, and conversely.

2. For each sequence $\{z_n\}$ below, name the limit points of the
    sequence and the limit points of the set of the points repre-
    sented by the elements of the sequence.
    (a) $1/1, 1/2, 2/1, 1/3, 2/2, 3/1, \ldots, 1/k, 2/(k-1), \ldots, (k-1)/2,$
         $k/1, \ldots,$
         which includes all of the positive rational numbers
         (each, indeed, an infinite number of times);
    (b) $\{i^n\}$;
    (c) $\{i^n/n\}$;
    (d) $\{[1 + 1000/n]\}$, where the symbol $[p]$ means the greatest
         integer which is not greater than p;

    (e) $0, 3/2, 0, 5/4, \ldots, \dfrac{1 + (-1)^{n+1}}{2} \dfrac{n+2}{n+1}, \ldots$

*3. Show that z_0 is a limit point of a set S if and only if in every
     neighborhood of z_0 lies a point of S different from z_0.

*4. Show that Z is a limit point of a sequence $\{z_n\}$ if and only if
     in every neighborhood of Z lies an element z_n of $\{z_n\}$ with n
     arbitrarily large.

5. Name the limit points of each of the sets S of points $z \equiv x + iy$
    that satisfy the conditions below.
    (a) $|z| < 2$,
    (b) x is rational and y is integral,
    (c) either $|z| \geq 1$ or z is a positive irrational real,
    (d) $x \neq 0$ and $y = \sin(1/x)$.

6. What are the limit points of the set S that consists of the
    positive integers plus the reciprocals of the negative integers?

7. The limit points of a sequence necessarily include the limit
    points of the set of the points represented by the elements of
    the sequence. Why?

6-4. Singular Points.

Given a function $f(z)$, a point z_0 is said to be a *singularity*, or a *singular
point*, of $f(z)$ if in every neighborhood of z_0 are regular points of $f(z)$,
whereas z_0 itself is not a regular point of $f(z)$. An *isolated singular point*
z_0 is a singular point throughout some neighborhood of which $f(z)$ is
regular except at z_0 itself. [Following an unfortunate but well-established
terminology, one calls a neighborhood of a point z_0 from which z_0 itself
has been deleted a *deleted neighborhood* of z_0. Thus an isolated singular

point is a singular point throughout some deleted neighborhood of which $f(z)$ is regular.]

EXAMPLE 1. The function $f(z) = 1/(1 - z)$ has one and only one singular point, $z = 1$. It is an isolated singularity.

EXAMPLE 2. The function $f(z) = \operatorname{cosec} 1/z$ has an isolated singular point at $z = 1/n\pi$ for $n = \pm 1, \pm 2, \ldots$. The point $z = 0$ is also a singularity, but it is not an isolated one.

6-5. Problems.

1. Show that a limit point of singularities of a function $f(z)$ is a (non-isolated) singularity of $f(z)$.

2. What are the singular points of the function $f(z)$ defined as
   (a)   sech z?
   (b)   sin $(1/z)$?
   (c)   sec $(1/z)$?
   (d)   0 if z is real and positive, and 1 otherwise?
   (e)   0 if $R(z) < 0$ and 1 if $R(z) \geq 0$?

*3. Show that the singular points of the function $f(z) = \operatorname{Ln} z$ compose the non-positive part of the x axis. What are the singular points of the function $f(z)$ defined as Ln z for $-\pi/2 < \operatorname{Arg} z \leq \pi$ and as Ln $z + 2\pi i$ for $-\pi < \operatorname{Arg} z \leq -\pi/2$? Note the artificiality of the singularities here—except the point $z = 0$—in connection with the multi-valued function Ln z.

4. What are the singularities of the function
$$f(z) = 1 + z + z^2 + \cdots + z^n + \cdots, \quad |z| < 1$$
   for
   (a) $|z| \leq 1$?
   (b)   all z?

   A certain artificiality is involved here, since the definition of $f(z)$ can be *extended* in such a way that the only singularity in the plane is the point $z = 1$. (See Example 1 of §6-4.)

6-6. The Laurent Expansion.

A "doubly infinite" series $\sum_{-\infty}^{\infty} z_n$ is said to *converge* if and only if each of the two series $\sum_{0}^{\infty} z_n$ and $\sum_{1}^{\infty} z_{-n}$ converges; its *value*, in case it converges, is defined to be the sum of the values of these two series. Thus the series $\sum_{-\infty}^{\infty} 2^{-|n|}$ converges; its value is 3.

THEOREM 6-1.   (Laurent's Series)   (Fig. 6-1)   *Let two circles,* $K: |z - z_0| = r_0$ *and* $k: |z - z_0| = r_1$, *where* $0 < r_1 < r_0$, *and the annular open region A between them lie in an open region R of*

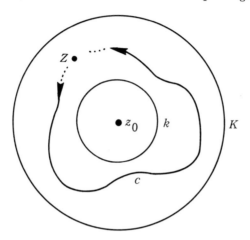

Figure 6-1

regularity of a function $f(z)$. *Let c be any simple closed path in A that contains k on its interior.* *Then, for every Z in A,*

$$f(Z) = \sum_{-\infty}^{\infty} a_n (Z - z_0)^n, \tag{6-1}$$

where

$$a_n = \frac{1}{2\pi i} \oint_{(c)} \frac{f(z)dz}{(z - z_0)^{n+1}}, \quad n = \ldots, -1, 0, 1, \ldots. \tag{6-2}$$

This is the *Laurent expansion* of $f(Z)$ about z_0, or the *Laurent series* for $f(Z)$ in powers of $Z - z_0$, for Z in A.   Note that the behavior of $f(z)$—even its definition—within the neighborhood of z_0 is entirely irrelevant.

Proof.   Reviewing the proof of Theorem 5-13, we see that

$$f(Z) = \frac{1}{2\pi i} \oint_{(K)} \frac{f(z)dz}{z - Z} - \frac{1}{2\pi i} \oint_{(k)} \frac{f(z)dz}{z - Z}. \tag{6-3}$$

Now, as in the proof of Theorem 5-3, we may assume that $f(z)$ is bounded on both K and k, so that there is a number B such that

$|f(z)| \leq B$ for all z on K or k. The first term on the right-hand side of (6-3) is therefore expressible as

$$\frac{1}{2\pi i}\oint_{(K)}\frac{f(z)dz}{z-Z} = \sum_{0}^{\infty} a_n(Z-z_0)^n, \quad a_n = \frac{1}{2\pi i}\oint_{(K)}\frac{f(z)dz}{(z-z_0)^{n+1}}, \quad (6\text{-}4)$$

the derivation being precisely that in the proof of Theorem 5-3. As for the second term on the right-hand side of (6-3), we may proceed in a fashion suggested by that proof:

$$\frac{1}{z-Z} = -\frac{1}{(Z-z_0)-(z-z_0)} = -\frac{1}{(Z-z_0)\left(1-\dfrac{z-z_0}{Z-z_0}\right)}$$

$$= -\frac{1}{Z-z_0}\left[1 + \frac{z-z_0}{Z-z_0} + \left(\frac{z-z_0}{Z-z_0}\right)^2\right.$$

$$\left. +\cdots+\left(\frac{z-z_0}{Z-z_0}\right)^{n-1} + \frac{\left(\dfrac{z-z_0}{Z-z_0}\right)^n}{1-\dfrac{z-z_0}{Z-z_0}}\right],$$

so that

$$-\frac{1}{2\pi i}\oint_{(k)}\frac{f(z)dz}{z-Z} = \frac{1}{2\pi i}\oint_{(k)}f(z)dz(Z-z_0)^{-1}$$

$$+\frac{1}{2\pi i}\oint_{(k)}(z-z_0)f(z)dz(Z-z_0)^{-2}$$

$$+\cdots+\frac{1}{2\pi i}\oint_{(k)}(z-z_0)^{n-1}f(z)dz(Z-z_0)^{-n}$$

$$+ R_{n+1}(Z),$$

where

$$R_{n+1}(Z) = \frac{1}{2\pi i}\oint_{(k)}\frac{(z-z_0)^n f(z)dz}{(Z-z_0)^{n+1}\left(1-\dfrac{z-z_0}{Z-z_0}\right)}$$

$$= \frac{1}{2\pi i}\oint_{(k)}\left(\frac{z-z_0}{Z-z_0}\right)^n\frac{f(z)dz}{Z-z}.$$

Putting $r_2 = |Z-z_0|$ and using Theorem 4-1, we see that

$$|R_{n+1}(Z)| \leq \frac{1}{2\pi}2\pi r_1\left(\frac{r_1}{r_2}\right)^n\frac{B}{r_2-r_1} = \frac{Br_1}{r_2-r_1}\left(\frac{r_1}{r_2}\right)^n,$$

and, therefore, that $R_{n+1}(Z) \to 0$ as $n \to \infty$. Exactly as in the proof of Theorem 5-3 at the corresponding point, we may conclude that

$$-\frac{1}{2\pi i}\oint_{(k)}\frac{f(z)dz}{z-Z} = \sum_1^\infty a_{-n}(Z-z_0)^{-n},\tag{6-5}$$

$$a_{-n} = \frac{1}{2\pi i}\oint_{(k)}\frac{f(z)dz}{(z-z_0)^{n+1}}.$$

Finally, by Theorem 5-1, both K and k in the formulas (6-4) and (6-5) for the a_n may be replaced by c. Substitution in (6-3) of the expansions in (6-4) and (6-5), with these replacements, completes the proof.

Writing, in the Laurent expansion just derived,

$$f_+(z) = \sum_0^\infty a_n(z-z_0)^n,\tag{6-6}$$

$$f_-(z) = \sum_1^\infty a_{-n}(z-z_0)^{-n},\tag{6-7}$$

one has $f(z) = f_+(z) + f_-(z)$. Since the series in (6-6) converges for certain values of z for which $|z-z_0|$ is less than r_0 but arbitrarily close to r_0, the radius of convergence of that series is at least r_0, so that $f_+(z)$ is regular for all z on the interior of K. And if one puts $w = 1/(z-z_0)$ in (6-7), then

$$f_-(z) = \sum_1^\infty a_{-n}w^n.\tag{6-8}$$

But the series in (6-7) converges for certain values of z for which $|z-z_0|$ is greater than r_1 but arbitrarily close to r_1, so that the series in (6-8) converges for certain values of w for which $|w|$ is less than $1/r_1$ but arbitrarily close to $1/r_1$. Hence the radius of convergence of the series in (6-8) is at least $1/r_1$, so that $f_-(z)$ is a regular function of w for all z for which $|w| < 1/r_1$. But $f_-(z)$ is therefore a regular function of z for all z on the exterior of the circle k.

It is to be noted that, if $a_{-1} = a_{-2} = \cdots = 0$, then $f(z) = f_+(z)$ for z in A, so that the Laurent series may be regarded as a generalization of the Taylor series.

6-7. Uniqueness of the Laurent Expansion.

As is the case with the Taylor series, the Laurent series for a given function is unique.

THEOREM 6-2.   *Let two circles,*

$$K: |z - z_0| = r_0$$

and

$$k: |z - z_0| = r_1,$$

where $0 < r_1 < r_0$, and the annular open region A between them lie in an open region R of regularity of a function $f(z)$. If $f(z)$ can be represented by a doubly infinite series of the form

$$f(z) = \sum_{-\infty}^{\infty} b_n(z - z_0)^n \tag{6-9}$$

for every z in A, then $b_n = a_n$ for $n = \ldots, -1, 0, 1, \ldots,$ where the a_n are given by (6-2).

Proof.   Let K' be the circle $|z - z_0| = r'$, where r' is any number between r_1 and r_0, and write $f(z) = g_+(z) + g_-(z)$, where

$$g_+(z) = \sum_{0}^{\infty} b_n(z - z_0)^n, \tag{6-10}$$

$$g_-(z) = \sum_{1}^{\infty} b_{-n}(z - z_0)^{-n}. \tag{6-11}$$

If the analysis which we applied above to the series in (6-6) and (6-7) is now applied to the series in (6-10) and (6-11), we must conclude, in particular, that $g_+(z)$ is regular within and on K' and that the series in (6-11) is absolutely convergent for z on K':

$$\sum_{1}^{\infty} |b_{-n}| r'^{-n} \text{ converges.} \tag{6-12}$$

The regularity of $g_+(z)$ implies that $\oint_{(K')} g_+(z)dz = 0$, so that $\oint_{(K')} g_-(z)dz$ exists and we have

$$\oint_{(K')} f(z)dz = \oint_{(K')} g_-(z)dz.$$

It follows that, for arbitrary $n > 0$,

$$\oint_{(K')} f(z)dz = \sum_{1}^{n} b_{-k} \oint_{(K')} (z - z_0)^{-k}dz + R_{n+1}, \tag{6-13}$$

where

$$R_{n+1} = \oint_{(K')} \sum_{n+1}^{\infty} b_{-k}(z - z_0)^{-k}dz.$$

Since

$$|R_{n+1}| \le \oint_{(K')} \sum_{n+1}^{\infty} |b_{-k}| r'^{-k}ds = 2\pi r' \sum_{n+1}^{\infty} |b_{-k}| r'^{-k},$$

we see, by (6-12), that $R_{n+1} \to 0$ as $n \to \infty$ and hence, by (6-13), that

$$\oint_{(K')} f(z)dz = \sum_{1}^{\infty} b_{-n} \oint_{(K')} (z - z_0)^{-n}dz. \tag{6-14}$$

(That is, the series may be "integrated termwise" around K'.) Reference to problem 14 of §5-4 now shows that all but the first of the integrals on the right-hand side of (6-14) vanish, leaving

$$\oint_{(K')} f(z)dz = b_{-1}2\pi i.$$

But then

$$b_{-1} = \frac{1}{2\pi i} \oint_{(K')} f(z)dz,$$

which equals a_{-1} as given by (6-2) with K' in the role of c.

Let us next multiply (6-9) by $(z - z_0)^{-k-1}$ for $k = \pm 1, \pm 2, \ldots$ and separate the doubly infinite series for $(z - z_0)^{-k-1}f(z)$, which results in a series with non-negative exponents and one with negative exponents [just as we separated the series (6-9) itself]. But then, exactly as in the preceding paragraph, we conclude that

$$b_k = \frac{1}{2\pi i} \oint_{(K')} \frac{f(z)dz}{(z - z_0)^{k+1}},$$

which equals a_k as given by (6-2), again with K' in the role of c. The proof is complete.

Let R_0 be the radius of convergence of the series (6-6) and $1/R_1$ that of the series (6-8) (in powers of w)—admitting the possibilities $R_0 = \infty$ and $1/R_1 = \infty$ (the latter then meaning that $R_1 = 0$). The Laurent series (6-1) then diverges for those values of z (if any) for which $|z - z_0| > R_0$ or $|z - z_0| < R_1$. But this means that $f(z)$ cannot be regular at all points z for which $R_1' < |z - z_0| < R_0'$ for any non-negative number R_1' that is less than R_1 or any number R_0' that is greater than R_0. Otherwise the derivation of the Laurent series would have led to a smaller value for R_1 or a larger value for R_0. (Compare problem 19 of §5-4.) Thus *the annular open region $R_1 < |z - z_0| < R_0$ is the largest such region which includes the region* $r_1 < |z - z_0| < r_0$ and within which the function $f(z)$ of Theorem 6-1 can be regular. (It is to be noted that this implies the impossibility of "redefining" $f(z)$ outside the circle $|z - z_0| = R_0$ or inside the circle $|z - z_0| = R_1$ so as to secure a larger such region.) In Chapter 9 it is proved that there is a singularity of $f(z)$ on the circle $|z - z_0| = R_0$ if R_0 is finite and one on the circle $|z - z_0| = R_1$ if $R_1 > 0$.

EXAMPLE 1.   The function $f(z) = 1/(z^2 - z)$ is regular for $0 < |z| < 1$ and for $|z| > 1$.   But $f(z) = 1/(z - 1) - 1/z$, so that

$$f(z) = -\frac{1}{1-z} - \frac{1}{z}$$

$$= -z^{-1} - 1 - z - z^2 - \cdots - z^n - \cdots \quad \text{for } 0 < |z| < 1,$$

$$f(z) = \frac{1}{z} \frac{1}{1 - 1/z} - \frac{1}{z} = \frac{1}{z}\left(1 + \frac{1}{z} + \frac{1}{z^2} + \cdots + \frac{1}{z^n} + \cdots\right) - \frac{1}{z}$$

$$= z^{-2} + z^{-3} + \cdots + z^{-n-1} + \cdots \quad \text{for } |z| > 1.$$

These are the (unique) Laurent expansions of this function in the relevant open regions.

EXAMPLE 2.   The function $f(z) = e^{1/z}$ is regular for $|z| > 0$. Hence the (unique) Laurent series for $f(z)$ here is

$$1 + \frac{1}{z} + \frac{1}{2!z^2} + \cdots + \frac{1}{n!z^n} + \cdots.$$

6-8.   Problems.

1.   Evaluate

(a) $\displaystyle\sum_{-\infty}^{\infty} \frac{\sin nx}{n^2 + 1}$,

(b) $\displaystyle\sum_{-\infty}^{\infty} 3^{-|n+1|}$.

2.   Show that a doubly infinite series $\sum_{-\infty}^{\infty} z_n$ converges if and only if $\sum_{N}^{\infty} z_n$ and $\sum_{-\infty}^{N-1} z_n$ both converge for every integer N, and that its value (in the case of convergence) is the sum of the values of these two series.

3.   Show that, if the region R of Theorem 6-1 is the annular open region between two circles

$$K^*: |z - z_0| = r_0^* \quad \text{and} \quad k^*: |z - z_0| = r_1^* (r_1^* < r_0^*),$$

then there is a Laurent expansion of $f(z)$ about the point z_0 for every z in R.

4.   Making use of problem 3, describe the annular open regions centered at the origin within which the function $f(z) = \tan z$ has Laurent expansions about the origin.   (See problem 6 of §2-12.)

5.   May the path c in (6-2) be replaced by k?   By K?

6. Find the Laurent expansions in the relevant annular open regions for the functions $f(z)$ given by
   (a) $1/(z^2 + z)$ if $z_0 = 0$, if $z_0 = -1$;
   (b) $1/(z^2 + 1)$ if $z_0 = 0$;
   (c) $1/(z - 1)$ if $z_0 = 0$, if $z_0 = 1$, if $z_0 = 2$;
   (d) $z/(z^2 - 1)$ if $z_0 = 0$;

   (e) $\dfrac{z + 2}{z(z^2 - 1)}$ if $z_0 = 0$, if $z_0 = 1$;

   (f) $\dfrac{z - 1}{z^2(z + 1)}$ if $z_0 = 0$.

7. What is the Laurent expansion about the origin for the function $f(z) = \sin 1/z$ in the region $|z| > 0$?

6-9. Analysis of Isolated Singular Points.   Decomposition of Rational Functions into Partial Fractions.

One of the principal uses of the Laurent expansion of a function $f(z)$ is to determine the natures of the isolated singularities of $f(z)$.   Suppose that $f(z)$ is regular in a deleted neighborhood of a point z_0.   Then the circle k in the derivation of the Laurent expansion can be taken as small as desired, so that $f_-(z)$ as given by (6-8) is an entire function of w.   Since $f_+(z)$, defined as a_0 when $z = z_0$, is regular at z_0, whereas every term in $f_-(z)$ as given by (6-7), for which $a_{-n} \neq 0$, becomes numerically infinite as $z \to z_0$, one speaks of $f_-(z)$ as the *principal part* of $f(z)$ in the neighborhood of z_0.   Cases will now be considered according to the number of non-vanishing coefficients a_{-n} in (6-7).

CASE 1.   If all of the a_{-n} are zero, then $f(z) = f_+(z)$ in a deleted neighborhood of z_0.   Hence, if z_0 is a singularity of $f(z)$, it is such only because either $f(z_0)$ is undefined or $f(z_0)$, though defined, is not equal to a_0.   By defining (or "redefining," as the case may be) $f(z_0)$ as a_0, the singularity can therefore be "removed."   In this case, then, z_0 is said to be an *isolated removable singularity*.   Hereafter the functions in this book will be assumed to have had "removed" such isolated removable singularities as they may have had.

Before the other cases are listed, it is necessary to extend the concept of "order of becoming infinite" introduced in §5-9.   Let two functions $f(z)$ and $g(z)$ be defined in a deleted neighborhood of a point z_0 and both become numerically infinite as $z \to z_0$.   If there are two positive numbers A and B such that $0 < A \leq |f(z)/g(z)| \leq B$ whenever $|z - z_0|$ is sufficiently small but different from zero, one says that $f(z)$ *becomes infinite to the same order (of magnitude) as* $g(z)$, or that $f(z)$ *is of the order of* $g(z)$ as z tends to z_0.

CASE 2. If a_{-n} is not zero for some positive n but $a_{-k} = 0$ for all $k > n$, then

$$f_-(z) = \frac{a_{-1}}{z - z_0} + \frac{a_{-2}}{(z - z_0)^2} + \cdots + \frac{a_{-n}}{(z - z_0)^n}$$
$$= a_{-1}w + a_{-2}w^2 + \cdots + a_{-n}w^n,$$

where, again, $w = 1/(z - z_0)$. Hence $f_-(z)$ is of the order of w^n as w becomes infinite, which is to say that $f_-(z)$ is of the order of $(z - z_0)^{-n}$ as z tends to z_0. One abbreviates by saying that $f_-(z)$ *becomes infinite to the nth order* as $z \to z_0$. In this case z_0 is said to be a *pole of nth order*. A pole of the first order is called a *simple pole*.

CASE 3. If an infinite number of the a_{-n} are different from 0, then $f_-(z)$ as given by (6-8) is an entire transcendental function of w, as is therefore also $g(w) \equiv a_0 + f_-(z)$. Hence $g(w)$ takes on values arbitrarily close to every (complex) number outside every circle. But this means that $a_0 + f_-(z)$ takes on values arbitrarily close to every (complex) number in every deleted neighborhood of z_0. Since moreover the function $f_+(z) - a_0$ is arbitrarily close to zero in the neighborhood of z_0, it is clear that $f(z)$ itself takes on values arbitrarily close to every (complex) number in every deleted neighborhood of z_0. This result, like the corresponding one for transcendental entire functions, is credited to Casorati and Weierstrass. There is also a Picard theorem that states that, when $f_-(z)$ has an infinite number of non-vanishing coefficients, $f(z)$ actually takes on every (complex) value in every deleted neighborhood of z_0, with at most one exception. In Case 3 the point z_0 is said to be an *isolated essential singularity*.

Thus if a function $f(z)$ is regular in a deleted neighborhood of a point z_0, it either is regular at z_0, becomes infinite to a positive integral order as $z \to z_0$, or takes on values arbitrarily close to every (complex) number in every deleted neighborhood of z_0.

It is now possible to give a simple proof of the partial fractions decomposition theory of elementary calculus. (See also problem 8 of §6-11.)

THEOREM 6-3. (Partial Fractions Decomposition of Rational Functions) *If* $f(z)$ *is the rational function* $P_m(z)/P_n(z)$, *where* $P_m(z)$ *and* $P_n(z)$ *are relatively prime polynomials (that is, having no common, non-constant, polynomial factor) of degrees* m *and* n, *respectively, and where* $P_n(z) = a(z - z_1)^{n_1}(z - z_2)^{n_2}\cdots(z - z_k)^{n_k}$,

*a ≠ 0, the z_j being all different and the n_j being positive integers,
then*

$$f(z) = \frac{a_{11}}{z - z_1} + \frac{a_{12}}{(z - z_1)^2} + \cdots + \frac{a_{1n_1}}{(z - z_1)^{n_1}}$$

$$+ \frac{a_{21}}{z - z_2} + \frac{a_{22}}{(z - z_2)^2} + \cdots + \frac{a_{2n_2}}{(z - z_2)^{n_2}}$$

$$+ \qquad \cdot \quad \cdot \quad \cdot \quad \cdot \quad \cdot \qquad (6\text{-}15)$$

$$+ \frac{a_{k1}}{z - z_k} + \frac{a_{k2}}{(z - z_k)^2} + \cdots + \frac{a_{kn_k}}{(z - z_k)^{n_k}}$$

$$+ P(z),$$

where (i) *none of* $a_{1n_1}, a_{2n_2}, \ldots, a_{kn_k}$ *is zero*, (ii) $P(z)$ *vanishes identically if* $m < n$, *and* (iii) $P(z)$ *is a polynomial of degree* $m - n$ *if* $m \geq n$.

Proof. Since $f(z)$ becomes infinite to the n_jth order at $z = z_j$ for $j = 1, 2, \ldots, k$, the z_j are poles of order n_j, respectively. The principal part of $f(z)$ at z_j is therefore of the form

$$\frac{a_{j1}}{z - z_j} + \frac{a_{j2}}{(z - z_j)^2} + \cdots + \frac{a_{jn_j}}{(z - z_j)^{n_j}},$$

with $a_{jn_j} \neq 0$, for $j = 1, 2, \ldots, k$, so that the function

$$P(z) \equiv f(z) - \sum_1^k \left(\frac{a_{j1}}{z - z_j} + \frac{a_{j2}}{(z - z_j)^2} + \cdots + \frac{a_{jn_j}}{(z - z_j)^{n_j}} \right) \qquad (6\text{-}16)$$

is entire. If now $m < n$, then $\lim_{|z| \to \infty} P(z) = 0$, so that $P(z) \equiv 0$. If $m \geq n$, then $P(z)$ is of the order of z^{m-n} as $|z| \to \infty$ and is therefore a polynomial of degree $m - n$. Solving (6-16) for $f(z)$ completes the proof.

Theorem 6-3 may obviously be rephrased thus: *A proper rational function* ($m < n$) *is the sum of its principal parts, and an improper rational function* ($m \geq n$) *is the sum of its principal parts and a polynomial.* A still shorter rephrasing is suggested in Problem Set 6-11.

6-10. The Point at Infinity.

The behavior as $|z| \to \infty$ of functions $f(z)$ that are regular for all z of sufficiently large magnitude resembles somewhat the behavior as $z \to z_0$ of functions $g(z)$ that are regular in a deleted neighborhood of z_0. One may take advantage of this resemblance by using such phrases as "$f(z)$ behaves

...at infinity" to signify that $f(1/z)$ behaves...at the origin, by writing $f(\infty)$ to indicate $\lim_{|z| \to \infty} f(z)$ when this limit exists, and by speaking of "infinity" or "the infinite point" as a regular point, pole, or isolated essential singularity according as the origin is such a point for $f(1/z)$. [It is to be recalled that removable singularities were to be supposed already "removed"; if $f(1/z)$ is regular in a deleted neighborhood of the origin, the origin is necessarily a singularity without this agreement, on the basis of failure of definition alone.]   One writes $z \to \infty$ to signify that $1/z \to 0$ (which is the same as saying that $|z| \to \infty$) and defines a *neighborhood* of the point at infinity as the set of all points for which $1/z$ lies in a neighborhood of the origin, plus the point at infinity itself.   A neighborhood of the point at infinity is therefore the *exterior* of any circle with center at the origin, plus the point at infinity.   A deleted neighborhood of the point at infinity is a neighborhood of that point, itself excepted.   All of this explains such phrases as "the finite plane" (which omits the point at infinity), "for all finite z" (excluding the point at infinity), and so on, which are often used.   The finite plane with the point at infinity adjoined is sometimes called the *closed plane*.   The "north pole" of the complex sphere (the point N in Fig. 1-2) is conventionally regarded as that point on the sphere whose projection is the point at infinity.   It is clear that the point at infinity does not enjoy all of the properties of "finite points"; it has neither argument, modulus, nor components.

To extend the ideas of §6-9 to the point at infinity, suppose that a function $f(z)$ is regular in a deleted neighborhood of the infinite point, so that $f(1/z)$ has a Laurent expansion $f(1/z) = \sum_{-\infty}^{\infty} a_n z^n$ in a neighborhood of the origin.   But this means that $f(z) = \sum_{-\infty}^{\infty} a_n z^{-n}$ in a neighborhood of the point at infinity.   The principal part there is $\sum_{-\infty}^{-1} a_n z^{-n} = \sum_{1}^{\infty} a_{-n} z^n$, so that

1. $f(z)$ is regular at the infinite point if the a_{-n} are all zero, and $f(\infty) = a_0$;

2. $f(z)$ has a pole of nth order at infinity if a_{-n} is not zero for some positive n but $a_{-k} = 0$ for all $k > n$, and $f(z)$ is of the order of z^n as $z \to \infty$;

3. $f(z)$ has an isolated essential singularity at infinity if an infinite number of the a_{-n} are different from zero, and $f(z)$ takes on values arbitrarily close to every (complex) number in every neighborhood of infinity.

EXAMPLE 1.   Every polynomial of degree $n > 0$ has exactly one singularity in the closed plane: a pole of order n at infinity.

EXAMPLE 2.   Every transcendental entire function has exactly one singularity in the closed plane: an isolated essential singularity at infinity.

EXAMPLE 3. Every rational function has only poles as singularities in the closed plane.

In summary: if z_0 is a finite point throughout a deleted neighborhood of which a function $f(z)$ is regular, then z_0 is a regular point if and only if $\lim_{z \to z_0} f(z)$ exists finite; z_0 is a pole of positive integral order n if and only if $\lim_{z \to z_0} (z - z_0)^n f(z)$ exists finite and non-zero; and z_0 is an isolated essential singularity if and only if $f(z)$ takes on values arbitrarily close to every (complex) number in every neighborhood of z_0. Notice that, since these three mutually exclusive situations exhaust all of the possibilities, any one of them is forced to occur by failure of the other two.

In further summary: if a function $f(z)$ is regular throughout a deleted neighborhood of the point at infinity, then the infinite point is a regular point if and only if $\lim_{z \to \infty} f(z)$ exists finite; the infinite point is a pole of positive integral order n if and only if $\lim_{z \to \infty} f(z)/z^n$ exists finite and non-zero; and the infinite point is an isolated essential singularity if and only if $f(z)$ takes on values arbitrarily close to every (complex) number in every neighborhood of the point at infinity. Again, any one of these mutually exclusive and exhaustive situations must occur if the other two fail.

EXAMPLE 4. Since

$$\lim_{z \to \pi/2} (z - \pi/2) \sec z = \lim_{z \to \pi/2} \frac{z - \pi/2}{-\sin (z - \pi/2)} = -1,$$

$\sec z$ has a pole of first order at the point $z = \pi/2$.

6-11. Problems.

*1. Describe a procedure for finding the a_{jk} in (6-15), the first step in which is to find $\lim_{z \to z_1} (z - z_1)^{n_1} f(z) \equiv a_{1n_1}$ and then to put $f_{1n_1} = f(z) - a_{1n_1}/(z - z_1)^{n_1}$.

2. Let $f(z)$ be regular in a deleted neighborhood of a finite point z_0. Make the best statement possible about the sort of point that z_0 is for $f(z)$ if, for *every* sequence of points $z_1, z_2, \ldots$ with z_0 as (sole) limit point, we have as $n \to \infty$

   (a) $f(z_n) \to 7$,
   (b) $f(z_n) \to \infty$,
   (c) $(z_n - z_0)^n f(z_n) \to -2$,
   (d) $(z_n - z_0)^2 f(z_n) \to 0$.

3. Let $f(z)$ be regular in a deleted neighborhood of a finite point z_0. Make the best statement possible about the sort

of point that z_0 is for $f(z)$ if, for *some particular* sequence of different points $z_1, z_2, \ldots$ with z_0 as (sole) limit point, we have as $n \to \infty$

(a) $f(z_n) \to 7$,
(b) $f(z_n) \to \infty$,
(c) $(z_n - z_0)^2 f(z_n) \to -2$,
(d) $(z_n - z_0)^2 f(z_n) \to 0$,
(e) $(z_n - z_0)^n f(z_n) \to 2$.

4. Let $f(z)$ have a pole of order $n > 0$ at a finite point z_0, and let $g(z)$ have a pole of order $m \geq n$ at z_0. Make the best statement possible about the sort of point that z_0 is for the function

(a) $f(z)g(z)$;
(b) $f(z)/g(z)$;
(c) $g(z)/f(z)$;
(d) $f(z) + g(z)$, taking special care with the case $m = n$.

5. Let $f(z)$ be regular for all finite z of modulus greater than $1/2$. Make the best statement possible about the sort of point that the point at infinity is for $f(z)$ if, as $n \to \infty$ (n is a positive integer),

(a) $f(n) \to 0$,
(b) $f(n)/n \to 0$,
(c) $f(n)/n^{3/2} \to 0$,
(d) $nf(n) \to 0$.

*6. If z_0 is a pole of positive order n of a function $f(z)$, show that there is a function $g(z)$ which is regular at z_0, for which $g(z_0) \neq 0$, and such that $f(z) = g(z)/(z - z_0)^n$ in a deleted neighborhood of z_0.

7. What sorts of singularities are the following points for the associated functions?

(a) The infinite point for $\cos z$.
(b) The origin for $\operatorname{cosech} z$.
(c) The origin for $\operatorname{cosec}^2 z$.
(d) The point $z = 1$ for $1/\operatorname{Ln} z$.
(e) The general finite singularity of $\tan z$ for that function.
     (See problem 6 of §2-12.)

*8. The partial fractions decomposition, which is familiar from elementary calculus, has terms of the form

$$\frac{(ax + b)}{(cx^2 + dx + e)^p},$$

where p is a positive integer. Reconcile this decomposition with that displayed in (6-15).

9. Give meanings to the following statements from the "arithmetic of (complex) infinity." By a is meant "a finite number."

(a) $\infty \pm a = \infty$,
(b) $\infty\, a = \infty$ if $a \neq 0$,
(c) $\infty\, \infty = \infty$,
(d) $a/0 = \infty$ if $a \neq 0$,
(e) $\infty\, 0$ is undefined,
(f) $\infty \pm \infty$ is undefined.

*10. Shorten the rephrasing of Theorem 6-3 by making use of the concept of the principal part at infinity of a function that has an isolated singularity there.

11. Let $g(z) = 1/f(z)$, where $f(z)$ has an isolated essential singularity at a point z_0.

(a) Show that z_0 is not necessarily an isolated singularity of $g(z)$.

(b) What sort of singularity of $g(z)$ is z_0 if it *is* an isolated singularity?

(c) Construct a function $f(z)$ such that z_0 is an isolated singularity for both $f(z)$ and $g(z)$.

6-12. Zeros.

"Order of approaching zero" may be defined in the same manner as "order of becoming infinite." Let two functions $f(z)$ and $g(z)$ be defined in a deleted neighborhood of a point z_0 (or of the infinite point) and both tend to zero as $z \to z_0$ (or as $z \to \infty$). If there are two positive numbers A and B such that $0 < A \leq |f(z)/g(z)| \leq B$ whenever z is in some deleted neighborhood of z_0 (or the infinite point), one says that $f(z)$ *approaches zero to the same order (of magnitude)* as $g(z)$, or that $f(z)$ *is of the order of* $g(z)$ *as z tends to* z_0 (*or becomes infinite*). Thus a polynomial whose constant term is zero approaches zero as $z \to 0$ to the same order as its non-vanishing term of lowest degree.

If $f(z)$ approaches 0 as $z \to z_0$ to the same order as $(z - z_0)^n$ for some positive number n, then $f(z)$ is said, more briefly, to approach zero *to the nth order*. And if $f(z)$ approaches zero as $z \to \infty$ to the same order as $1/z^n$, one says again that $f(z)$ approaches zero *to the nth order*.

If a function $f(z)$, defined in a neighborhood of a point z_0 but not constant in any neighborhood of z_0, vanishes when $z = z_0$, then one calls z_0

a *zero* of $f(z)$; and if, for a function $f(z)$ that is defined in a neighborhood of the infinite point but not constant in any neighborhood of that point, it is true that $\lim_{z \to \infty} f(z) = 0$, then one says that the point at infinity is a *zero* of $f(z)$. A zero of $f(z)$ is said to be *of the nth order* if $f(z)$ approaches zero to the nth order as z tends to the zero. In particular, a zero of the first order is called a *simple zero*.

THEOREM 6-4. *If a non-constant function $f(z)$ is regular at one of its zeros, say z_0, then $f(z)$ tends to zero as $z \to z_0$ to a positive integral order n; indeed $\lim_{z \to z_0} f(z)/(z - z_0)^n$ exists, finite and nonzero.*

Proof. In a neighborhood of z_0 we have

$$f(z) = a_n(z - z_0)^n + a_{n+1}(z - z_0)^{n+1} + \cdots,$$

where $n > 0$ and $a_n \neq 0$. Hence the limit asserted in the theorem exists and equals a_n.

There is an interesting relationship between zeros and poles.

THEOREM 6-5. *If a non-constant function $f(z)$ is regular in a deleted neighborhood of a point z_0 and z_0 is a pole (or a zero) of nth order of $f(z)$, then $g(z) \equiv 1/f(z)$ is regular in a deleted neighborhood of z_0, and z_0 is a zero (or a pole) of nth order of $g(z)$. In this statement "the point at infinity" may be read for "z_0."*

Proof. If z_0 is a finite, nth order pole of $f(z)$, then

$$\lim_{z \to z_0} (z - z_0)^n f(z) \text{ exists, finite and non-zero.}$$

That is,

$$\lim_{z \to z_0} \frac{(z - z_0)^n}{g(z)} \text{ exists, finite and non-zero,}$$

so that

$$\lim_{z \to z_0} \frac{g(z)}{(z - z_0)^n} \text{ exists, finite and non-zero.}$$

But this means, precisely, that z_0 is an nth order zero of $g(z)$. Interchanging the roles of $f(z)$ and $g(z)$ and reversing the steps in this argument, we may prove the remainder of the theorem for finite z_0. The proof for the infinite point is deferred to the problems in §6-13.

The following is a curious consequence of all of this. Let $f(z)$ be regular in a deleted neighborhood of a point z_0. If z_0 is a regular point and

$f(z_0) \neq 0$, then z_0 may be called a pole or a zero of *zeroth order*; and if z_0 is a zero (or a pole) of nth order, then z_0 may be called a pole (or a zero) of *negative order* $-n$. For these are the conclusions to which one is led if in the criteria for poles and zeros in terms of $\lim_{z \to z_0} (z - z_0)^n f(z)$ and $\lim_{z \to z_0} f(z)/(z - z_0)^n$ one permits n to have non-positive values. The analogous situations obtain with reference to the infinite point: The matter will not be pursued further in this book.

6-13. Problems.

*1. Prove the proposition of Theorem 6-5 for the point at infinity.

2. Determine the orders of the several zeros of the following functions:

    (a) $z \tan^2 z$,

    (b) $z^2 \cotan z$,

    (c) $\operatorname{Ln} (z^2 - 1)$.

3. Let $f(z)$ have a zero of order n at a regular point z_0 and let $g(z)$ have a pole of order m at z_0. Make the best statement possible about the sort of point that z_0 is for the function

    (a) $f(z)g(z)$,

    (b) $f(z)/g(z)$,

    (c) $g(z)/f(z)$.

4. Show that, if z_0 is a regular point and a zero of a non-constant function $f(z)$, it is isolated from other zeros of $f(z)$—that is, that there is a circle about z_0 within which z_0 is the only zero of $f(z)$.

5. Let a function $f(z)$ be defined in a deleted neighborhood of the origin and suppose that $\lim_{z \to 0} |f(z)|/\sqrt{|z|} = 1$.

    (a) Show that $f(z)$ cannot be regular at the origin.

    (b) Determine whether $f(z)$ can be regular throughout the deleted neighborhood in which it is defined.

6. If $f(z)$ has a pole of positive order m at the origin and a zero of positive order n at infinity and is elsewhere regular, state as an inequality the relationship between m and n.

7. Let the origin be a zero of order n and the point at infinity a pole of order m of an entire function $f(z)$. Without making use of the fact that $f(z)$ must be a polynomial, determine the

sorts of points that the origin and the infinite point are for the function $g(z) \equiv 1/f(1/z)$ where this expression has meaning.

*8. If z_0 is a regular point and a zero of positive order n of a function $f(z)$, show that there is a function $g(z)$ that is regular at z_0, for which $g(z_0) \neq 0$, and such that $f(z) = (z - z_0)^n g(z)$ in a neighborhood of z_0.

9. Let $g(z) = 1/f(z)$, where $f(z)$ is entire.
    (a) Prove that the only singularities that $g(z)$ can have in the finite plane are poles.
    (b) Prove that, if $f(z)$ is also transcendental, then the infinite point cannot be either a regular point or a pole for $g(z)$.

10. Consider the function $F(z) = 1/[f(z) + g(z)]$, where z_0 is a pole of order n for the function $g(z)$.
    (a) What sort of point is z_0 for $F(z)$ if $f(z)$ is regular at z_0?
    (b) To what extent may the restriction on $f(z)$ be relaxed without changing the answer to part (a)?

11. Generalize the preceding problem by considering the function $G(z) = h(z)/[f(z) + g(z)]$, where $f(z), g(z)$, and $h(z)$ are all regular in a deleted neighborhood of z_0.

12. (a) Let z_0 be a limit point of poles of a function $f(z)$. Show that $f(z)$ takes on values arbitrarily close to every (complex) number w_0 in every neighborhood of z_0. [Consider the function $g(z) = 1/[f(z) - w_0]$.]
    (b) Need the singularities of $f(z)$ of which z_0 is a limit point in part (a) above be poles in order for the conclusion to hold? Why?

13. Defining an *essential singularity* of a function $f(z)$ in general as a point z_0 such that $g(z) \equiv (z - z_0)^n f(z)$ fails for each positive integer n to be regular at z_0, show that, if z_0 is a limit point of singularities of $f(z)$, then it is an essential singularity of $f(z)$.

*14. Referring to §5-6, explain how to find by long division the Laurent expansion of $f(z)/g(z)$ about the point $z = 0$ if $f(z)$ and $g(z)$ are regular in a deleted neighborhood of that point and $f(z)$ has a zero or a pole of order k and $g(z)$ has a zero or a pole of order l there. (Four cases.)

15. Using the theory developed in problem 14, find the terms, through the one in z^2, of the Laurent series near the origin for the function $f(z)$ given by

(a) $z/\sin z$,
(b) $z^2/\sin z$,
(c) $z/\sin^2 z$,
(d) $\cot z/\mathrm{Ln}\,(1 + z)$.

6-14. Residues.

If a function $f(z)$ is regular in a deleted neighborhood of a point z_0, and c is a simple closed path in that neighborhood with z_0 on its interior, one speaks of the value of

$$\frac{1}{2\pi i}\oint_{(c)} f(z)dz$$

as the *residue* of $f(z)$ at z_0. By (6-2), this residue equals the coefficient a_{-1} of $1/(z - z_0)$ in the Laurent expansion of $f(z)$ in the neighborhood of z_0; it is, of course, independent of c.

EXAMPLE 1.   The residue at z_0 of a function $f(z)$ that is regular at z_0 is zero.

EXAMPLE 2.   The residue at the origin of the function

$$f(z) = \frac{\sin z}{z^4} \equiv \frac{1}{z^3} - \frac{1}{6z} + \frac{z}{120} - \cdots$$

is $-1/6$.

EXAMPLE 3.   To evaluate $\oint_{(k)} f(z)dz$, where

$$f(z) = \frac{2(z^2 - 1)}{(z^2 + 1)^2}$$

and k is a sufficiently small circle with center at $z = i$, we may write

$$f(z) = \frac{1}{(z - i)^2} + \frac{1}{(z + i)^2} = \frac{1}{(z - i)^2} + a_0 + a_1(z - i)$$
$$+ a_2(z - i)^2 + \cdots,$$

where the values of the a's are of no consequence. Since the coefficient of $1/(z - i)$ is zero, the integral vanishes.

In case $f(z)$ has a simple pole at z_0, then

$$f(z) = a_{-1}(z - z_0)^{-1} + a_0 + a_1(z - z_0) + \cdots$$

in the neighborhood of z_0, so that the residue of $f(z)$ at z_0 is given by $\lim_{z \to z_0} (z - z_0)f(z)$.

EXAMPLE 4.   The residue at the origin of the function $f(z) = $ cotan z equals $\lim_{z \to 0} z$ cotan $z \equiv \lim z/\sin z = 1$.

6-15. Problems.

1. Let $f(z)$ be regular at the point z_0 and $g(z)$ have a simple zero there.   Show that the residue of the function $f(z)/g(z)$ at z_0 is $f(z_0)/g'(z_0)$.

2. Find the residue at the origin of the function
   (a) $f(z) = \sin (1/z)$;
   (b) $f(z) = \cos (1/z)$;
   (c) $f(z) = \text{cotanh } z$;
   (d) $f(z) = \sin z/z^3$;
   (e) $f(z) = \cos z/z^3$;
   (f) $f(z) = e^z/z^n$, where n is a positive integer.

3. Evaluate $\oint_{(k)} e^{1/z}dz$, where k is any circle with the origin on its interior.

4. Find the residue at the point $z = 1$ of the function
$$f(z) = \frac{Az^2 + Bz + C}{(z^2 - 1)(z - 1)},$$
where A, B, and C are constants.

5. Find the residue of the function $f(z) = \tan z$ at the point $z = \pi/2$.

6. Let $g(z)$ be regular at z_0 and $f(z)$ have a simple pole there with residue a_{-1}.   What is the residue at z_0 of the function $F(z) \equiv g(z)f(z)$?

7. Use the result of problem 6, along with the answers to problems 2(c) and 5, to find the residue of the function
   (a) e^z cotanh z at the origin,
   (b) $\sinh z \tan z$ at the point $z = \pi/2$.

*8. If a function $f(z)$ has a pole of order $n > 1$ at the point z_0, describe a method for finding the residue of $f(z)$ at z_0, the first step of which is to find $\lim_{z \to z_0} (z - z_0)^n f(z) \equiv a_{-n}$ and the next to put $f_n(z) = f(z) - a_{-n}/(z - z_0)^n$.   (Compare problem 1 of §6-11.)   Use this method to solve problem 4.

9. If $f(z)$ has a pole of order n at the point z_0, then the residue of $f(z)$ at z_0 is given by $g^{(n-1)}(z_0)/(n-1)!$, where $g(z) = (z - z_0)^n f(z)$.   Prove this and use it to solve problem 4.

10. Solve problems 13–16 of §5-4 by means of residue theory.

6-16.   The Residue Theorem.   The Principle of the Argument.   Rouché's Theorem.

Theorem 5-1 leads immediately to a relationship of first importance in residue theory.

THEOREM 6-6.   (Residue Theorem) *If $f(z)$ is regular in a simply connected open region R, except possibly at a finite number of points $z_1, z_2, \ldots, z_n$, and c is a simple closed path in R with these points on its interior, then*

$$\oint_{(c)} f(z)dz = 2\pi i \sum \operatorname{res}_j [f(z)],$$

where $\operatorname{res}_j [f(z)]$ means the residue of $f(z)$ at the point z_j, $j = 1, 2, \ldots, n$.

EXAMPLE.   Let us evaluate

$$\oint_{(k)} \frac{z^2 - 2}{z^2(z - 1)}\, dz,$$

where k is a circle with center at the origin and radius greater than one.   First, the residue of the integrand at $z = 1$ equals

$$\lim_{z \to 1} (z - 1)\frac{z^2 - 2}{z^2(z - 1)} = -1.$$

To find the residue at $z = 0$, we use the method suggested in problem 8 of §6-15: since

$$\lim_{z \to 0} z^2 \frac{z^2 - 2}{z^2(z - 1)} = 2,$$

the sought residue equals

$$\lim_{z \to 0} z \left[\frac{z^2 - 2}{z(z - 1)} - \frac{2}{z^2} \right] = 2.$$

Hence the original integral equals $2\pi i(-1 + 2) = 2\pi i$.

The reason for the title of the next theorem will be given after the proof of *Rouché's theorem* (Theorem 6-8).

THEOREM 6-7.   (Principle of the Argument) *Let $f(z)$ be regular in a simply connected open region R, except at (at most) a finite number of poles, $z_1, z_2, \ldots, z_m$, and let the zeros (if any) of $f(z)$*

in R be finite in number, $z_1', z_2', \ldots, z_n'$. If c is any simple closed path in R with these poles and zeros on its interior, then

$$\oint_{(c)} \frac{f'(z)}{f(z)} \, dz = 2\pi i(N - M),$$

where N is the number of the n zeros, each counted according to its multiplicity (the order of a pole or a zero is often called its multiplicity), and M is the number of the m poles, also so counted.

Proof. By problem 6 of §6-11 and problem 8 of §6-13, if z_0 is any one of the z_j or the z_j', then $f(z) = (z - z_0)^k g(z)$ in a deleted neighborhood of z_0, where $g(z)$ is regular at the point z_0, $g(z_0) \neq 0$, and k is numerically equal to the order of the pole or zero and is positive if z_0 is a zero and negative if z_0 is a pole. Hence

$$\frac{f'(z)}{f(z)} = \frac{g'(z)}{g(z)} + \frac{k}{z - z_0} \qquad (6\text{-}17)$$

in a deleted neighborhood of z_0. Since the first term on the right-hand side of (6-17) is regular at z_0, for sufficiently small circles K with center at z_0 we have

$$\oint_{(K)} \frac{f'(z)}{f(z)} \, dz = \oint_{(K)} \frac{k}{z - z_0} \, dz = 2\pi i k,$$

so that the residue of $f'(z)/f(z)$ at z_0 is k. Since the z_j and the z_j' are the only singularities of $f'(z)/f(z)$ in R, application of the residue theorem completes the proof.

THEOREM 6-8. (Rouché's Theorem) *Let $f(z)$ and $g(z)$ be regular within and on a simple closed path c, except for (at most) a finite number of poles and zeros within c, let $|g(z)| < |f(z)|$ for all z on c, and put $\varphi(z) = f(z) + g(z)$. If N and M have the meanings for $f(z)$ assigned to them in Theorem 6-7 and N_φ and M_φ have the corresponding meanings for $\varphi(z)$, then $N_\varphi - M_\varphi = N - M$.*

Proof. Noting first that the conditions of Theorem 6-7 are satisfied by both $f(z)$ and $\varphi(z)$,† we may write

$$\oint_{(c)} \frac{\varphi'(z)}{\varphi(z)} \, dz = \oint_{(c)} \frac{f'(z) + g'(z)}{f(z) + g(z)} \, dz$$

$$= \oint_{(c)} \left\{ \frac{f'(z)}{f(z)} + \frac{f(z)g'(z) - f'(z)g(z)}{[f(z)]^2} \, \frac{1}{1 + g(z)/f(z)} \right\} dz$$

$$= \oint_{(c)} \frac{f'(z)}{f(z)} \, dz + \oint_{(c)} \frac{h'(z)}{h(z)} \, dz,$$

† That $\varphi(z)$ cannot have an infinite number of zeros within c is a consequence of certain conclusions reached in Chapter 9.

where $h(z) = 1 + g(z)/f(z)$. Since

$$R[h(z)] = 1 + R\left[\frac{g(z)}{f(z)}\right] \geq 1 - \left|\frac{g(z)}{f(z)}\right| > 0$$

on c,

$$\oint_{(c)} \frac{h'(z)}{h(z)} \, dz = \text{Ln } h(z)\Big]_{z_0}^{z_0} = 0,$$

where z_0 is any point on c. Hence

$$2\pi i(N_\varphi - M_\varphi) \equiv \oint_{(c)} \frac{\varphi'(z)}{\varphi(z)} \, dz = \oint_{(c)} \frac{f'(z)}{f(z)} \, dz \equiv 2\pi i(N - M)$$

from which the conclusion follows.

The question naturally arises, why can it not be said that $\oint_{(c)} f'(z)dz/f(z)$ vanishes for the same reason that $\oint_{(c)} h'(z)dz/h(z)$ does so? The answer is that, while an indefinite integral of $f'(z)/f(z)$ is indeed $\text{Ln } f(z)$ for "most" values of z, this is not necessarily the case when $f(z)$ is non-positive real. On the other hand, for *every* value of z for which $f(z) \neq 0$ an indefinite integral of $f'(z)/f(z)$ is

$$\ln f(z) \equiv \text{Ln } |f(z)| + i \arg f(z)$$

for an appropriate determination of the multi-valued argument function. In fact, if z_0 is an arbitrary point on c, then

$$\oint_{(c)} \frac{f'(z)}{f(z)} \, dz = \text{Ln } |f(z_0)| + i \arg f(z_0) - \text{Ln } |f(z_0)| - i \arg^* f(z_0)$$
$$\equiv i[\arg f(z_0) - \arg^* f(z_0)],$$

where "arg*" signifies an argument which is in general different from that denoted here by "arg." In view of Theorem 6-7 it may therefore be concluded that $2\pi(N - M)$ is precisely equal to the total change in a continuously varying argument of $f(z)$ as z traverses c; it is for this reason that Theorem 6-7 is often called the *principle of the argument*.

6-17. Problems.

1. Find the residues of the integrand in the example of §6-16 by writing

$$\frac{z^2 - 2}{z^2(z - 1)} = \frac{A}{z} + \frac{B}{z^2} + \frac{C}{z - 1}$$

and solving for A and C by the method of undetermined coefficients.

2. Evaluate $\oint_{(K)} dz/(z^2 - 1)$ if K is the circle
   (a) $|z - 1| = 1$,
   (b) $|z + 1| = 1$,
   (c) $|z| = 2$.

3. Evaluate

$$\oint_{(c)} \frac{z^3 - z - 1}{z^2(z^2 - 1)}\, dz$$

   if c is a square of side 3 with center at the origin.

4. Evaluate $\oint_{(K)} z^k \sin z\, dz$, where k is an integer and K is any circle with center at the origin.

5. Let $f(z)$ have an isolated essential singularity at the point z_0 and be otherwise regular throughout the finite plane. Suppose also that the Laurent expansion of $f(z)$ about z_0 has only a finite number k of terms in the "ascending" part of the series (that is, the terms with non-negative exponents). Describe a method, suggested by problem 8 of §6-15, for finding the residue of $f(z)$ at z_0.

6. Find the several values of

$$\oint_{(K)} \frac{e^z}{(z - 1)(z - 2)(z - 3)}\, dz,$$

   where K represents the general circle whose center is at the origin and which passes through no singularity of the integrand.

7. If $P(z) = a(z - z_1)(z - z_2) \cdots (z - z_n)$, where the z_j are all distinct, $a \neq 0$, and $n > 1$, find the value of $\oint_{(K)} dz/P(z)$, where K is a circle with certain of the z_j—say $z_1, z_2, \ldots, z_m$ $(m \leq n)$—on its interior and none on its circumference. Establish a certain numerical identity by considering the case in which $m = n$ and using the last statement in problem 18 of §5-4.

8. By using Theorem 6-7, evaluate $\oint_{(K)} \cotan z\, dz$, where K is the circle $|z| = r$ and r is equal to no integral multiple of π.

9. Using Theorem 6-7, state a criterion, in terms of integration around circles, that an entire function $f(z)$ never takes on some particular (complex) value a.

*10. Use Rouché's theorem to prove the fundamental theorem of algebra in the form *an nth degree polynomial $P_n(z)$ has*

exactly n zeros, each being counted according to its multiplicity.
(Compare §5-10.) [Write the polynomial

$$P_n(z) \equiv a_0 + a_1 z + \cdots + a_{n-1} z^{n-1} + a_n z^n$$

as $f(z) + g(z)$, where $f(z) = a_n z^n$.]

11. Prove the fundamental theorem of algebra as stated in the preceding problem by deducing that $P_n'(z)/P_n(z)$ has a Laurent expansion of the form

$$\frac{n}{z} + \frac{b_2}{z^2} + \frac{b_3}{z^3} + \cdots + \frac{b_k}{z^k} + \cdots$$

at least for all z of sufficiently large magnitude and then making use of the parenthetical remark following (6-14).

12. Let $f(z)$ be regular within and on the unit circle c: $|z| = 1$, let $|f(z)| < 1$ for all z on c, let n be a non-negative integer, and put $g(z) = f(z) - z^n$.

(a) Use Rouché's theorem to show that $g(z)$ has exactly n zeros (multiplicity taken into account) within c.

(b) Does Rouché's theorem tell us anything that is non-trivial in case n is a negative integer?

6-18. Residue Theory in the Evaluation of Certain Real Integrals.

Sometimes trigonometric integrals of the form

$$\int_0^{2\pi} f(\sin \theta, \cos \theta) d\theta \tag{6-18}$$

and improper integrals of the form

$$\int_0^\infty f(x) dx \tag{6-19}$$

can be evaluated by applying residue theory to the integration of appropriate regular functions around appropriate closed paths. This procedure is often called "contour integration," the contour involved being the path of integration.

The integral in (6-18) can be transformed into a contour integral by expressing the circular functions in exponential form and then putting $z = e^{i\theta}$:

$$\int_0^{2\pi} f(\sin \theta, \cos \theta) d\theta = \int_{\theta=0}^{2\pi} F(z) dz, \quad F(z) \equiv f\left(\frac{z - z^{-1}}{2i}, \frac{z + z^{-1}}{2}\right) \frac{1}{iz}.$$

But this means that

$$\int_0^{2\pi} f(\sin \theta, \cos \theta) d\theta = \oint_{(K)} F(z) dz,$$

where K is the unit circle $|z| = 1$, so that the evaluation can be carried out if $F(z)$ is such that residue theory is applicable here.

EXAMPLE 1. To evaluate $\int_0^{2\pi} d\theta/(2 - \sin \theta)$ we make the substitution indicated above, obtaining

$$\int_0^{2\pi} \frac{d\theta}{2 - \sin \theta} = \oint_{(K)} \frac{dz}{iz\left(2 - \dfrac{z - z^{-1}}{2i}\right)} = 2 \oint_{(K)} \frac{dz}{4iz - z^2 + 1},$$

where K is the unit circle $|z| = 1$. The roots of the denominator of the integrand being $(2 \pm \sqrt{3})i$, we may conclude that the original integral equals $4\pi i$ times the residue of $1/(4iz - z^2 + 1)$ at the point $z = (2 - \sqrt{3})i$. That is,

$$\int_0^{2\pi} \frac{d\theta}{2 - \sin \theta} = 4\pi i \lim_{z \to (2-\sqrt{3})i} \frac{z - (2 - \sqrt{3})i}{4iz - z^2 + 1}$$

$$= 4\pi i \lim_{z \to (2-\sqrt{3})i} \frac{-1}{z - (2 + \sqrt{3})i} = 2\pi/\sqrt{3}.$$

EXAMPLE 2. To evaluate $\int_0^\infty dx/(1 + x^2)$ by means of residue theory, let us first construct a path c consisting of segments c_1 and c_2, where c_1 is the portion of the x axis from $-R$ to R and c_2 is the upper half of the circle $|z| = R$ from R back to $-R$, R being any real number greater than one (Fig. 6-2). Since the function

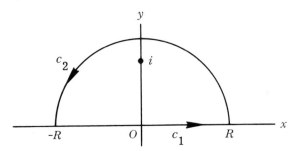

Figure 6-2

$1/(1 + z^2)$ has the single pole $z = i$ within c and its residue there is $\lim_{z \to i} (z - i)/(1 + z^2) = 1/2i$, we have $\oint_{(c)} dz/(1 + z^2) = \pi$. Now

$$\int_{(c_1)} \frac{dz}{1 + z^2} = 2 \int_0^R \frac{dx}{1 + x^2},$$

so that

$$\int_0^R \frac{dx}{1 + x^2} = \frac{\pi}{2} - \frac{1}{2} \int_{(c_2)} \frac{dz}{1 + z^2},$$

and from this it follows that $\int_0^\infty dx/(1 + x^2)$ exists and equals

$$\frac{\pi}{2} - \lim_{R \to \infty} \int_{(c_2)} \frac{dz}{1 + z^2},$$

provided only that this last limit exists. But this limit does exist, and is in fact zero, for

$$\left| \int_{(c_2)} \frac{dz}{1 + z^2} \right| \leq \int_{(c_2)} \frac{ds}{|1 + z^2|}$$

$$\leq \int_{(c_2)} \frac{ds}{R^2 - 1} = \int_0^\pi \frac{R d\theta}{R^2 - 1} = \frac{\pi R}{R^2 - 1} \to 0.$$

Thus we recapture the familiar result, $\int_0^\infty dx/(1 + x^2) = \pi/2$.

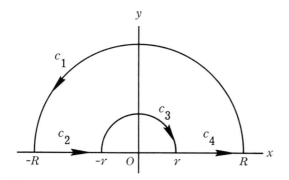

Figure 6-3

EXAMPLE 3. Evaluation of the integral $\int_0^\infty \sin x \, dx/x$ involves some tricks, the first of which is to calculate a contour integral of e^{iz}/z rather than, as one might expect, $\sin z/z$. Starting with any two numbers r and R for which $0 < r < R$, let us construct a path c consisting of segments c_1, c_2, c_3, and c_4, where c_1 is the semicircle $z = Re^{i\theta}$ with $0 \leq \theta \leq \pi$, c_2 is the line segment $y = 0$ with $-R \leq x \leq -r$, c_3 is the semicircle $z = re^{i\theta}$ with $\pi \geq \theta \geq 0$, and c_4 is the line segment $y = 0$ with $r \leq x \leq R$ (Fig. 6-3). We have

$$\oint_{(c)} \frac{e^{iz}}{z} \, dz = 0. \tag{6-20}$$

Now on c_2 and c_4 we have

$$\frac{e^{iz}}{z} \, dz = \frac{e^{ix}}{x} \, dx = \frac{\cos x + i \sin x}{x} \, dx,$$

so that, since $\cos x/x$ is an odd function and $\sin x/x$ is an even function,

$$\int_{(c_2)} \frac{e^{iz}}{z} \, dz + \int_{(c_4)} \frac{e^{iz}}{z} \, dz = 2i \int_r^R \frac{\sin x}{x} \, dx.$$

Hence from (6-20) we have (canceling out a factor i)

$$2 \int_r^R \frac{\sin x}{x} \, dx = \int_0^\pi e^{ir(\cos \theta + i \sin \theta)} d\theta - \int_0^\pi e^{iR(\cos \theta + i \sin \theta)} d\theta. \qquad (6\text{-}21)$$

Since for $0 < \theta \le \pi/2$ we have

$$\sin \theta \equiv \theta - \frac{\theta^3}{3!} + \cdots > \theta - \frac{\theta^3}{6} = \theta\left(1 - \frac{\theta^2}{6}\right) > \theta\left(1 - \frac{2^2}{6}\right) = \frac{\theta}{3},$$

the second integral on the right-hand side of (6-21) is not numerically greater than

$$\int_0^\pi e^{-R \sin \theta} d\theta = 2 \int_0^{\pi/2} e^{-R \sin \theta} d\theta < 2 \int_0^{\pi/2} e^{-R\theta/3} d\theta$$

$$= \frac{6}{R}(1 - e^{-R\pi/6}) < \frac{6}{R}.$$

If therefore we let $R \to \infty$ in (6-21) we find that

$$\int_r^\infty \frac{\sin x}{x} \, dx = \frac{1}{2} \int_0^\pi e^{-r \sin \theta}[\cos (r \cos \theta) + i \sin (r \cos \theta)] d\theta$$

$$= \frac{1}{2} \int_0^\pi e^{-r \sin \theta} \cos (r \cos \theta) d\theta. \qquad (6\text{-}22)$$

Our final step is to let $r \to 0$. Since the integrand in the last member of (6-22) is nearly equal to 1 for small r and all values of θ, it is to be suspected that that member tends to $\pi/2$, and we are therefore led to consider the difference

$$\frac{\pi}{2} - \frac{1}{2} \int_0^\pi e^{-r \sin \theta} \cos (r \cos \theta) d\theta = \frac{1}{2} \int_0^\pi [1 - e^{-r \sin \theta} \cos (r \cos \theta)] d\theta. \qquad (6\text{-}23)$$

The integrand in the right-hand side of (6-23) being non-negative, if $r \le \pi/2$ we have

$$0 < \frac{\pi}{2} - \frac{1}{2} \int_0^\pi e^{-r \sin \theta} \cos (r \cos \theta) d\theta$$

$$\le \frac{1}{2} \int_0^\pi (1 - e^{-r} \cos r) d\theta = \frac{\pi}{2}(1 - e^{-r} \cos r),$$

and the last expression does indeed tend to zero as $r \to 0$. Letting $r \to 0$ in (6-22), then, we obtain $\int_0^\infty \sin x\, dx/x = \pi/2$.

6-19. Problems.

Evaluate the following integrals by means of residue theory.

1. $\int_0^{2\pi} d\theta/(2 + \cos\theta)$.

2. $\int_0^{2\pi} d\theta/(2 + \sin\theta + \cos\theta)$.

3. $\int_0^{2\pi} d\theta/(1 + \sin^2\theta)$.

4. $\int_0^{2\pi} d\theta/(2 + \sin\theta)^2$.

5. $\int_0^{2\pi} e^{3i\theta} d\theta/(1 - 4e^{2i\theta})$.

6. $\int_0^\infty dx/(x^2 + x + 1)$.

7. $\int_0^\infty dx/(1 + x^4)$.

8. $\int_0^\infty dx/(x^4 - 2x^2 + 3)$.

9. $\int_0^\infty dx/(1 + x^2)(4 + x^2)$.

10. $\int_0^\infty dx/(1 + x^2)^2$.

11. $\int_0^\infty dx/(1 + x^2)^n$, n a positive integer.

12. $\int_0^\infty \cos x\, dx/(1 + x^2)$ by integrating $e^{iz}/(1 + z^2)$ around the contour c of Example 2, §6-18. [Note that $|e^{iz}| \equiv e^{-y} \leq 1$ on c.]

13. $\int_0^\infty \cos x\, dx/(1 + x^4)$, using the suggestions given in the preceding problem.

14. $\int_0^\infty \cos x\, dx/(1 + x^2)^2$.

15. $\int_0^\infty \sin^2 x\, dx/x^2$.

6-20. Inverse Functions.

A theorem on inverse functions in real calculus reads as follows:
If $y = f(x)$ is a continuously differentiable function in an interval containing a point x_0 for which $f'(x_0) \neq 0$, then there are two intervals, $I: |x - x_0| < a$ on the x axis and $I': |y - y_0| < b$ on the y axis, where $y_0 = f(x_0)$, such that

the equation $y = f(x)$ is satisfied for each y in I' by one and only one x in I—so that, for these values of y and x, x is a function of y: $x = f^{-1}(y)$. More-over, dx/dy exists for each y in I' and is given by

$$\frac{dx}{dy} = \frac{1}{dy/dx}.$$

There is an analogous theorem for complex functions.

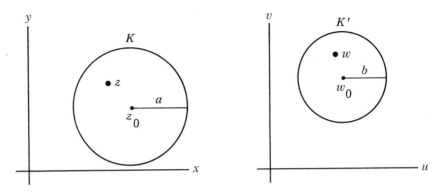

Figure 6-4

THEOREM 6-9.   (Fig. 6-4)   *If $w = f(z)$ is a regular function at a point z_0 for which $f'(z_0) \neq 0$, then there are two circles, K: $|z - z_0| = a$ in the z plane and K': $|w - w_0| = b$ in the w plane, where $w_0 = f(z_0)$, such that the equation $w = f(z)$ is satisfied for each w on the interior of K' by one and only one z on the interior of K—so that, for these values of w and z, z is a function of w: $z = f^{-1}(w)$. [One describes this situation by saying that the function $w = f(z)$ has locally a unique inverse in the neighborhood of w_0.]   Moreover, dz/dw exists for each w on the interior of K' and is given by*

$$\frac{dz}{dw} = \frac{1}{dw/dz}.$$

Proof.   Let us first take a so small that the following conditions are satisfied on the interior of K: $f(z)$ is regular,

$$|f'(z) - f'(z_0)| < |f'(z_0)|,$$

and there is a positive number B such that

$$|f(z) - w_0| > B|z - z_0|.   \tag{6-24}$$

[That condition (6-24) can be brought about follows from the facts that $f(z) - w_0 = f'(z_0)(z - z_0) + \cdots$ for small values of $|z - z_0|$

and that $f'(z_0) \neq 0$.] If, now, z_1 and z_2 are any two points on the interior of K, and we take l as the line segment joining z_1 and z_2, we have

$$
\begin{aligned}
|f(z_2) - f(z_1)| &= \left| \int_{z_1 (l)}^{z_2} f'(z)dz \right| \\
&= \left| \int_{z_1 (l)}^{z_2} \{f'(z_0) + [f'(z) - f'(z_0)]\}dz \right| \\
&\geq \left| \int_{z_1 (l)}^{z_2} f'(z_0)dz \right| - \left| \int_{z_1 (l)}^{z_2} [f'(z) - f'(z_0)]dz \right| \\
&> |(z_2 - z_1)f'(z_0)| - \int_{z_1 (l)}^{z_2} |f'(z_0)|ds \\
&= |z_2 - z_1| |f'(z_0)| - |z_2 - z_1| |f'(z_0)| = 0.
\end{aligned}
$$

That is, $f(z)$ cannot take on any given value at *more* than one point on the interior of K. Hence denial of the first part of the conclusion of the theorem with the circle K fixed as above means that for every positive number b there is a point w_b on the interior of the corresponding circle K' such that the function $\varphi_b(z) \equiv f(z) - w_b$ vanishes at *no* point on the interior of K.

In particular, $\varphi_b(z)$ vanishes at no point within *or on* the circle $K_1: |z - z_0| = a/2$, and so

$$
\oint_{(K_1)} \frac{\varphi_b'(z)}{\varphi_b(z)} \, dz = 0.
$$

Therefore, by the principle of the argument, we have both

$$
\frac{1}{2\pi i} \oint_{(K_1)} \frac{f'(z)}{f(z) - w_b} \, dz = 0, \qquad \frac{1}{2\pi i} \oint_{(K_1)} \frac{f'(z)}{f(z) - w_0} \, dz = 1,
$$

whence

$$
\frac{1}{2\pi i} \oint_{(K_1)} \left[\frac{f'(z)}{f(z) - w_0} - \frac{f'(z)}{f(z) - w_b} \right] dz = 1. \tag{6-25}
$$

Taking $b < Ba/2$ and supposing $|f'(z)| < M$, say, for all z on K_1, we may deduce from (6-25) and (6-24) that

$$
\begin{aligned}
1 &\leq \frac{1}{2\pi} \oint_{(K_1)} \frac{|f'(z)| \, |w_0 - w_b|}{|f(z) - w_0| \, |f(z) - w_b|} \, ds \\
&< \frac{Mb}{2\pi} \oint_{(K_1)} \frac{ds}{|f(z) - w_0| \, ||f(z) - w_0| - |w_b - w_0||} \\
&\leq \frac{Mb}{2\pi} \oint_{(K_1)} \frac{ds}{B|z - z_0|(B|z - z_0| - b)} \\
&= \frac{Mb}{2\pi} 2\pi \frac{a}{2} \frac{1}{B\frac{a}{2}\left(B\frac{a}{2} - b\right)} = \frac{Mb}{B\left(B\frac{a}{2} - b\right)}.
\end{aligned}
$$

If we now let b tend to zero, we arrive at the contradiction $1 \leq 0$.

This establishes the existence of the inverse asserted in the theorem.

To show that this inverse has a derivative dz/dw for each w on the interior of K', let us take an arbitrary point w_1 on the interior of K' and put $z_1 = f^{-1}(w_1)$. Since $f'(z)$ does not vanish on the interior of K (as constructed above), the part of the theorem just proved shows that there are two circles, $k: |z - z_1| = c$ in the z plane and $k': |w - w_1| = d$ in the w plane such that the equation $w = f(z)$ is satisfied for each w on the interior of k' by one and only one z on the interior of k. Since c and d can be taken arbitrarily small, let us choose them so that the interiors of k and k' lie on the interiors of K and K', respectively. Hence the inverse of $f(z)$ in the neighborhood of w_1 must be the same as the inverse previously discovered. Let us also take c so small that, for some $B_1 > 0$,

$$|f(z) - w_1| > B_1 |z - z_1| \qquad (6\text{-}26)$$

for each z on the interior of k. Let w be any point other than w_1 in k' and consider the difference quotient $(z - z_1)/(w - w_1)$, where $z = f^{-1}(w)$. Since, by (6-26), $z \to z_1$ as $w \to w_1$, we have

$$\lim_{w \to w_1} \frac{z - z_1}{w - w_1} = \frac{1}{\lim\limits_{z \to z_1} (w - w_1)/(z - z_1)} = \frac{1}{dw/dz},$$

and the proof is complete.

EXAMPLE. If $w = f(z) = z^3$, let us express the inverse function $z = f^{-1}(w)$ in the neighborhood of w_0 in terms of Ln w if $z_0 = (-1 + \sqrt{3}i)/2$. Since we have $z = e^{(\operatorname{Ln} w + 2n\pi i)/3}$ for $n = 0$ or 1 or 2, it suffices to discover which of these values for n satisfies the condition

$$\frac{(-1 + \sqrt{3}i)}{2} = e^{(\operatorname{Ln} w_0 + 2n\pi i)/3}$$

with $w_0 \equiv z_0{}^3 = 1$. This value is clearly $n = 1$, so that

$$f^{-1}(w) = w^{(\operatorname{Ln} w + 2\pi i)/3}$$

That the derivative of this function at $w = w_0$ is indeed

$$\frac{dz}{dw}\bigg]_{w_0} = \frac{1}{dw/dz]_{z_0}} = \frac{1}{3z_0{}^2}$$

should be checked by the student.

An important extension of the first part of Theorem 6-9 is taken up in problem 10 of §9-20.

6-21. Problems.

1. The *value* of $z = f^{-1}(w)$ for fixed w is a zero of the function $F(z) \equiv f(z) - w$. Show that, if this w is on the interior of the circle K' and the zero is on the interior of the circle K of the proof of Theorem 6-9, then the zero is a simple one.

2. Express the second and third derivatives of a function $z = f^{-1}(w)$ that is inverse to the function $w = f(z)$ in terms of the derivatives of $f(z)$.

3. If $w = f(z) = e^z$, express the inverse $z = f^{-1}(w)$ in the neighborhood of w_0 in terms of Ln w if

   (a) $z_0 = \pi i$,
   (b) $z_0 = 3\pi i/2$,
   (c) $z_0 = -\pi i/2$.

4. If $w = f(z) = z^2$, express the inverse $z = f^{-1}(w)$ in the neighborhood of w_0 in terms of Ln w if

   (a) $z_0 = 2$,
   (b) $z_0 = -2$.

5. If $w = f(z) = \sin z$, find an explicit expression for the inverse $z = f^{-1}(w) \equiv \sin^{-1} w$ in the neighborhood of the point $z_0 = 5\pi/4$.

6. In the neighborhoods of which points w_0 does Theorem 6-9 guarantee the existence of a locally unique inverse $z = f^{-1}(w)$ if

   (a) $f(z) = e^z$?
   (b) $f(z) = \cos z$?
   (c) $f(z) = z^2 - 4z$?
   (d) $f(z) = 1/z$?
   (e) $f(z) = z^3 + 3z$?

7. Find the values of the derivatives of the inverse functions in problem 6 above at the point w where $z = 2i$.

Analytic Continuation

7

7-1. Analytic Continuation from Open Regions.

Suppose that a function $f(z)$ is defined in one of the following ways:

(a) $f(z) = z + \dfrac{z^2}{2!} + \cdots + \dfrac{z^n}{n!} + \cdots$ in R: $|z| < \frac{1}{2}$,

(b) $f(z) = z + z^2 + \cdots + z^n + \cdots$ in R: $|z| < \frac{1}{2}$,

(c) $f(z) = z + \dfrac{z^2}{2} + \cdots + \dfrac{z^n}{n} + \cdots$ in R: $|z| < \frac{1}{2}$.

In each case there are (i) a connected open region S that includes R and is more extensive than R and (ii) a function $F(z)$ that is regular throughout S and coincides with $f(z)$ throughout R. In case (a), S may be taken as the entire finite plane and $F(z)$ as the function $e^z - 1$; in case (b), S may be taken as the entire closed plane, except the point $z = 1$, and $F(z)$ as the function $z/(1 - z)$; in case (c), S may be taken as the entire finite plane, except that part of the x axis for which (make the substitution $w = 1 - z$ and refer to problem 6 of §5-4) $x \geq 1$, and $F(z)$ as the function $-\operatorname{Ln}(1 - z)$.

In each case it has been possible to extend or "continue" the definition of the initial regular function $f(z)$ into a more extensive connected open region S than that—R—in which it was initially defined, in such a way that it was regular throughout S. The process of so doing for any function $f(z)$ initially defined and regular throughout an open connected set R is called *analytic continuation*, and the function $F(z)$ so obtained for maximal (the meaning of this term will be clarified in §7-3) S is called the *analytic function* of which $f(z)$ is an *element*.

It will be instructive to add one more example to the list in the first paragraph of this section:

(d) $f(z) = a_0 + a_1 z + \cdots + a_n z^n + \cdots$ in R: $|z| < \frac{1}{2}$,

where the radius of convergence of the series is 1, and *nothing more* is known about the a_n. There are, surely, a connected open region S_0 that includes R and is more extensive than R, and a function $F_0(z)$ that is regular throughout S_0 and coincides with $f(z)$ throughout R; indeed, such an S_0 is the interior of the circle $|z| = 1$, and such an $F_0(z)$ is the function $a_0 + a_1 z + \cdots + a_n z^n + \cdots$. But do a still more extensive S and a corresponding $F(z)$ exist? This was the case in examples (b) and (c) above. The answer is "not necessarily," as will now be seen.

7-2. An Analytic Function with a Natural Boundary.

An example of type (d) for which S_0 is without doubt the maximal S is given by the classic example

$$f(z) = g(z) \equiv z + z^2 + z^6 + \cdots + z^{n!} + \cdots. \qquad (7\text{-}1)$$

For if z is of the form $z = re^{2\pi i p/q}$, where p and q are positive integers and r is a positive number less than 1, then

$$|f(z)| = \left| \sum_1^{q-1} r^{n!} e^{2\pi i n! p/q} + \sum_q^\infty r^{n!} \right| \geq \sum_q^\infty r^{n!} - (q-1),$$

and the right-hand member of this inequality becomes infinite as $r \to 1$. (In fact, if N is any positive integer, the finite sum $\sum_q^{q+2N} r^{n!}$ alone will be greater than N whenever r is so close to 1 that $r^{(q+2N)!}$ is greater than $\frac{1}{2}$.) Therefore, if there are a connected open region S that is more extensive than S_0 and a function $F(z)$ that is regular throughout S and coincides with $g(z)$ throughout S_0 then, in every neighborhood of every point z_0 in S that is on the circle $|z| = 1$, there are points z, namely those of the form $z = e^{2\pi i p/q}$, where p and q are positive integers, at which $F(z)$ is not continuous—let alone differentiable—so that z_0 could not be a regular point for $F(z)$, contrary to the presumption. Here the circle $|z| = 1$ is, as one says, a *natural boundary*.

7-3. Generation of an Analytic Function from an Element.

This section is devoted to a (generally theoretical) procedure for finding the analytic function $F(z)$ and its open region S of definition of maximum extension, of which a given regular function $f(z)$ defined throughout a connected open region R is an element.

About each point z_1 in R the function $f(z)$ has a Taylor expansion.   If the corresponding series,

$$\sum a_n(z - z_1)^n, \tag{7-2}$$

converges only for z in R, it may be said that no continuation of $f(z)$ from z_1 has been effected.   Thus if $f(z) = 1 + z + z^2 + \cdots + z^n + \cdots$ in $R\colon |z| < 1$ no continuation from $z_1 = \frac{1}{2}$ is effected.   If no continuation of $f(z)$ is effected for *any* z_1 in R, then one says that $f(z)$ is *not continuable* outside of R.   Thus the function $g(z)$ of (7-1) is not continuable outside of the interior of the circle $|z| = 1$.   But, if for some z_1 in R the series (7-2) converges for some values of z that are not in R, it may be said that a continuation of $f(z)$ from z_1 has been effected and that this continuation is the regular function $f_1(z)$ defined by the series (7-2) on the interior R_1 of the circle of convergence of that series.   The uniqueness of this continuation follows from Theorem 5-6.

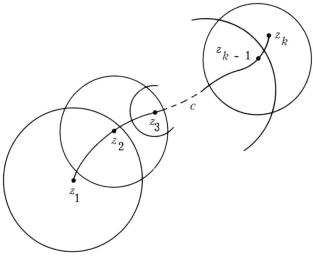

Figure 7-1

If R_1 is the entire finite plane, then the continuation is completely accomplished.   If it is not, one next considers the Taylor expansion about the points z_2 of R_1.   If the series represented by these expansions converge for no z that is in neither R nor R_1, it may be said that $f(z)$ is *not further continuable* from z_1.   In the alternative case there is a continuation of $f(z)$, via $f_1(z)$, to a function $f_2(z)$, which is regular on the interior R_2 of a circle with center at z_2 and which has certain points in neither R nor R_1. As before, the continuation of $f_1(z)$ from R_1 to $f_2(z)$ in R_2 is unique.

One proceeds in this way, either indefinitely or until $f(z)$ is not further continuable from z_1 via z_2 via...via z_n, say.   [If in the process of continuation an R_k overlaps an R_j, $k > j$, the portion P of R_k that is also in R_j

must be regarded as a *new* part of the domain of z if $f_k(z)$ does not coincide with $f_j(z)$ throughout P. Such apparently paradoxical situations will be clarified in §7-5.] And one does this for *every* z_1 in R, for *every* z_2 in the corresponding R_1, and so on. If $z_1, z_2, \ldots, z_k$ is a particular finite succession of points in this process and c is a path starting at z_1, passing in order through $z_2, z_3, \ldots, z_{k-1}$, and terminating at z_k, all points of which, between z_j and z_{j+1}, lie on the interior R_j of the circle of the described construction with center at z_j, it is said that the continuation from $f(z)$ to $f_1(z)$ to...to $f_{k-1}(z)$ is the analytic continuation of $f(z)$ *along the path c* (Fig. 7-1). Evidently, analytic continuation along a given path is unique.

7-4. Problems.

1. Letting $f(z)$ be defined by the series below in $R: |z| < 1$, find by inspection [as we did in examples (a) and (b) of §7-1] the analytic continuation $F(z)$ and its connected open region S of definition.

   (a) $f(z) = 1 - z^2 + z^4 - \cdots + (-1)^n z^{2n} + \cdots$;

   (b) $f(z) = z + z^3/3! + \cdots + z^{2n+1}/(2n+1)! + \cdots$;

   (c) $f(z) = 1 - z + z^2 - \cdots + (-1)^n z^n + \cdots + g(z)$, where $g(z)$ is the function of (7-1);

   (d) $f(z) = 1 - z + z^2 - \cdots + (-1)^n z^n + \cdots + g(z/2)$, where $g(z)$ is the function of (7-1).

2. Starting with $f(z)$ and R as in example (b) of §7-1, we may take z_1 as 0, so that R_1 is the interior of the circle $|z| = 1$. Knowing that $f(z) = z/(1 - z)$ for all z in R, give the equation of the circle whose interior is R_2 if we pick z_2 as $i/2$.

3. Given $f(z) = 1 + z^2 + z^4 + \cdots + z^{2n} + \cdots$ in $R: |z| < 1$, describe a succession of interiors R_j of circles by means of which we can continue $f(z)$ along a portion of the y axis that includes the interval $0 \le y \le y_0$ for given $y_0 > 0$.

4. Starting with the element $f(z) = 1 + z/3 + z^2/3^2 + \cdots + z^n/3^n + \cdots + g(1/z)$, where $g(z)$ is the function of (7-1), find the corresponding analytic function $F(z)$ and its maximal open region of definition.

5. Show that the unit circle $|z| = 1$ is a natural boundary for the function $h(z) = z + z^2 + z^4 + \ldots + z^{2^n} + \ldots$, $|z| < 1$. [Observe first that in every neighborhood of every point on the unit circle lies one of the $2^{n\text{th}}$ roots of 1 for some n. Letting z_0 be such a root, show that $\lim_{r \to 1^-} |f(rz_0)| = \infty$.]

7-5. Multi-valued Analytic Functions.

It may happen in the process of continuation just described that one of the regions R_n will overlap another, say R_m, with which it is not consecutive. The question then arises, do $f_n(z)$ and $f_m(z)$ necessarily coincide throughout the set of points common to R_n and R_m? In example (b) of §7-1 the answer is yes, since Theorem 5-6 requires that $f_k(z) = z/(1 - z)$ for all z in R_k, for every k. But in example (c) of §7-1 the answer is no, as will now be seen.

The analysis may be somewhat easier to follow if, instead of the function in example (c), which led to the continuation $F(z) = -\operatorname{Ln}(1 - z)$, one starts with

$$f(z) = (z - 1) - \frac{(z - 1)^2}{2} + \cdots + (-1)^{n+1} \frac{(z - 1)^n}{n} + \cdots$$

$$\text{in } R: |z - 1| < 1 \quad (7\text{-}3)$$

and continues it as $F(z) = \operatorname{Ln} z$ for all z except the points on the non-positive part of the x axis. Using the general procedure outlined above and taking $z_1 = 3/2$, $z_2 = 2$, $z_3 = 3, \ldots, z_k = k, \ldots$, one does indeed "generate" $\operatorname{Ln} z$ in the entire half-plane $x > 0$; if, instead, one takes $z_1 = 1 + i/2$, $z_2 = i/2$, and the subsequent z_k tending to infinity along the positive y axis, one extends this generation into the quarter-plane for which $x \leq 0$ and $y > 0$; finally, if one takes $z_1 = 1 - i/2$, $z_2 = -i/2$, and continues to infinity along the negative y axis, one completes the generation of $\operatorname{Ln} z$ as the continuation that was before named by inspection.

But if, in some "chain of circles" used in continuing $f(z)$ as given by (7-3), one picks a z_j in the upper part of the half-plane $x < 0$, z_j being the first of the z_k with negative abscissa, the corresponding R_j will be the interior of the circle $|z - z_j| = |z_j|$, so that $f_j(z) = F_1(z)$ throughout R_j, where

$$F_1(z) = \begin{cases} \operatorname{Ln} z \text{ for } y \geq 0 \\ \operatorname{Ln} z + 2\pi i \text{ for } y < 0 \end{cases} \text{ in } R_j,$$

since $F_1(z)$ is regular throughout R_j. Similarly, if the process of continuation leads to a first z_j with negative abscissa, and z_j lies in the lower part of the half-plane $x < 0$, then $f_j(z)$ will equal $F_2(z)$ throughout the corresponding R_j, where

$$F_2(z) = \begin{cases} \operatorname{Ln} z \text{ for } y < 0 \\ \operatorname{Ln} z - 2\pi i \text{ for } y \geq 0 \end{cases} \text{ in } R_j,$$

since $F_2(z)$ is regular throughout R_j.

Thus, continuation of the element of $\operatorname{Ln} z$ given by (7-3) across the negative x axis is $\operatorname{Ln} z \pm 2\pi i$ in the neighborhood of any point on that axis, the sign depending on the direction of crossing. Since the function

Ln z + constant is regular wherever Ln z is, this means that, in a complete circuit (that is, continuation around a simple closed path) about the origin, a continued element of Ln z returns to its original value augmented or decreased by $2\pi i$ according as the circuit is made in the positive or the negative sense; and this in turn means that in n circuits about the origin—all in the same sense—an original element $f(z)$ of Ln z will be continued into $f(z) \pm 2n\pi i$, the sign being determined as before.

Whenever there is an analytic continuation $f^*(z)$ of an element $f(z)$ of an analytic function $F(z)$ from a connected open region R back into R that does not coincide with $f(z)$ throughout R, $F(z)$ may evidently be regarded as multiple-valued in R; for each z in R, $f(z)$ and $f^*(z)$ are two of its (generally distinct) values. If the maximum number of distinct functional values that can be obtained at any point of R by continuation is n, then $F(z)$ is n-valued in R—this terminology being used even if some of the values "coincide" at some of the points of R. If, finally, there is no maximum number of such values, $F(z)$ is infinitely many-valued in R. One speaks of the several functions $f(z), f^*(z), \ldots$ as the *branches* of $F(z)$ in R.

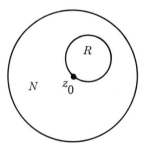

Figure 7-2

EXAMPLE 1.   The analytic continuation of the element $f(z)$ of (7-3) is clearly the function $\ln z$ of §2-9.   It is infinitely many-valued throughout the finite plane, except the origin.

EXAMPLE 2.   If in $R: |z - 1| < 1$ we define $f(z)$ as the principal value of $z^{1/2}$ as defined in §2-9, then $f(z) = e^{\frac{1}{2}\mathrm{Ln}\,z}$ in R, and we see that a single circuit about the origin brings us to the continuation $f^*(z) = e^{\frac{1}{2}(\mathrm{Ln}\,z \pm 2\pi i)} = -f(z)$ in R. In this case, however, the analytic function $F(z)$ of which $f(z)$ in R is an element is merely double-valued in R, since no circuit that is not taken about the origin continues $f(z)$ back to a different function in R, and since n circuits in the same sense about the origin continue $f(z)$ back to $e^{\frac{1}{2}(\mathrm{Ln}\,z \pm 2n\pi i)} = (-1)^n f(z)$—that is, to either $f(z)$ or $f^*(z)$. Here $F(z)$ is the double-valued function $z^{1/2}$.

Next, suppose there is a point z_0 and a function $F(z)$ that is analytic in a deleted neighborhood of z_0. If, for every sufficiently small deleted neighborhood N of z_0 and arbitrary circle whose interior R is in N and which passes through z_0 (Fig. 7-2), it happens that successive continuations of an element $f(z)$ of $F(z)$ from R around every circuit in N about z_0 generate an n-valued (or infinitely many-valued) function in R, then z_0 is called a *branch point of $F(z)$ of $(n - 1)$th (infinite) order*. Thus, the origin is a branch point of order 1 for the function $F(z) = z^{1/2}$ and a branch point of infinite order for the function $F(z) = \ln z$.

7-6.   Riemann Surfaces.

For the two multiple-valued functions used as illustrations above, namely $z^{1/2}$ and $\ln z$, the non-positive half of the x axis figured as a "dividing line" between the principal values of these analytic functions and the other values. Visualization of the transition from these principal values in S, the "slit plane" from which this part of the x axis has been removed, to the other branches of the analytic functions is facilitated by the following mental construction. One imagines at his disposal an infinite number of these slit planes—with the non-positive half of the x axis, however, restored and attached to the upper part of the half-plane $x \le 0$. In the case of the function $F(z) = z^{1/2}$ one supposes that two of these planes are placed, point for point, one under the other; one then supposes the upper edge of the slit in the lower plane pasted onto the lower edge of the slit in the upper plane, and the lower edge of the slit in the lower plane pasted onto the upper edge of the slit in the upper plane. (Here mental power needs to exceed physical capability! It is instructive to make a paper model, as best one can.) If one agrees that for all z on the lower plane $z^{1/2}$ shall mean the principal value and that for all z on the upper plane $z^{1/2}$ shall mean the negative of the principal value, then analytic continuations along all paths that cross the slit, or *cut*, as it is often called, lead to the other branch of $z^{1/2}$ in a way that makes this double-valued function on the single plane *single-valued* on the *double plane*.

A *Riemann surface of two sheets* has been "constructed."

In the case of the function $F(z) = \ln z$ one supposes an infinite number of the slit planes piled in order—$p_1, p_2, \ldots$—on top of an initial plane p_0, and an infinite number piled similarly below p_0—$p_{-1}, p_{-2}, \ldots$; one then supposes the upper edge of the slit in each plane p_n pasted onto the lower edge of the slit in the plane p_{n+1} for $n = 0, \pm 1, \pm 2, \ldots$. If it is now agreed that, for all z on the plane p_n, $\ln z$ shall mean $\mathrm{Ln}\, z + 2n\pi i$, there results a single-valued function on a *Riemann surface of infinitely many sheets*.

The general idea of the Riemann surface is to replace multiple-valuedness in the z plane by single-valuedness in a "multiple" z plane. The ramifications in the cases of many functions can be very complicated. It may be instructive to consider one more example: construction of a Riemann surface for the function $(z^2 - 1)^{1/2} \equiv \sqrt{r_1 r_2} e^{i\varphi}$, where $r_1 = |z - 1|$, $r_2 = |z + 1|$, and 2φ is the sum of a polar angle θ_1 of $z - 1$ and a polar angle θ_2 of $z + 1$. Let R be taken as the interior of any circle that encloses neither of the points $z = 1$, $z = -1$, and the element $f(z)$ as $\sqrt{r_1 r_2} e^{i\Phi}$, where Φ is some particular choice of φ and varies continuously as z moves about in R. Continuation of $f(z)$ around any circuit about both of the points $z = 1$ and $z = -1$ leads upon completion to $f^*(z) = \sqrt{r_1 r_2} e^{i\varphi}$ where, since both θ_1 and θ_2 have increased or decreased by 2π, $\varphi = \Phi \pm 2\pi$; that is, $f^*(z) = f(z)$: the initial element has been returned to. But if $f(z)$ is continued around any circuit about only one of the points $z = 1$ and $z = -1$, then one of the angles θ_1 and θ_2 increases or decreases by 2π while the other returns to its original value; thus $f(z)$ returns to $f^{**}(z) = \sqrt{r_1 r_2} e^{i(\Phi \pm \pi)} = -f(z)$, and z is on a sheet of the Riemann surface different from the one on which R lay. The two sheets may be thought of as the z plane slit along the portion $-1 \le x \le 1$ of the x axis and its duplicate. These are to be attached along the slit so that, whenever it is crossed, passage is effected from one sheet to the other. On one of these sheets $F(z)$ may be identified with $\sqrt{r_1 r_2} e^{i\varphi}$ for some continuously varying determination of φ and on the other with $-\sqrt{r_1 r_2} e^{i\varphi}$.

7-7. Problems.

1. Show that, although the analytic function $w = \ln z$ is many-valued, its derivative is not. Is the same true of the analytic function $w = z^{1/2}$?

2. In terms of Ln z, describe the several branches of $z^{1/3}$ in the open region R consisting of those points z for which
    (a) $|z - 1| < 1$,
    (b) $|z + 1| < 1$.

3. Show that the function $F(z) = g(1/z) + \ln z$, where $g(z)$ is the function of (7-1) and the definition is as wide as possible, is infinitely many-valued but has no branch points.

4. Describe a Riemann surface for the function
    (a) $F(z) = z^{1/3}$,
    (b) $F(z) = (z - z^2)^{1/2}$.

5. Using the Riemann surface described in the text for the function $F(z) = z^{1/2}$, show that the function

$$G(z) = \frac{1}{1 + z^{1/2}}$$

is regular at the point $z = 1$ on one of the sheets and has a singular point there on the other sheet. Of what sort is this singularity?

6. Show that the function $G(z) = 1/\ln z$ has, except the origin, exactly one singularity among all of the points on the several sheets described in the text for the function $F(z) = \ln z$. What is the residue of $G(z)$ there?

7. The choice of the slit or slits in imagining a Riemann surface is very largely arbitrary.

    (a) If the slit or cut in the z plane that was used to construct the surface for $\ln z$ had been the non-negative part of the y axis, how would the branch of $\ln z$ have been defined on that sheet on which this branch would equal $\operatorname{Ln} x$ when $z = x > 0$?

    (b) In what respect would the Riemann surface for $\ln z$ constructed as suggested in part (a) be different from that constructed in the text?

    (c) If the cut in the z plane that was used to construct the surface for $z^{1/2}$ had been that suggested in part (a), how would the branch of this function have been defined on that sheet on which this branch would equal the positive square root of x when $z = x > 0$?

    (d) In what respect would the Riemann surface for $z^{1/2}$ constructed as suggested in part (c) be different from that constructed in the text?

    (e) Describe some cut in the z plane other than a rectilinear one by means of which a Riemann surface could be constructed for $\ln z$.

8. Starting with the element $f(z) = \operatorname{Ln} z + g(2/z)$ in $R: |z - 3| < 1$, where $g(z)$ is the function of (7-1), discuss the possibilities of analytic continuation and construction of a Riemann surface for the resulting analytic function.

9. (a) Repeat problem 8 for the element

$$f(z) = \sqrt{r_1 r_2}\, e^{i\Phi} + g(2/z),$$

where the notation is that of the last illustration of Riemann surface in §7-6.

(b) Comment on the "definition"

$$F(z) = (z^2 - 1)^{1/2} + g(2/z).$$

7-8. Analytic Continuation from a Line Segment.

Suppose there is a sequence of distinct points $z_1, z_2, \ldots, z_n, \ldots$ with a limit point z_0 and a function $g(z)$ defined on these points. If there is a function $f(z)$ that is regular at z_0 and for which $f(z_n) = g(z_n)$ for $n = 1, 2, \ldots$ (or for merely all sufficiently large n), then it is unique, by Theorem 5-6. It may therefore be said that such a function and the analytic function $F(z)$ of which it is an element are *determined* by the values $g(z_n)$. In particular, given a function $g(z)$ defined on a line segment L—finite or infinite—either there is no function $f(z)$ that is regular at each point of L and coincides with $g(z)$ for all z on L, or there is exactly one such function. In the latter case one says that the analytic function $F(z)$ of which $f(z)$ is an element is the *analytic continuation of $g(z)$ from L*.

It is essentially for the aforementioned reason that one defines e^z as $\sum_0^\infty z^n/n!$ rather than as, say, $\sum_0^\infty [R(z)]^n/n!$ Both of these "continuations" from the real axis coincide with e^x whenever $z = R(z) = x$, but only the definition that has been accepted above is the *analytic* continuation of e^x. The accepted definitions of the other elementary functions are similarly motivated. (On the other hand, many functions of a real variable—most of them in a technical sense—cannot be analytically continued at all.)

EXAMPLE 1. The real function $g(x) = |x|$ of the real variable x on L: $0 < x < 1$ is analytically continuable from L into the entire finite plane as $F(z) = z$.

EXAMPLE 2. The real function $g(x) = |x|$ of the real variable x on L: $-1 < x < 1$ is not analytically continuable from L, since a function $f(z)$ that is regular at each point of L and coincides with $g(z)$ for all z on L must equal z in a neighborhood of the origin since this is the (unique) continuation of $g(x)$ for $z = x$ with $0 \le x < 1$, whereas $f(z)$ must also equal $-z$ in a neighborhood of the origin by a similar argument involving the fact that $g(z) = -z$ for $z = x$ with $-1 < x \le 0$.

7-9. Problems.

1. Is the real function $g(x) = |x|$ of the real variable x on L: $-1 < x < 0$ analytically continuable from L?

2. What is the analytic continuation of the real function $g(x) = \sum_1^\infty x^{n!}$ of the real variable x on $L: -1 < x < 1$?

3. Is the real function $g(x) = e^{|x|}$ of the real variable x on $L: -\infty < x < \infty$ analytically continuable from L?

4. Is the real function $g(x) = \cos |x|$ of the real variable x on $L: -\infty < x < \infty$ analytically continuable from L?

5. What is the analytic continuation of the real function $g(x)$ of the real variable x on $L: 0 < x < 1$ if
   (a) $g(x) = \text{Ln } x + \sqrt{x}$,
   (b) $g(x) = \text{Ln } x - \sqrt{x}$?

6. What is the analytic continuation of the real function $g(x) = \sum_0^\infty (-x)^n$ of the real variable x on $L: |x| \leq \epsilon$, where ϵ is any positive number less than 1?

7. Is the function $g(x)$ of the real variable x on $L: 0 < x < 1$ analytically continuable if
   (a) $g(x) = R(\sin ix)$,
   (b) $g(x) = |\sin ix|$,
   (c) $g(x) = \overline{\sin ix}$?

8. Is the real function $g(y) = \sin y$ of the real variable y on $L: 0 < y < 1$, where $z = x + iy$, analytically continuable?

9. The function $f(z) = \sin(1/z)$ vanishes at each of the infinite set of points $z = 1/n\pi$, $n = 1, 2, \ldots$. So does the function $g(z) \equiv 0$. Why then can we not conclude that $\sin(1/z) \equiv 0$? (Compare problem 2 of §5-8.)

10. Given an entire function $f(z)$ such that $f(n) = e^n$ for $n = 1, 2, \ldots$, can we conclude that $f(z) = e^z$ for all finite z?

11. Given a function $f(z)$ that is regular at infinity, if $f(n) = 1/n$ for all sufficiently large n, can we conclude that $f(z) = 1/z$ in the neighborhood of infinity?

12. Given that a function $f(z)$ has a pole of order n at a point z_0, do the values of $f(z)$ on an infinite set of points with z_0 as a limit point determine $f(z)$ throughout a deleted neighborhood of z_0?

7-10. Persistence of Functional Relationships.

In elementary trigonometry it is easy to construct geometric proofs of the familiar formulas for $\sin(A \pm B)$ and $\cos(A \pm B)$ if $0 < A < \pi/4$

and $0 < B < \pi/4$. Addition of a bit of limit theory in elementary calculus then leads without difficulty to the differentiation formulas for the functions $\sin x$ and $\cos x$ when $0 < x < \pi/4$. Finally, application of an "extended law of the mean" in a later calculus course yields the expansions

$$\sin x = \sum \frac{(-1)^n x^{2n+1}}{(2n+1)!} \quad \text{and} \quad \cos x = \sum \frac{(-1)^n x^{2n}}{2n!}$$

for $0 < x < \pi/4$. At this point the technique of §7-8 may be introduced to obtain in a single step the entire functions $\sin z$ and $\cos z$. (Note that this procedure does not *of itself* identify these functions for real $z = x$, outside of the range $0 < x < \pi/4$, with the functions $\sin x$ and $\cos x$ as defined geometrically for x outside of that range.)

It will now be shown that the relationship

$$\sin (A + B) = \sin A \cos B + \cos A \sin B, \tag{7-4}$$

only assumed to be true if $0 < A < \pi/4$ and $0 < B < \pi/4$, is true for *all* real A and B. First, observe that, for fixed real B such that $0 < B < \pi/4$, the entire function $f(z) = \sin (z + B) - (\sin z \cos B + \cos z \sin B)$ vanishes for all $z = x$ on the segment $0 < x < \pi/4$ of the x axis. Uniqueness of analytic continuation from this segment therefore proves that $\sin (z + B) - (\sin z \cos B + \cos z \sin B)$ vanishes for each real B such that $0 < B < \pi/4$ and all finite z. But this is to say that, for each fixed z, the entire function $F_z(w) = \sin (z + w) - (\sin z \cos w + \cos z \sin w)$ of w vanishes for all $w = u$ on the segment $0 < u < \pi/4$ of the u axis (in the w plane). Appealing once more to the uniqueness of analytic continuation (this time in the w plane), one concludes that

$$\sin (z + w) - (\sin z \cos w + \cos z \sin w)$$

vanishes for all finite z and w. That (7-4) is true for all real A and B is now a trivial corollary.

Thus has been established, in the case of (7-4), what is called *persistence of functional relationship* or *permanence of form*: the relationship (7-4), established for A and B in certain limited domains, *persists* when A and B are permitted to take values in wider domains; the form of the relationship is *permanent*.

7-11. Problems.

1. Supposing the relationship

$$\cos (A + B) = \cos A \cos B - \sin A \sin B$$

to have been proved if $0 < A < \pi/4$ and $0 < B < \pi/4$, argue that it holds for all real A and B.

2. Supposing the relationship $e^A e^B = e^{A+B}$ to have been proved for all real numbers A and B, argue that $e^z e^w = e^{z+w}$ for all finite complex numbers z and w.

3. Supposing the relationship

$$\tan (A + B) = \frac{\tan A + \tan B}{1 - \tan A \tan B}$$

to have been proved for all real numbers A and B for which $\tan A$ and $\tan B$ are defined and $\tan A \tan B \neq 1$, show directly by the method of §7-10 that

$$\tan (z + w) = \frac{\tan z + \tan w}{1 - \tan z \tan w}$$

for all finite complex numbers z and w for which $\tan z$ and $\tan w$ are defined and $\tan z \tan w \neq 1$.

4. Although the series

$$\sum_0^\infty \frac{n - 1}{n!} z^n,$$

representing a function which we shall call $f(z)$, has infinite radius of convergence, the series $\sum_0^\infty z^n$, representing the function $1/(1 - z)$ where convergent, has radius of convergence 1, so that development of a series for the function $f(z)/(1 - z)$ by multiplication of the two series given is meaningless for values of z not numerically less than 1. However, this development is meaningful and valid for all z which *are* numerically less than 1 and leads (give the details) to the relationship $f(z)/(1 - z) = -e^z$ for such z. From the validity of this relationship, thus proved only for $|z| < 1$, how can we conclude that $f(z) = (z - 1)e^z$ for *all* finite z?

5. One constructs problems like the preceding by "starting with the answer" (of course!). Construct such a problem in which $f(z)$ is given as the Taylor expansion about the origin of $(1 + z^2) \sin z$. Discover this formula for $f(z)$ by first multiplying the series by the Taylor expansion about the origin of of the function $1/(1 + z^2)$ where this process is valid.

Conformal Mapping

8

8-1. Mappings or Transformations.

Given a single-valued function $f(z)$, the relationship

$$w = f(z) \qquad\qquad (8\text{-}1)$$

assigns to each point z of the domain S a unique point w of the range T. For this reason (8-1) is often called a *mapping* or *transformation* of S onto T. Under this transformation the point w determined by (8-1) for a given point z is called the *image* of z, and if S' is any set of points z in S, and T' is the set of the images w of these points, then T' is called the *map* of S'.

EXAMPLE 1. The transformation $w = iz + 2$ maps the closed z plane onto the closed w plane.

EXAMPLE 2. The transformation $w = |z|^2$ maps the finite z plane onto the non-negative real axis in the w plane.

EXAMPLE 3. The transformation $w = z^2$ maps the closed z plane onto the closed w plane, each point w in the w plane except the origin and the point at infinity being the image of two distinct points z in the z plane.

EXAMPLE 4. The transformation $w = Az$, where A is an arbitrary non-zero complex number, maps circles into circles and lines into lines, because the locus $|z - z_0| = a$ in the z plane is equivalent to the locus $|w/A - z_0| = a$, or $|w - Az_0| = |A|a$ in the w plane, and the locus $z = z_0 + tz_1$ (z_0 and z_1 fixed complex numbers and t a real parameter) in the z plane is equivalent to the locus $w/A = z_0 + tz_1$ or $w = Az_0 + tAz_1$ in the w plane.

8-2. Problems.

In problems 1–11, describe in geometric terms the map T if

1. $w = iR(z)$, and S is
    (a) the finite z plane,
    (b) the interior of the circle $|z| = 1$;

2. $w = 1/z$, and S is
    (a) the interior of the circle $|z| = 1$,
    (b) the closed z plane;

3. $w = \bar{z}$, and S is the interior of the circle
    (a) $|z - i| = 1$,
    (b) $|z - i| = 2$,
    (c) $|z| = 1$;

4. $w = z + (i - 1)$, and S is
    (a) the interior of the first quadrant,
    (b) the closed z plane;

5. $w = z(i - 1)$, and S is
    (a) the interior of the first quadrant,
    (b) the closed z plane;

6. $w = z^2$, and S is
    (a) the interior of the circle $|z| = 1$,
    (b) the set of points z for which $0 \leq \text{Arg } z < \pi$, plus the
         origin;

7. $w = (z - 1)(z - 2)$, and S is the closed z plane;

8. $w = x^2 + iy$, where $z = x + iy$, and S is the finite z plane;

9. $w = e^z$, and S is the infinite strip
    (a) $0 \leq R(z) \leq 1$,
    (b) $0 \leq I(z) \leq 1$;

10. $w = \sin z$, and S is the infinite strip $0 \leq R(z) < 2\pi$;

11. w is the decimal $.a_1b_1a_2b_2\ldots a_nb_n\ldots$, and S is the interior of
     the square in the z plane bounded by the axes and the lines
     $x = 1$, $y = 1$, decimal representations of x and y (agreed
     to be taken as non-terminating) being $.a_1a_2\ldots a_n\ldots$ and
     $.b_1b_2\ldots b_n\ldots$, respectively.   Is any point w in T the image
     of more than one point z in S?

12. What is the image of the point $z = \frac{1}{2} + \frac{1}{2}i$ under each of the transformations above?

13. For each of the transformations 1–8 above, find the map of the portion of the line $z = (1 + i)t$ that lies in S.

*14. Show that the transformation $w = z + B$, where B is an arbitrary complex number, maps circles into circles and lines into lines.

8-3. Mappings or Transformations, Continued.

Those mappings (8-1) are of special interest that satisfy at certain points $z \equiv x + iy$ of S the conditions

(CD) $\qquad$ $u(x, y)$ and $v(x, y)$ are continuously differentiable functions of x and y, $\qquad$ (8-2)

(R) $\qquad$ $\dfrac{\partial u}{\partial x}\dfrac{\partial v}{\partial y} - \dfrac{\partial v}{\partial x}\dfrac{\partial u}{\partial y} \neq 0,$

where, as usual,

$$w = u + iv \equiv u(x, y) + iv(x, y).$$

(The properties expressed by these conditions and their analogs in the theory of mapping in n dimensions in general are often called, respectively, "continuous differentiability" and "regularity" of the mappings, but so to call them here would clearly invite confusion.) The usefulness of conditions (CD) and (R) appears in the next theorem.

THEOREM 8-1. *If c is a curve of class C_1 in the z plane, and if the mapping (8-1) satisfies conditions (CD) and (R) at every point on c, then the map d of c in the w plane is also a curve of class C_1.*

Proof. Let $x = x(t)$, $y = y(t)$, $t_0 \leq t \leq T$, be a parameterization of c for which $x'(t)$ and $y'(t)$ are continuous and never vanish simultaneously for $t_0 < t < T$. Then a parameterization of d is given by $u = u(t) \equiv u[x(t), y(t)]$, $v = v(t) \equiv v[x(t), y(t)]$, and $u'(t) \equiv u_x x'(t) + u_y y'(t)$ and $v'(t) \equiv v_x x'(t) + v_y y'(t)$ are continuous. Moreover, $u'(t)$ and $v'(t)$ cannot vanish simultaneously at any point of d for which $t_0 < t < T$, for if they did, the resulting equations,

$$\begin{aligned} u_x x'(t) + u_y y'(t) &= 0, \\ v_x x'(t) + v_y y'(t) &= 0, \end{aligned}$$ (8-3)

would imply that $x'(t)$ and $y'(t)$ vanished simultaneously at the corresponding point of c, since by (R) of (8-2) the determinant of the coefficients of these quantities in (8-3) is not zero. Thus d is of class C_1.

8-4. Conformal Mapping.

Roughly speaking, the mapping (8-1) is said to be *conformal* if the map T^* of a set S^* is "nearly similar" to S^* in the oriented sense whenever the latter is "small." (One says that two figures are similar *in the oriented sense* if uniform magnification and/or rotation *without reflection* brings one into congruence with the other.) This idea may be made precise in a variety of ways, generally suggested by conditions under which two triangles are similar in the oriented sense (Fig. 8-1). Thus conformality at a

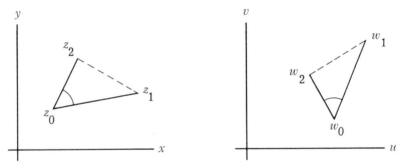

Figure 8-1

point z_0 of S could be defined with the conditions involving two sides and the included angle in mind; the requirements could then be stated as follows. [Here $f(z_j)$ is denoted by w_j. The angle $\angle w_2 w_0 w_1$ in (8-5) is defined for z_1 and z_2 sufficiently close to z_0, by (8-4).]

$$\lim_{z_1 \to z_0} \left| \frac{w_1 - w_0}{z_1 - z_0} \right| = r \neq 0, \tag{8-4}$$

$$\lim_{z_1, z_2 \to z_0} (\angle w_2 w_0 w_1 - \angle z_2 z_0 z_1) = 0 \bmod 2\pi, \tag{8-5}$$

it being understood that the variables z_1 and z_2 are points of S, both different from z_0.

As will shortly appear, however, if the transformation satisfies the conditions (CD) and (R) of (8-2), then the condition (8-4) is a *consequence* of condition (8-5). Indeed, both conditions (8-4) and (8-5) are then consequences of the single condition that, if k_1 and k_2 are any two curves of class C_1 through z_0 in the z plane, and l_1 and l_2 are their respective maps, then the angle from l_1 to l_2 at w_0 equals the angle from k_1 to k_2 at z_0. The mapping (8-1) is therefore said to be *conformal at z_0 if this angle-preserving condition is satisfied*.

To discover what is implied by conditions (CD) and (R) of (8-2) and conformality at an arbitrary point $z_0 \equiv x_0 + iy_0$ in S, observe that (1) the maps of the lines $x = x_0$ and $y = y_0$ in the z plane must be orthogonal at the image w_0 in the w plane of z_0, and (2) the angle from the map of the line $y = y_0$ to the map of the line $y = y_0 + (x - x_0)$ must be $45°$ at w_0 (Fig. 8-2).

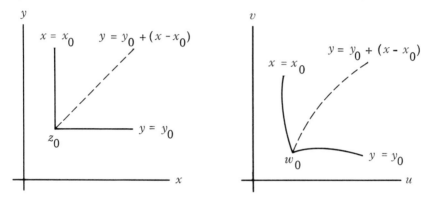

Figure 8-2

The equations that follow, through (8–10), are to be interpreted as holding at z_0. From (1) it follows that

$$\frac{\dfrac{d}{dx} v(x, y_0)}{\dfrac{d}{dx} u(x, y_0)} = -\frac{\dfrac{d}{dy} u(x_0, y)}{\dfrac{d}{dy} v(x_0, y)}$$

if neither denominator vanishes, and in any case that

$$u_x u_y + v_x v_y = 0. \tag{8-6}$$

And from (2) it follows that

$$\frac{\dfrac{\dfrac{d}{dx} v[x, y_0 + (x - x_0)]}{\dfrac{d}{dx} u[x, y_0 + (x - x_0)]} - \dfrac{\dfrac{d}{dx} v(x, y_0)}{\dfrac{d}{dx} u(x, y_0)}}{1 + \left\{ \dfrac{\dfrac{d}{dx} v[x, y_0 + (x - x_0)]}{\dfrac{d}{dx} u[x, y_0 + (x - x_0)]} \right\} \left\{ \dfrac{\dfrac{d}{dx} v(x, y_0)}{\dfrac{d}{dx} u(x, y_0)} \right\}} = 1,$$

or that

$$\frac{\dfrac{v_x + v_y}{u_x + u_y} - \dfrac{v_x}{u_x}}{1 + \left(\dfrac{v_x + v_y}{u_x + u_y}\right)\left(\dfrac{v_x}{u_x}\right)} = 1,$$

if no denominator vanishes, and in any case that

$$u_x v_y - u_y v_x = u_x{}^2 + v_x{}^2 + u_x u_y + v_x v_y,$$

which, by (8-6), reduces to

$$u_x v_y - u_y v_x = u_x{}^2 + v_x{}^2. \tag{8-7}$$

Now by condition (R) of (8-2), at least one of the partials in (8-6) does not vanish. If, as may be supposed, such a one is u_x, then (8-6) yields

$$u_y = -\frac{v_x v_y}{u_x}, \tag{8-8}$$

and substitution from (8-8) in (8-7) results in

$$v_y(u_x{}^2 + v_x{}^2) = u_x(u_x{}^2 + v_x{}^2),$$

or

$$u_x = v_y. \tag{8-9}$$

But then (8-8) says that

$$u_y = -v_x. \tag{8-10}$$

Since (8-9) and (8-10) are the Cauchy-Riemann equations, it follows from condition (CD) of (8-2) that the function $f(z)$ of (8-1) is differentiable at z_0 and hence regular in S. Moreover, the condition (R) of (8-2) can now be written as

$$u_x{}^2 + v_x{}^2 \neq 0,$$

which is precisely to say that $f'(z) \neq 0$ in S.

The necessity part of the following theorem has thus been proved.

THEOREM 8-2. *A necessary and sufficient condition that a mapping* (8-1) *in an open region S satisfy the conditions* (CD) *and* (R) *of* (8-2) *and be conformal is that* $f(z)$ *be regular in S and possess a derivative which does not vanish in S.*

Proof of the sufficiency is considerably simpler. First, the mapping satisfies condition (CD) because of the infinitely manifold differentiability of the function $f(z)$. Next, condition (R) is satisfied by virtue of the Cauchy-Riemann equations and the non-vanishing of $f'(z)$. Finally, condition (8-5) is met, since

$$\lim_{z_1, z_2 \to z_0} (\angle w_2 w_0 w_1 - \angle z_2 z_0 z_1) \bmod 2\pi$$

$$= \lim \{[\text{Arg}(w_2 - w_0) - \text{Arg}(w_1 - w_0)]$$
$$- [\text{Arg}(z_2 - z_0) - \text{Arg}(z_1 - z_0)]\} \bmod 2\pi$$

$$= \lim \left(\text{Arg}\frac{w_2 - w_0}{z_2 - z_0} - \text{Arg}\frac{w_1 - w_0}{z_1 - z_0}\right) \bmod 2\pi$$

$$= [\text{Arg}f'(z_0) - \text{Arg}f'(z_0)] \bmod 2\pi$$

$$= 0 \bmod 2\pi.$$

The mapping is therefore conformal.

The condition (8-4) is often verbalized thus: the *limiting magnification* of the mapping (8-1) at the point z_0 is r. To interpret the condition (8-5), suppose z_2 lying on a curve c of class C_1 that passes through z_0, and z_1 lying on the horizontal line l that passes through z_0 (Fig. 8-3). Then

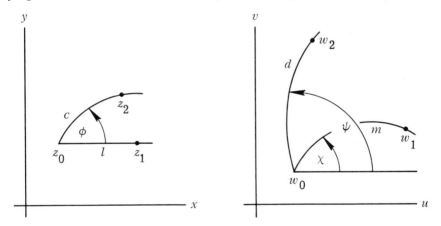

Figure 8-3

w_2 will lie on the map d of c and w_1 on the map m of l. If χ is the inclination of m at w_0, it may be said that (8-1) "rotates" the curve l through angle χ. Similarly, if φ is the inclination of c at z_0 and ψ is the inclination of d at w_0, (8-1) rotates the curve c through angle $\psi - \varphi$. Condition (8-5) now requires that $\psi - \chi = \varphi$, which is to say that $\psi - \varphi = \chi$: every curve of class C_1 that passes through z_0 is rotated by the mapping (8-1) through the same angle χ at z_0. This effect of the condition (8-5) may therefore be verbalized thus: the *rotation* of the mapping (8-1) at the point z_0 is χ. The next theorem follows from the facts that $r = |f'(z_0)|$ and

$$\chi = \lim \text{Arg} \, (w_1 - w_0) \bmod 2\pi$$
$$= \lim \, [\text{Arg} \, (w_1 - w_0) - \text{Arg} \, (z_1 - z_0)] \bmod 2\pi$$
$$= \lim \text{Arg} \, \frac{w_1 - w_0}{z_1 - z_0} \bmod 2\pi$$
$$= \text{Arg} \, f'(z_0) \bmod 2\pi.$$

THEOREM 8-3.   *If in the mapping (8-1) S is an open set, $f(z)$ is regular in S, and $f'(z)$ does not vanish in S, then at each point z in S the limiting magnification of the mapping is $|f'(z)|$ and the rotation is $\text{Arg} \, f'(z_0) \bmod 2\pi$.*

EXAMPLE.   The transformation $w = f(z) = z - 2/z$ is conformal except at $z = 0$, where $f(z)$ has a pole, and at $z = \pm \sqrt{2}i$, where $f'(z) \equiv 1 + 2/z^2$ vanishes.   Examining the mapping at the particular point $z = 1 + i$, where $f'(z) = 1 - i$, we find that there the rotation is $-\pi/4$ and the limiting magnification is $\sqrt{2}$.

8-5.   Problems.

1.   For each of problems 1–10 in §8-2, determine where
   (a)   the function of the mapping is regular,
   (b)   condition (CD) of (8-2) is satisfied,
   (c)   condition (R) of (8-2) is satisfied.

2.   Find the rotations and limiting magnifications of the following mappings at the point z_0 indicated.
   (a) $w = (1 + i)z - 2$, z_0 arbitrary;
   (b) $w = z^n$, $z_0 = i - 1$;
   (c) $w = e^z$, $z_0 = \pi i$, $1 + \pi i/2$;
   (d) $w = \ln z$, $z_0 = -1 + i$, $2 - 3i$;
   (e) $w = \sin z$, $z_0 = \pi$, i;
   (f) $w = z^3 - 3$, $z_0 = 2 + 3i$.

3.   In simple geometric terms, describe the locus of the points in the z plane for which (i) the limiting magnification, (ii) the rotation, is constant for each of the following transformations.
   (a) $w = z^2$;
   (b) $w = z^2 + 3z$;
   (c) $w = 1/z$;
   (d) $w = e^z$;
   (e) $w = z^n$, where n is an arbitrary (complex) constant;
   (f) $w = az^2 + bz + c$, where a, b, and c are arbitrary (complex) constants.

4. The mapping $w = z^2$ is not conformal at the origin. If the point z_1 tends to the origin in such a way that Arg z_1 approaches a limit φ mod 2π, what happens to Arg w_1? Does this mapping have a limiting magnification at the origin?

5. Proceeding in a fashion suggested by problem 4, investigate the mapping $w = f(z)$ at a point z_0 of regularity of $f(z)$ which is a zero of order n.

6. Show that, if the mapping (8-1) satisfies conditions (CD) and (R) of (8-2) and is conformal in an open set S, then the map of S is also open. (This result will be improved upon in §9-20.) (Use Theorem 6-9.)

8-6. Streamlines for Harmonic Equipotential Curves.

Let a mapping (8-1) be given in which S is an open set, $f(z)$ is regular throughout S, and $f'(z)$ vanishes at no point in S. As shown in Chapter 6, if z_0 is an arbitrary point in S, then for each w in the neighborhood of the point $w_0 = f(z_0)$ the equation $w = f(z)$ determines z uniquely in the neighborhood of z_0 and the function

$$z = f^{-1}(w) \tag{8-11}$$

thereby defined is regular at w_0. Moreover, for this inverse function $dz/dw \neq 0$ at w_0. Hence in the neighborhood of every point w_0 of T the mapping (8-1) defines a (local) *inverse mapping* (8-11) in the neighborhood of each associated z_0 which is conformal. In particular, since the lines $u = u_0$ and $v = v_0$ in the w plane intersect orthogonally at the point $w_0 \equiv u_0 + iv_0$, their inverse maps $u(x, y) = u_0$ and $v(x, y) = v_0$ in the z plane in the neighborhood of each point z_0 for which $w_0 = f(z_0)$ will also intersect orthogonally at z_0.

It will be recalled (problem 7 of §2-7) that the real and imaginary parts of a function that is regular at a point are harmonic there. Now in many kinds of two-dimensional fluid flow a function $u(x, y)$ for which the curves $u(x, y) = $ constant are the *equipotential curves*† is harmonic in an open region S. If, then, there is a function $f(z)$ that is regular and has a non-vanishing derivative in S and for which $R[f(z)] = u(x, y)$, the preceding paragraph and a uniqueness theorem from the theory of differential equation show that the curves $v(x, y) \equiv I[f(z)] = $ constant will be the streamlines, since they are everywhere in S orthogonal to the equipotential curves.

† These are curves which are everywhere perpendicular to the *streamlines*, or curves of flow. Briefly, the equipotential curves and the streamlines are *orthogonal trajectories*.

Thus the finding of the streamlines is essentially the finding of the imaginary part of a regular function, once the real part is known—*provided* that a harmonic function $u(x, y)$ is always the real part of a regular function.

To show that this is indeed the case, the *harmonic conjugate* $v(x, y)$, as it is called, of such a function $u(x, y)$ will now be exhibited. This is a function of x and y such that $f(z) \equiv u(x, y) + iv(x, y)$ is regular throughout S. Since a harmonic function has continuous second partials and the expression

$$- \frac{\partial u}{\partial y} \, dx + \frac{\partial u}{\partial x} \, dy$$

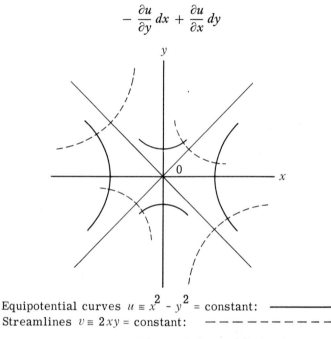

Equipotential curves $u \equiv x^2 - y^2$ = constant: ——————————
Streamlines $v \equiv 2xy$ = constant: — — — — — — — — —

Figure 8-4

is an exact differential† throughout S, the expression may be tentatively identified with dv and v obtained (for example, by line integration). But then the relationships $\partial v/\partial x = -\partial u/\partial y$ and $\partial v/\partial y = \partial u/\partial x$ follow at once; and these are precisely the Cauchy-Riemann equations and show, with the continuities of these derivatives, that $f(z) \equiv u(x, y) + iv(x, y)$ is regular throughout S, as was to be proved.

EXAMPLE 1.   Given the equipotential curves $u(x, y) = constant$ where u is the harmonic function $x^2 - y^2$, and S is the finite plane

† See problem 4 of §4-9. In problem 5 of §8-7 it is shown that a function which is harmonic throughout an open region has derivatives of all orders there.

except the origin [where $\partial u/\partial x = \partial u/\partial y = 0$, so that $f'(0) = 0$], if we put $dv = 2y\,dx + 2x\,dy$, then we obtain by inspection $v = 2xy + constant$. The streamlines are therefore the curves $xy = constant$. Here

$$f(z) = (x^2 - y^2) + 2xyi + constant = z^2 + constant \quad \text{(Fig. 8-4)}.$$

EXAMPLE 2. Given the equipotential curves $u(x, y) = constant$, where u is the harmonic function $e^{-y}\cos x$ and S is the finite plane, if we put $dv = e^{-y}\cos x\,dx - e^{-y}\sin x\,dy$, then we obtain by line integration

$$v = \int_0^x e^0 \cos x\,dx + \int_0^y (-e^{-y}\sin x)\,dy + constant$$
$$= \sin x + e^{-y}\sin x - \sin x + constant$$
$$= e^{-y}\sin x + constant.$$

Here, then, the streamlines are the curves $e^{-y}\sin x = constant$; and

$$f(z) = e^{-y}\cos x + ie^{-y}\sin x + constant$$
$$= e^{-y+ix} + constant = e^{iz} + constant.$$

8-7. Problems.

1. Given the following harmonic functions $u(x, y)$ and regions S, find the streamlines $v(x, y) = constant$ for the equipotential curves $u(x, y) = constant$ and express the function $f(z) \equiv u(x, y) + iv(x, y)$ in a simple form. In parts (a) and (b), sketch a few of the equipotential curves and the streamlines.

(a) $u(x, y) = x/(x^2 + y^2)$, S: the finite plane except the origin. [To find $v(X, Y)$ suppose $Z \equiv X + iY$ in the upper half-plane $y > 0$ and integrate from i to Z along the path consisting of, first, a vertical line segment and then a horizontal line segment; deduce the form of $v(x, y)$ for the general point (x, y) different from the origin by applying the principles of analytic continuation to the function $f(z)$ that you obtain for $I(z) > 0$.]

(b) $u(x, y) = \arctan y/x$, S: the finite plane except the non-positive x axis. Pick branches of the arctangent function that make $u(x, y)$ continuous in S when appropriate values are assigned where $x = 0$.

(c) $u(x, y) = 3x^2y - y^3$, S: the finite plane except the origin.

(d) $u(x, y) = \sin x \cosh y$, S: the finite plane except what points?

(e) $u(x, y) = x^3y + axy^3$, where a is so determined that u is harmonic, S: the finite plane except what point?

(f) $u(x, y) = e^x(A \cos y + B \sin y)$, where A and B are arbitrary but not both zero, S: the finite plane.

2. Show directly that the curves $u(x, y) = u_0$ and $v(x, y) = v_0$ in the z plane, which were discussed in the text, intersect orthogonally by examining their slopes and using the Cauchy-Riemann equations.

3. The finding of streamlines can equally well be carried out by assuming the harmonic function $u(x, y)$ of the text to be the *imaginary* part of a regular function $f^*(z)$ and proceeding to find the real part of that function, say $v^*(x, y)$. [The streamlines will then, of course, be given by $v^*(x, y) = constant$.] Give the details of this procedure, and find the relationship between $v^*(x, y)$ and the function $v(x, y)$ of the text.   How is the function $f^*(z)$ related to the function $f(z)$ of the text?

4. If $f(z)$ is regular in a neighborhood of the point z_0, and $F(w)$ is regular in a neighborhood of the point $w_0 = f(z_0)$, then $R\{F[f(z)]\}$ and $I\{F[f(z)]\}$ are harmonic in a neighborhood of z_0. Why?   Illustrate in case $F(w) = e^w$, $w \equiv f(z) = z^2$, and z_0 is an arbitrary point.

*5. Using the fact—to be proved in Chapter 9—that a regular function has derivatives of all orders, show that, for a function $u(x, y)$ that is harmonic in an open region R, $\partial^{m+n}u/\partial x^m \partial y^n$ exists in R for every pair of non-negative integers m and n.

8-8.   The General Bilinear Transformation.

It is traditional in a discussion of conformal mapping to give a geometric interpretation of the *bilinear transformation*

$$w = \frac{az + b}{cz + d}, \qquad \begin{vmatrix} a & b \\ c & d \end{vmatrix} \neq 0. \tag{8-12}$$

[The non-vanishing of the determinant in (8-12) is simply a formal way of requiring that the transformation be defined for at least some values of z and not reduce to a constant.]

It will first be shown that (8-12) is equivalent to a succession of mappings of the three basic forms

$$w = z + B, \tag{8-13}$$

$$w = Az, \tag{8-14}$$

$$w = \frac{1}{z}. \tag{8-15}$$

If $c = 0$, then $w = Az + B$, where $A = a/d$ and $B = b/d$; that is, $w = z' + B$, where $z' = Az$. In this case, then, (8-12) is equivalent to a transformation of type (8-14) followed by a transformation of type (8-13). If $c \neq 0$, then $w = A/(cz + d) + B$, where $A = (bc - ad)/c$ and $B = a/c$; that is, $w = z'''' + B$, where $z'''' = Az'''$, $z''' = 1/z''$, $z'' = z' + d$, and $z' = cz$. In this case, then, (8-12) is equivalent to two transformations each of types (8-13) and (8-14) and one transformation of type (8-15) in this order: (8-14), (8-13), (8-15), (8-14), and (8-13).

It remains to analyze the transformations (8-13), (8-14), and (8-15). Since for every $z \equiv x + iy$ addition of the constant $B \equiv b' + ib''$ to z is the same as increasing x by b' units and y by b'' units, (8-13) amounts to *translating* the plane b' units to the right and b'' units up. Noting that $|Az| = |A| |z|$ and Arg $Az = ($Arg $A +$ Arg $z)$ mod 2π, one sees that (8-14) is equivalent to *expanding* the plane in the ratio $|A|:1$ and *rotating* it through the angle Arg A. Finally, from the facts that $|1/z| = 1/|z|$ and Arg $1/z = -$ Arg z mod 2π, one is able to interpret (8-15) as *inversion* of the plane with respect to the unit circle $|z| = 1$ followed by *reflection* of the plane in the x axis. (The *inverse* of a point P with respect to a circle with center Q and radius R is the point P' such that Q, P, and P' are collinear, Q is not between P and P', and $\overline{QP} \cdot \overline{QP'} = R^2$. *Inversion* is the process of determining inverses.)

EXAMPLE.   The mapping

$$w = \frac{2z + (1 - i)}{(1 + i)z - 1} \equiv \frac{2 - 2i}{(1 + i)z - 1} + (1 - i)$$

is effected by expanding the z plane in the ratio $\sqrt{2}:1$ and rotating it through $45°$ $[z' = (1 + i)z]$, translating the z' plane one unit to the left $[z'' = z' - 1]$, inverting the z'' plane in the unit circle $|z''| = 1$ and reflecting it in the real axis of that plane $[z''' = 1/z'']$, expanding the z''' plane in the ratio $2\sqrt{2}:1$ and rotating it through $-45°[z'''' = (2 - 2i)z''']$, and translating the z'''' plane one unit to the right and one unit down $[w = z'''' + (1 - i)]$. In particular, the point $z = 4 + 3i$ is transformed successively into the points $z' = 1 + 7i$, $z'' = 7i$, $z''' = -i/7$, $z'''' = -2/7 - 2i/7$, and $w = 5/7 - 9i/7$.

To determine the image of the point at infinity under the bilinear transformation (8-12), we observe that

$$\lim_{z \to \infty} w = \lim_{z \to \infty} \frac{a + b/z}{c + d/z},$$

which gives us the point a/c if $c \neq 0$ and (since if $c = 0$, neither a nor d can vanish) the infinite point if $c = 0$.

8-9. Problems.

1. Each of the transformations (8-14) and (8-15) involves two operations, one involving magnitude and one involving argument. Are these two operations in each case commutative?

2. Which, if any, *pair* of the transformations (8-13), (8-14), and (8-15) are commutative?

3. As in the example of §8-8, describe in geometric terms and in order each of the five basic transformations whose successive applications result in the bilinear transformation given below. Also, list the successive images of the point named.

   (a) $w = \dfrac{(1 + i)z - 1}{iz - i}$, $z = 1 - i$;

   (b) $w = \dfrac{iz + i}{z + i}$, $z = 2$;

   (c) $w = \dfrac{z + 1}{2z + 3}$, $z = i$;

   (d) $w = \dfrac{(1 + 2i)z + (2 + i)}{(1 - 2i)z + (2 - i)}$, $z = 0$.

4. Is the mapping

$$w = \frac{(1 + 2i)z + (2 - i)}{(2 + i)z + (1 - 2i)}$$

   a bilinear transformation according to the definition in the text? What is the map of the unit circle $|z| = 1$ under this transformation?

5. The infinite point is what sort of point for the mapping function if in the general bilinear transformation (8-12) we have

   (a) $a = 0$?
   (b) $c = 0$?

6. (a) Show that the inverse of a bilinear mapping function exists and is also a bilinear mapping function.
   (b) Under what circumstances do a bilinear mapping function and its inverse coincide?

7. What is the point in the z plane whose image under the general bilinear transformation (8-12) is the infinite point in the w plane?

8. If z is a bilinear function of ζ, and w is a bilinear function of z, then w is a bilinear function of ζ. Prove this.

9. Determine the circumstances under which a bilinear transformation maps real points into real points.

10. Show that the limiting magnification of a bilinear mapping never vanishes.

11. Show that the general bilinear transformation maps circles into circles (straight lines regarded as special cases). (Recall Example 4 of §8-1 and problem 14 of §8-2 and consider the second paragraph in §8-8.)

8-10. Fixed Points of the General Bilinear Transformation.

A *fixed point* of a mapping is a point whose image is itself when the w plane is imagined as coinciding with the z plane. Thus it has just been seen that the infinite point is a fixed point of the general bilinear transformation (8-12) when and only when $c = 0$. The finite fixed points of that transformation can be found by putting $w = z$ in (8-12) and solving the resulting equation:

$$cz^2 + (d - a)z - b = 0. \tag{8-16}$$

From (8-16) it is seen that, if $c = 0$ and $d \neq a$, there is one finite fixed point, $z = b/(d - a)$. If $c = 0$ and $d = a$, there are two extreme cases: with $b \neq 0$ there are no finite fixed points, but with $b = 0$, (8-12) reduces to the *identity transformation*, $w = z$, for which all points in the closed plane are fixed points. If $c \neq 0$, the fixed points are the two (possibly "coincident") roots of the quadratic equation (8-16).

EXAMPLE. Given that, under a bilinear transformation (8-12), the image of the infinite point is the origin, $z = -1$ is a fixed point, and the image of the point 1 is the point i, what is the other fixed point, if any? The first condition requires that $a = 0$. From the second we therefore find that $-1 = b/(-c + d)$, so that

$$w = \frac{c - d}{cz + d}.$$

The last condition now states that $i = (c - d)/(c + d)$, or that

$d = -ci$. The transformation is therefore

$$w = \frac{c + ci}{cz - ci} \equiv \frac{1 + i}{z - i},$$

and (8-16) becomes $z^2 - iz - (1 + i) = 0$, whose roots are $z = -1$ and $1 + i$. The solution to our problem is thus $z = 1 + i$.

8-11. Problems.

1. Find the fixed points and the image of the infinite point for each of the mappings below.

   (a) $w = \dfrac{z + 1}{z - 1}$,

   (b) $w = \dfrac{z}{2z + 1}$,

   (c) $w = z + i$,

   (d) $w = \dfrac{i}{z + i}$.

2. Determine the bilinear mapping for which the infinite point is a fixed point and which maps the points i and $-i$ into the points 1 and -1, respectively. What is the other fixed point, if any?

3. Determine the bilinear mapping for which the image of the infinite point is 2 and the fixed points are 1 and i. What is the point whose image is the infinite point?

8-12. Other Mappings by Analytic Functions.

The mapping $w = z^2$ transforms the half-plane P: $0 < \operatorname{Arg} z \leq \pi$, the origin included, into the entire w plane; it also so transforms the half-plane P_φ obtained by rotating P through the arbitrary angle φ about the origin. It therefore maps the finite z plane, except the origin, *twice* onto the w plane (or once onto a two-sheeted Riemann surface for $z = w^{1/2}$)— a circumstance in agreement with the discussion of the inverse function in Chapter 6.

The mapping $w = e^z$ maps the infinite strip $\varphi \leq y < \varphi + 2\pi$ (φ arbitrary) onto the entire w plane, except the point $w = 0$. This follows from the solvability of the equation $e^z = w \neq 0$ for z and the periodicity of the function e^z.

The transformation $w = z^{1/2}$ maps a two-sheeted Riemann surface for the function $f(z) = z^{1/2}$ onto the finite w plane. It transforms either single sheet onto a half of the w plane—conventions having been duly adopted as to inclusion or exclusion of the cut and its map.

The transformation $w = \ln z$ transforms each sheet of a Riemann surface for the function $f(z) = \ln z$ onto a horizontal strip of width 2π, one edge included and one excluded, so that the aggregate of all the sheets of the Riemann surface maps onto the entire finite w plane.

Given an analytic mapping $w \equiv u + iv \equiv u(x, y) + iv(x, y) = f(z)$, where $z = x + iy$, a significance of the loci $u(x, y) = $ constant and $v(x, y) = $ *constant* in the z plane has already been mentioned in §8-6. These loci also provide insight into the mapping itself. Figure 8-4 exhibits a few of them for the mapping $w = z^2$. It is also helpful to consider the loci $x = $ *constant* and $y = $ *constant* in the w plane.

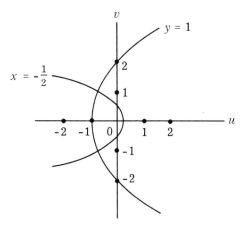

Figure 8-5

EXAMPLE 1.   The transformation just mentioned, $w = z^2$, is conformal for all z except $z = 0$, where $dw/dz = 0$. Here $u = x^2 - y^2$ and $v = 2xy$, so that: the map of the line $x = a$ is the curve

$$u = a^2 - y^2,$$
$$v = 2ay,$$

where y plays the role of a parameter; and the map of the line $y = b$ is the curve

$$u = x^2 - b^2,$$
$$v = 2xb,$$

where x serves as a parameter.   In this simple example it is easy to eliminate the parameter in each of these pairs of equations. The line $x = a$ maps into the parabola $u = a^2 - v^2/4a^2$ if $a \neq 0$ and into the half-line $v = 0$ with $u \leq 0$ if $a = 0$.   Similarly, the line $y = b$ maps into the parabola $u = v^2/4b^2 - b^2$ if $b \neq 0$ and into the half-line $v = 0$ with $u \geq 0$ if $b = 0$. The origin is the common focus of all of these parabolas—the image of precisely that point in the z plane where the mapping is not conformal. The maps of the lines $x = -\frac{1}{2}$ and $y = 1$ are shown in Figure 8-5. These maps (curves) intersect orthogonally, as could have been predicted (How?).

EXAMPLE 2.   The transformation

$$w = \cos z \equiv \cos x \cosh y - i \sin x \sinh y$$

maps the strip $\varphi \leq x < \varphi + 2\pi$ with $-\infty < y < \infty$ in the z plane, for arbitrary, constant real φ, into the entire open w plane and is conformal for all z except $z = n\pi$ for integral n, where $dw/dz = 0$. Here $u = \cos x \cosh y$ and $v = -\sin x \sinh y$, so that

$$\frac{u^2}{\cos^2 x} - \frac{v^2}{\sin^2 x} = 1,$$

$$\frac{u^2}{\cosh^2 y} + \frac{v^2}{\sinh^2 y} = 1.$$

Hence the lines $x = a$ are mapped into halves (since $\cosh y > 0$) of confocal hyperbolas with foci at $z = \pm 1$ if $a \neq n\pi/2$ for integral n, and the lines $y = b$ are mapped into confocal ellipses with the same foci as the hyperbolas if $b \neq 0$ (Fig. 8-6).   (What are the

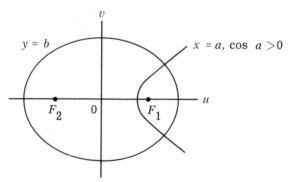

Figure 8-6

maps of the lines excluded in this discussion?)   A theorem from the theory of differential equations, to the effect that confocal ellipses and hyperbolas are orthogonal trajectories, is thus verified.

Students who wish to pursue the subject of conformal mapping further are advised to see Chapters VIII through X of R. V. Churchill: *Complex*

Variables and Applications, which is listed in the bibliography at the end of this book.

8-13. Problems.

1. If D is the domain of definition of the function $w = f(z)$ and R the range, find if possible a subset S of D such that the map of S is also R, where
    (a) $f(z) = iz$;
    (b) $f(z) = z^2 + 2z$;
    (c) $f(z) = e^{iz}$;
    (d) $f(z) = \sin z$;
    (e) $f(z) = 1/z$;
    (f) $f(z) = 1/z^2$;
    (g) $f(z) = z^n$, n a positive integer greater than 1.

2. Give, for each of the mappings in problem 1 above, equations for the maps of the lines $x = a$ and $y = b$—eliminating the parameter where this is feasible and, in these cases, sketching a few of the maps.

3. Sketch a few of the curves $R[f(z)] = constant$ and $I[f(z)] = constant$ in the z plane for the functions $f(z)$ in parts (a), (b), (c), and (f) of problem 1.

Some Techniques for More Penetrating Analysis

9

9-1. Epsilon-Delta and Related Techniques.

The proofs in §2-2 of the limit theorems on sums, products, and quotients of complex variables were thrown back onto similar theorems from real calculus. While this device enables passage from conviction of the truth of those theorems in real calculus to acceptance of their truth in complex calculus, yet their proof in real calculus by the ϵ–δ techniques demanded by current standards of rigor is quite as complicated as their direct proof in complex analysis by those same techniques. Since one purpose of this chapter is to take a second and critical look at some parts of the earlier chapters, it will now be illustrated how ϵ–δ techniques can be used directly in proving limit theorems by showing that, if $w \to w_0 \neq 0$ and $w^* \to w_0^*$ as $p \to 0$ $(p > 0)$, then $w^*/w \to w_0^*/w_0$. (Compare Example 4, §2-2.) First, there is a δ' such that $|w - w_0| < |w_0|/2$ whenever $0 < p < \delta'$, so that $|w| > |w_0|/2$ for such values of p and therefore

$$\left| \frac{w^*}{w} - \frac{w_0^*}{w_0} \right| \equiv \frac{|w^* w_0 - w w_0^*|}{|w w_0|} < \frac{2}{|w_0|^2} |w^* w_0 - w w_0^*|$$

$$\equiv \frac{2}{|w_0|^2} |w_0(w^* - w_0^*) - w_0^*(w - w_0)|$$

$$\leq \frac{2}{|w_0|^2} [|w_0| \, |w^* - w_0^*| + |w_0^*| \, |w - w_0|]$$

whenever $0 < p < \delta'$. Next, for arbitrary $\epsilon > 0$, there is a $\delta'' > 0$ such that

$$|w^* - w_0^*|, \, |w - w_0| < \frac{|w_0|^2 \epsilon}{2(|w_0| + |w_0^*|)}$$

whenever $0 < p < \delta''$. Hence, if $\delta = \min(\delta', \delta'')$ it follows that

$$\left| \frac{w^*}{w} - \frac{w_0^*}{w_0} \right| < \epsilon$$

whenever $0 < p < \delta$.

The next illustration of ϵ–δ techniques concerns real variables; it is proof of the theorem used in §5-7. Given that $F(x)$ is continuous for $a \leq x \leq b$ and $F(x) \leq M$ there, it is to be shown that $\int_a^b F(x)dx \leq M(b - a)$, with equality holding only if $F(x) = M$ throughout the interval. Since, for every subdivision of the interval, $\sum F(x_j')\Delta x_j \leq \sum M\Delta x_j \equiv M(b - a)$, the first conclusion of the theorem is immediate. To prove the second conclusion, suppose that $F(c) < M$ for some c such that $a \leq c \leq b$. Indeed, it may be supposed that $a < c < b$, since the continuity of $F(x)$ would force $F(a) = F(b) = M$ if $F(x) \equiv M$ for $a < x < b$. If $\epsilon = [M - F(c)]/2 > 0$, there is a $\delta > 0$ such that $a \leq c - \delta < c < c + \delta \leq b$ and $|F(x) - F(c)| < \epsilon$ whenever $c - \delta \leq x \leq c + \delta$, so that

$$F(x) < F(c) + \epsilon \equiv M - \epsilon$$

for such values of x. If, next, the interval $a \leq x \leq b$ is subdivided in such a way that $|\sum F(x_j')\Delta x_j - \int_a^b F(x)dx| < \epsilon\delta$ *and that the points of subdivision include the particular points* $c \pm \delta$, then

$$\sum F(x_j')\Delta x_j \leq M(b - a - 2\delta) + (M - \epsilon)2\delta \equiv M(b - a) - 2\epsilon\delta,$$

so that

$$M(b - a) - \int_a^b F(x)dx \equiv M(b - a) + \left[\sum F(x_j')\Delta x_j \right.$$
$$\left. - \int_a^b F(x)dx \right] - \sum F(x_j')\Delta x_j$$
$$> M(b - a) - \epsilon\delta - [M(b - a) - 2\epsilon\delta]$$
$$\equiv \epsilon\delta > 0.$$

That is, $M(b - a) > \int_a^b F(x)dx$. The proof is complete.

It is appropriate at this point to give the proof of Morera's theorem (Theorem 4-15) promised in §4-10. First, the hypothesis that the integral in the theorem vanishes for each closed path in R is equivalent to the hypothesis that, given any two points z_1 and z_2 in R, the integral $\int_{z_1(c)}^{z_2} f(z)dz$ has the same value for each path c in R that joins z_1 to z_2. (Why?) If, then, any point Z in R is fixed upon, a function $F(z)$ is defined for each z in R by the integral $F(z) \equiv \int_{Z(c)}^z f(\zeta)d\zeta$, where c is any path in R that joins Z to z. It is to be shown first that $F'(z)$ exists at each point z in R. Accordingly, let z be an arbitrary but fixed point in R. Then, for a variable point ζ in R, $f(\zeta) = f(z) + \eta(\zeta)$, where $\eta(\zeta)$ is a continuous function of ζ for ζ near z and tends to zero as $\zeta \to z$. It follows from this last property of

$\eta(\zeta)$ that, given arbitrary $\epsilon > 0$, there is a circle k with center at z whose interior lies in R and for which $|\eta(\zeta)| < \epsilon$ whenever ζ is within k.

Now, for all Δz of sufficiently small magnitude $F(z + \Delta z) - F(z) = \int_{z(l)}^{z + \Delta z} f(\zeta)d\zeta$, where l may be taken as the line segment from z to $z + \Delta z$. Hence

$$F(z + \Delta z) - F(z) = \int_{z(l)}^{z + \Delta z} [f(z) + \eta(\zeta)]d\zeta$$
$$= f(z)\Delta z + \int_{z(l)}^{z + \Delta z} \eta(\zeta)d\zeta,$$

so that, if $|\Delta z| < \delta$, where δ is the radius of k, then

$$\left| \frac{F(z + \Delta z) - F(z)}{\Delta z} - f(z) \right| \equiv \left| \int_{z(l)}^{z + \Delta z} \eta(\zeta)d\zeta \right| \frac{1}{|\Delta z|} < \frac{\epsilon|\Delta z|}{|\Delta z|} = \epsilon.$$

Thus $F(z)$ is regular throughout R, with $F'(z) = f(z)$. But, by Theorem 5-4, $F(z)$ has derivatives of all orders, so that, in particular, $F''(z)$ exists. And this is to say that $f'(z)$ exists, so that $f(z)$ itself is regular throughout R, which is what was to be proved.

In §2-2 it was seen how limiting situations could be reduced to the standard form $\lim_{p \to 0} q = 0, p > 0, q \ge 0$. One often prefers, however, to think, not of the behavior of the variables p and q as such, but of the behavior of other variables in terms of which p and q may be expressed. Thus in the situation $\lim_{z \to z_0} w = w_0$ one may choose to regard the conditions $|w - w_0| < \epsilon$ and $0 < |z - z_0| < \delta$ not merely as restrictions on two non-negative real variables but as restrictions on the positions of w and z in complex planes. A similar remark may be made about interpreting the situation $\lim_{z \to \infty} f(z) = A$, which means first: Given arbitrary $\epsilon > 0$, there is an $R > 0$ such that $|f(z) - A| < \epsilon$ whenever $|z| > R$. In fact, certain limiting situations can be described very neatly indeed in terms of *neighborhoods*.

EXAMPLE 1. The continuity condition, $\lim_{z \to z_0} f(z) = f(z_0)$ means that, given an arbitrary neighborhood N of $w_0 \equiv f(z_0)$, there is a neighborhood M of z_0 such that $w \equiv f(z)$ is in N whenever z is in M.

EXAMPLE 2. The condition $\lim_{z \to z_0} w = \infty$ means that, given an arbitrary neighborhood N of the infinite point, there is a deleted neighborhood M of z_0 such that w is in N whenever z is in M.

EXAMPLE 3. The condition $\lim_{z_1, z_2 \to z_0} f(z_1, z_2) = A$ means that, given an arbitrary neighborhood N of A, there is a neighborhood M of z_0 such that $w \equiv f(z_1, z_2)$ is in N whenever both z_1 and z_2 are in M and not both $z_1 = z_0$ and $z_2 = z_0$.

"Neighborhood proofs" or "ϵ-neighborhood proofs" are sometimes especially happy.

EXAMPLE 4. To prove that $F(z) \equiv f(z) + g(z)$ is continuous at $z = z_0$ if $f(z)$ and $g(z)$ are both continuous there, we may proceed as follows. Given arbitrary $\epsilon > 0$, there is a neighborhood M_1 of z_0 such that $|f(z) - f(z_0)| < \epsilon/2$ whenever z is in M_1, and there is a neighborhood M_2 of z_0 such that $|g(z) - g(z_0)| < \epsilon/2$ whenever z is in M_2. If then M is the smaller of M_1 and M_2, we have

$$|F(z) - F(z_0)| \leq |f(z) - f(z_0)| + |g(z) - g(z_0)|$$
$$< \epsilon/2 + \epsilon/2 \equiv \epsilon$$

whenever z is in M. This is an example of "ϵ-neighborhood proofs;" it is clearly equivalent to an ϵ-δ proof.

EXAMPLE 5. Let us prove by "neighborhood analysis" that a continuous function of a continuous function is continuous. We are given that $z = f(\zeta)$ is continuous at ζ_0 and that $w = F(z)$ is continuous at $z_0 \equiv f(\zeta_0)$, and we are to show that $w = F[f(\zeta)]$ is continuous at ζ_0. Now given an arbitrary neighborhood N of $w_0 \equiv F[f(\zeta_0)]$ there is a neighborhood M of z_0 such that w is in N whenever z is in M. But then there is also a neighborhood L of ζ_0 such that z is in M whenever ζ is in L. Hence w is in N whenever ζ is in L, and this is all that needed to be shown.

If x is a real variable, one defines a *neighborhood* of the point x_0 as the "open interval" consisting of those values of x for which $|x - x_0| < r$ for some positive number r; a *deleted neighborhood* of x_0 is a neighborhood of x_0 from which x_0 itself has been removed. With these additional definitions the limiting behavior of real functions of real or complex variables and of complex functions of real variables can be characterized without introducing new terms. For example, a complex function $f(x)$ of the real variable x is continuous at a point x_0 in a neighborhood of which it is defined if, given an arbitrary neighborhood N of $w_0 \equiv f(x_0)$, there is a neighborhood M of x_0 such that $w \equiv f(x)$ is in N whenever x is in M.

This section concludes with a somewhat different example of usage of the terms and symbols with which it is concerned. The example consists of two statements of the Casorati-Weierstrass theorem set forth as Theorem 5-15. An "ϵ-R" statement follows: *If $f(z)$ is a transcendental entire function, then, given an arbitrary (complex) number w_0 and two arbitrary positive numbers ϵ and R, there is a value z_0 of z for which $|z_0| > R$ and $|f(z_0) - w_0| < \epsilon$.* A "neighborhood" statement is this: *If $f(z)$ is a transcendental entire function, then, given an arbitrary (complex) number w_0*

and an arbitrary neighborhood N of w_0, in every neighborhood of the point at infinity there is a value z_0 of z for which $f(z_0)$ is in N.

9-2. Problems.

1. Given that $\lim_{z \to z_0} f(z) = A$, construct an ϵ–δ proof that

$$\lim_{z \to z_0} [-f(z)] = -A.$$

2. Characterize the following situations in terms of inequalities:
    (a) $\lim_{z \to z_0} f(z) = \infty$, $f(z)$ being defined in a deleted neighborhood of z_0;
    (b) $\lim_{z \to \infty} f(z) = \infty$, $f(z)$ being defined in a deleted neighborhood of the infinite point.

3. Characterize the situations of problem 2 in terms of neighborhoods.

4. Let a real function $f(z)$ of the complex variable z be defined in a deleted neighborhood of the point $z = i$. Express the proposition that $\lim_{z \to i} f(z) = 2$ using
    (a) ϵ–δ notation,
    (b) neighborhood terminology.

5. Give a direct "ϵ-neighborhood" proof that $ww^* \to w_0 w_0^*$ as $p \to 0 \ (p > 0)$ if $w \to w_0$ and $w^* \to w_0^*$ as $p \to 0 \ (p > 0)$.

6. Characterize the condition of Example 3 of §9-1 in ϵ–δ terms.

7. Assuming Theorem 5-15 in ϵ–δ terms, give an ϵ–δ proof of the Casorati-Weierstrass theorem set forth in Case 3, §6-9.

8. Let $f(z, \zeta)$ be defined whenever z is in the neighborhood of a point z_0 and ζ is in the neighborhood of the infinite point. Define "continuity of $f(z, \zeta)$ at (z_0, ∞)" in terms of
    (a) limits;
    (b) positive numbers of the sorts we have labeled ϵ, δ, and R;
    (c) neighborhoods.

*9. Prove that, if $\lim_{n \to \infty} z_n = z_0$, then $\lim_{n \to \infty} (\sum_1^n z_k)/n = z_0$. (Needing to show that, given arbitrary $\epsilon > 0$, there is a positive number N such that

$$D \equiv \left| \frac{1}{n} \sum_1^n z_k - z_0 \right| < \epsilon$$

whenever $n > N$, start with the fact that there is a positive number N' such that $|z_k - z_0| < \epsilon/2$ whenever $k > N'$.)

10. Use the methods of this section to prove that a function $f(z)$ that is continuous at a point z_0 is bounded in the neighborhood of z_0.

9-3. Closed, Null, and Bounded Point Sets.

Heretofore the book has been concerned with few types of point sets other than *open* ones—what in §4-6 were called open "regions." In order to prove some of the more subtle theorems of the general theory, it is necessary to consider other types, among which one of the most important is the *closed set*. A point set S is said to be closed if it contains all of its finite limit points. (Sometimes the infinite point is also taken into consideration, as in the phrase "the closed plane.") Thus the set S consisting of all points z for which $|z| \leq 1$ is closed; the set S consisting of all points z for which $0 < |z| \leq 1$ is not closed (nor open); the set of all points in the finite plane is both closed and open; every set consisting of only a finite number of points is closed (since it *does* contain all of its limit points). It is customary to regard the *null set* (which consists of no points at all) as both open and closed. The set $\bar{S}$ obtained by adjoining to a set S all of its limit points is called the *closure* of S. A set S all points of which lie within some circle is said to be *bounded*.

EXAMPLE 1. The set of the reciprocals of the positive integers is bounded; the set of the positive integers is not.

EXAMPLE 2. Let us show that, given any set S, the *derived set* S', which consists of all of the limit points of S, is closed. Evidently we need only show that, if z_0 is a limit point of S', then it is contained in S'. But in every deleted neighborhood N of z_0 is a point z_N of S', and in every deleted neighborhood M of z_N is a point of S—in particular this is so when M is small enough to be included in N (and therefore, of course, also to fail to contain z_0). That is, in every deleted neighborhood of z_0 is a point of S, so that z_0 is a limit point of S and is therefore contained in S', as was to be proved.

9-4. Problems.

1. State whether the set S is closed, open, or neither if S consists of all points $z \equiv x + iy$ for which

   (a) $R(z) \geq 0$;
   (b) $R(z) < 0$;

(c) $0 \le I(z) \le 1$;

(d) $0 < I(z) \le 1$;

(e) $y = x^2$

(i)   with no restriction on x,

(ii) with $|x| \le 1$,

(iii) with $|x| > 1$;

(f) $|z| = 1$;

(g) either $|z| \le 1$ or z lies in the open interval $1 < x < 2$ on the x axis;

(h) either $|z| \le a$ or both $-b < x < b$ and $-b < y < b$, where a and b are positive numbers;

(i) both $|z| \le a$, $-b < x < b$, and $-b < y < b$, where a and b are positive numbers;

(j) $x > 0$ except the points on the line segments $x = 1/n$, $-n \le y \le n, n = 1, 2, \ldots$;

(k) z lies on none of the line segments in part (j).

2. Which of the sets in problem 1 are bounded?

3. Prove that the closure $\bar{S}$ of any set S is itself closed.

9-5. Complementary Set.   Isolated Points. Boundary Points.   Interior Points.

The *complement* $C(S)$ of a set S *with respect to* a set T is the set of all of the points of T that remain after those points of T (if any) that are also in S have been removed.   The phrase "the complement of S" without qualification means the complement of S with respect to a set T whose composition is understood by the context; in complex variable theory this set T is usually understood to be the set of all points in the finite plane; in real variable theory it is usually understood to mean the set of all real numbers.   The null set and a given set T are complements of each other with respect to T.

An *isolated point* z_0 of a set S is a point of S in a deleted neighborhood of which are no points of S.

A *boundary point* of a set S is a point z_0 in every neighborhood of which are a point of S and a point of $C(S)$.   The point z_0 itself may or may not be a point of S.   By the *boundary* of a set S is meant the set of all of the boundary points of S.

An *interior point* of a set S is a point z_0, some neighborhood of which consists entirely of points of S.

EXAMPLE 1.   The boundary of the open half-plane $R(z) > 0$ is the y axis.

EXAMPLE 2. The boundaries of a set and of its complement coincide.

EXAMPLE 3. An isolated point of a set S is always a boundary point of S.

EXAMPLE 4. Every point of an open set S is an interior point of S.

In the preceding chapters the term "region" has been used only when modified by the adjective "open." A definition of the unqualified term follows. In this book a *region* will mean either a non-null open region or a non-null open region to which have been adjoined some or all of its boundary points. A region that includes all of its boundary points, being closed (Example 6 below), is appropriately called a *closed region*.

EXAMPLE 5. The set of points z for which $1 < |z| \le 2$ is a region; it is neither open nor closed.

EXAMPLE 6. The segment of the x axis for which $0 < x < 1$ is not a region.

EXAMPLE 7. To show that a region S that includes all of its boundary points is a closed set of points, we suppose that there is a limit point z_0 of S that is not in S. Then z_0 is in $C(S)$, while in every neighborhood of z_0 is a point of S. Hence z_0 is a boundary point of S and therefore is included in S, contrary to assumption.

9-6. Problems.

1. What is the boundary of the set S consisting of
    (a) the points $z = i^n/n$ for $n = 1, 2, \ldots$?
    (b) all points on the real axis?
    (c) all points in the finite plane?
    (d) all points on the interior of the unit circle $|z| = 1$, all points on the real axis for which $1 < x < 2$, and the points $z = 1, 2, \ldots$?
    (e) all points z for which $0 < |z| \le 1$?
    (f) all points z for which $0 \le |z| < 1$?
    (g) a finite number of points?

2. Name the isolated points, if any, of each of the sets of problem 1.

3. If z_0 is a limit point of a set S but not also a boundary point of S, how can z_0 be characterized more simply?

4. Prove that the set B of all of the boundary points of a given set S is closed.

5. A necessary and sufficient condition that a set S be closed is that it include all of its boundary points. Example 6 above establishes one part of this theorem. Prove the other part.

6. Show that a necessary and sufficient condition that a set S be closed is that $C(S)$ be open.

7. In every neighborhood of every point z_0 of a region S is an interior point of S. Why?

8. (a) If from the closure $\bar{S}$ of a given set S are removed all of the interior points of $\bar{S}$, do the points which remain constitute the boundary of S?
   (b) What if the points removed are the interior points of S rather than of $\bar{S}$?

9. State whether or not the set S is a region if S consists of all points $z \equiv x + iy$ for which
   (a) $0 < |z| \le 1$;
   (b) either $x > 0$ and $y > 0$ or $x < 0$ and $y \le 0$;
   (c) either $|z| < 1$ or $z = x$ and $-a \le x \le a$, where a is a positive number;
   (d) x is a rational number;
   (e) z lies on none of the line segments $x = 1/n$, $-n \le y \le n$, $n = 1, 2, \ldots$ [the set of problem 1(k) of §9-4].

9-7. The Elementary Algebra of Sets.

Although the sets for which the definitions of this section are made are sets of points z in the complex plane, these definitions can be construed as made for sets of elements of any sort. Given two sets of points S_1 and S_2 (Fig. 9-1), one says that they are equal and writes $S_1 = S_2$ if every point in S_1 is a point in S_2 and conversely; one symbolizes and defines the *sum* or *union* of S_1 and S_2 as the set $S_1 + S_2$ (or $S_1 \cup S_2$) consisting of all points which are in either S_1 or S_2, the *difference* between S_1 and S_2, in this order, as the set $S_1 - S_2$ consisting of all points which are in S_1 but not in S_2, and the *product* or *intersection* of S_1 and S_2 as the set $S_1 S_2$ (or $S_1 \cap S_2$) consisting of all points which are in both S_1 and S_2. By way of illustration of the use of these concepts, a formal proof is now given of the trivial fact that, for any two point sets S_1 and S_2,

$$C(S_1 + S_2) = C(S_1)C(S_2). \tag{9-1}$$

If z_l is an arbitrary point in the left-hand set of (9-1), then it is not in either S_1 or S_2 and so must be in the complement of each, which means that it is a point in the right-hand set of (9-1). And if z_r is an arbitrary point in the right-hand set of (9-1), then it is in the complements of both S_1 and S_2 and hence not in either S_1 or S_2, which means that it is a point in the left-hand set of (9-1).

It is clear that complements of equal sets are equal. Also that $C[C(S)] = S$ for every set S.

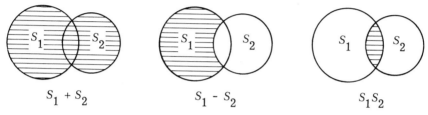

$$S_1 + S_2 \qquad\qquad S_1 - S_2 \qquad\qquad S_1 S_2$$

Figure 9-1

9-8. Problems.

1. Let the set S_1 consist of those points z for which $|z| \leq 1$ and the set S_2 of those points z for which both $-a < R(z) < a$ and $-a < I(z) < a$. State for which values of a
   (a) $S_1 + S_2$ is open,
   (b) $S_1 + S_2$ is closed,
   (c) $S_1 S_2$ is open,
   (d) $S_1 S_2$ is closed.

2. Given three sets, S_1, S_2, and S_3, is it always true that
   (a) $S_1(S_2 + S_3) = S_1 S_2 + S_1 S_3$?
   (b) $S_1(S_2 - S_3) = S_1 S_2 - S_1 S_3$?

*3. Given any two sets S_1 and S_2, show that $C(S_1) + C(S_2) = C(S_1 S_2)$
   (a) by the direct method used in proving (9-1),
   (b) by replacing S_1 and S_2 in (9-1) by $C(S_1)$ and $C(S_2)$, respectively, and taking complements in the resulting equation.

4. Given any two sets S_1 and S_2, show that $S_1 - S_2 = S_1 C(S_2)$.

5. Show that each of the following is, in general, false, and state under precisely what circumstances each is true:
   (a) the proposition that $(S_1 + S_2) - S_2 = S_1$,
   (b) the proposition that $(S_1 - S_2) + S_2 = S_1$.

6. Given any two sets S_1 and S_2, show that

$$S_1 + S_2 = S_1 C(S_2) + S_2 C(S_1) + S_1 S_2.$$

*7. Given two open sets S_1 and S_2, show that both $S_1 + S_2$ and $S_1 S_2$ are open.

*8. Given two closed sets S_1 and S_2, show that both $S_1 + S_2$ and $S_1 S_2$ are closed.

9. Given two sets S_1 and S_2, show that the conditions $S_1 + S_2 = S_1$ and $S_1 S_2 = S_2$ are equivalent.

10. Supposing that the difference $S_1 - S_2$ had been defined as "that set S_3 such that $S_1 = S_2 + S_3$," discuss the questions of existence and uniqueness of this difference and of the possible usefulness of the definition.

11. Given two sets S_1 and S_2, let the *quotient* of S_1 by S_2 be defined as "that set S_3 such that $S_1 = S_2 S_3$." Discuss the questions of existence and uniqueness of this quotient and of the possible usefulness of the definition.

9-9. The Elementary Algebra of Sets, Continued.

The ideas of the preceding paragraphs will now be extended. Given any number, finite or infinite, of point sets S, one symbolizes and defines their *sum* or *union* as the set $\sum S$ (or $\cup S$) consisting of all points that are in at least one of the S, and their *product* or *intersection* as the set $\prod S$ (or $\cap S$) consisting of all points which are in each of the S. As in the proof of (9-1) and problem 3 of §9-8, it can be shown that $C(\sum S) = \prod C(S)$ and $C(\prod S) = \sum C(S)$. And as in problems 7 and 8 of §9-8, it can be shown that $\sum S$ is open if all of the S are open and that $\prod S$ is closed if all of the S are closed. However, if there are an infinite number of the S, $\sum S$ may not be closed even when all of the S are closed; this is the case if the S are the sets of all z for which $|z| \le n/(n + 1)$ for $n = 1, 2, \ldots$; in fact, here $\sum S$ is open. And if there are an infinite number of the S, $\prod S$ may not be open even when all of the S are open; this is the case if the S are the sets of all z for which $|z| < a$ for each real number a that is greater than 1; here, indeed, $\prod S$ is closed. (It is to be noted that the *set* of the sets in a sum or product of infinitely many sets need not be *denumerable*. A set of infinitely many objects S is said to be "denumerable" if there exists an ordering of the objects of the sort $S_1, S_2, \ldots, S_n, \ldots$ in which each object appears once and only once.)

9-10. Problems.

1. Construct an example to show that a product of infinitely many open sets may not be open by taking complements in the example in the text to show that a sum of infinitely many closed sets may not be closed.

2. What situation is shown by taking complements in the example in the text to show that a product of infinitely many open sets may not be open? Do this.

3. Construct an example to show that a product of infinitely many open sets may be neither open nor closed.

4. Construct an example to show that a sum of infinitely many closed sets may be neither closed nor open.

5. Given a set S and an infinite number of sets T, is it necessarily true that $S \sum T = \sum ST$?

6. Given an infinite number of sets S and an infinite number of sets T, is it necessarily true that $(\sum S)(\sum T) = \sum ST$?

7. Given a denumerably infinite number of sets $S_1, S_2, \ldots$ and a denumerably infinite number of sets $T_1, T_2, \ldots$, is it necessarily true that $\prod S_n + \prod T_n = \prod (S_n + T_n)$?

9-11. Extreme Bounds on Real Sets.

If the student has suspected that some axiom is needed, in addition to those with which he is familiar, to establish many of the theorems whose proofs he has seen described in elementary courses as "beyond the scope of this book," he is justified. This section is concerned with such an axiom about real numbers.

A real set S is said to be *bounded on the right* if there is a number B such that $x \leq B$ for each x in S; any such number B is called an *upper bound* for S. Similarly, if there is a number b such that $x \geq b$ for each x in S, then S is said to be *bounded on the left*, and any such number b is called a *lower bound* for S. A real set is clearly bounded if it is bounded on both the right and the left. Consider the proposition:

$$\text{that every non-null set } S \text{ of real numbers that} \atop \text{has an upper bound has a } \textit{least upper bound.}\dagger \qquad (9\text{-}2)$$

If the student is willing to accept the truth of proposition (9-2), he may take it as the axiom mentioned at the beginning of this section. If not, in

† That is, the set of all upper bounds of S has a smallest member.

order to speak the language of contemporary mathematics, he will have to accept the truth of some other axiom, of which (9-2) is a consequence; such an alternative axiom will shortly be stated. Since the truth of (9-2) is bound to be accepted one way or another, it is in order to say a few words about the least upper bound of a non-null set of real numbers that is bounded on the right. This number is often called the *supremum* of S and written sup S.

EXAMPLE 1.   The least upper bound of the set of all negative integers is -1; it is a member of S.

EXAMPLE 2.   If S is the set of all negative numbers, then sup $S = 0$; it is not a member of S.

The least upper bound or supremum, M, of a non-null set S of real numbers that is bounded on the right is characterized by these properties:

$$x \le M \text{ for } every \ x \text{ in } S; \tag{9-3}$$
$$\text{for every } \epsilon > 0, x > M - \epsilon \text{ for } some \ x \text{ in } S.$$

The first property states that M is an upper bound and the second states that there is no smaller upper bound. The properties (9-3) can be used to show that, if the least upper bound M of a non-null set S of real numbers that is bounded on the right is not in S, then it is a limit point of S. The second condition in (9-3), along with the fact that M itself is not in S, means that there is a point of S in every deleted neighborhood of M.

9-12. Problems.

1.   In problem 2 below it will be shown that a non-null set S of real numbers that is bounded on the left has a *greatest lower bound* (often called the *infimum* of S and written inf S). Characterize this number, m, by two properties analogous to those in (9-3).

2.   Prove the theorem quoted in problem 1. [Consider the set T of the negatives of the numbers that constitute S. Show first that T is bounded on the right. If $M = \sup T$, show by means of (9-3) that the number $m \equiv -M$ meets the characterization formulated in problem 1 for inf S.]

*3.   State, for each of the sets S below, whether it is bounded, bounded on the right, bounded on the left. Name sup S and inf S whenever they exist, and state whether they are members of S. The set S consists of

(a)   all positive integers;
(b)   the two points 0 and 1;
(c)   all real numbers x for which $0 < x \leq 1$;
(d)   all the negative numbers plus the point 3;
(e)   the numbers $1, 1/2, 1/3, \ldots, 1/n, \ldots$;
(f)   all non-negative rational numbers that are less than 1.

9-13.   The Axiom of Continuity.

The axiom offered as alternative to the truth of (9-2) is the truth of the proposition

> that, given two subsets L and R of the real numbers such that
> (i)   every real number is in either L or R,
> (ii) neither L nor R is null, and
> (iii) every number l in L is less than every number r in R,   (9-4)
> then there is a number c such that every number x that is less than c is in L and every number x that is greater than c is in R.

This is called the *Axiom of Continuity* and bears the name of Richard Dedekind, in whose systematic analysis of the real number system it occurs as a theorem.   The number c of the axiom of continuity is unique, for if there is a different number c' with the characteristic properties of c, then every number x between c and c' is a member of both L and R, contrary to provision (iii) of (9-4).   The number c itself may belong to either L or R: if L is the set of non-positive numbers, and R consists of the remaining real numbers, then $c = 0$ and belongs to L; if L is the set of negative numbers, and R consists of the remaining real numbers, then again $c = 0$, but now it belongs to R.   The separation of the real numbers into the subsets L and R is called a *Dedekind cut*, and c is called the *cut number* determined by this cut.

The following theorem from real variable theory is inserted to illustrate use of the axiom of continuity.

THEOREM 9-1.   *If a real function $f(x)$ of the real variable x is continuous on the closed interval $a \leq x \leq b$ and $f(b) \neq f(a)$, then $f(x)$ takes on every value between $f(a)$ and $f(b)$ on the open interval $a < x < b$.*

Proof.   Suppose for definiteness that $f(a) < f(b)$, and let N be any number such that $f(a) < N < f(b)$.   Putting $\varphi(x) = f(x) - N$, we see that $\varphi(a) < 0$ and $\varphi(b) > 0$ and that the theorem will be proved if we can show that $\varphi(x)$ vanishes for some x such that $a < x < b$. Let L be the set of all real numbers l that are either less than a or, if not less than a, then such that $\varphi(x) \leq 0$ for every x for which $a \leq x \leq l$. Let R consist of the remaining real numbers. All reals are included in L and R, by definition of R. Since a is in L, and b is in R, neither L nor R is null. Finally, any number x that is less than a number l in L belongs to L, so that every number r in R is greater than every number l in L. Let c be the cut number determined by this Dedekind cut.

We note first that $c > a$ (since there are points in L that are greater than a) and that $c < b$ (since there are points in R that are less than b). It remains only to show that $\varphi(c) = 0$. If $\varphi(c) < 0$, there are points in L that are greater than c, contrary to the nature of c; and if $\varphi(c) > 0$, there are points in R that are less than c, also contrary to the nature of c. The only remaining alternative is the desired conclusion. Incidentally, the cut number c belongs to L.

The next two theorems establish the equivalence of the least upper bound axiom and the cut axiom.

THEOREM 9-2. *Proposition (9-2) is implied by proposition (9-4).*

Proof. Let R consist of all of the upper bounds of S, and L of the remaining real numbers. All real numbers are included in L and R by definition of L. Since S has an upper bound, R is not null; and if x is any member of S, then the number $x - 1$ belongs to L, so that L is not null either. Finally, every number x that is greater than a number r in R belongs to R, so that every number l in L is less than every number r in R. The cut number c determined by this Dedekind cut is an upper bound of S, since otherwise there is a member x of S for which $x > c$, so that the number $(c + x)/2$ is in L, which is impossible since $(c + x)/2 > c$. Moreover, c is the *least* upper bound, since all upper bounds are in R. Clearly, c belongs to R.

THEOREM 9-3. *Proposition (9-2) is equivalent to proposition (9-4).*

Proof. In view of Theorem 9-2, we need only show that proposition (9-4) is implied by proposition (9-2). Assuming conditions (i), (ii), and (iii) of proposition (9-4) fulfilled, we see by (ii) and (iii) that the set L is non-null and bounded on the right. Proposition (9-2) therefore assures the existence of a least upper bound c' for L. Now let x be any real number different from c'.

If $x > c'$, then x cannot belong to L (since c' is an upper bound for L) and so, by (i), must belong to R.   And if $x < c'$, then there is a member l of L for which $l > x$ (since c' is the *least* upper bound for L), so that, by (i) and (iii), x belongs to L.   This completes the proof.

9-14. Problems.

Prove the following theorems by means of either the axiom of continuity or the truth of proposition (9-2).   The set L and the number c mentioned in problems 1 and 2 may be taken in the sense of proposition (9-4) in the one case and as the set S of proposition (9-2) and its least upper bound, respectively, in the other.

*1.   *If the real function $f(x)$ of the real variable x is continuous on the closed interval $a \leq x \leq b$, then $f(x)$ is bounded there.*   [Supposing the conclusion false, let L consist of the real numbers l that are either less than a or, if not less than a, then such that $f(x)$ is bounded for $a \leq x \leq l$, and let R consist of the remaining reals.   Then a is in L and b is in R.   Use the fact that $f(x)$ is bounded in the neighborhood of c.]

2.   ARCHIMEDES' THEOREM (actually, an *axiom* in the context of Archimedes' development): *If the real numbers a and b are positive, there is an integer n such that $na \geq b$.*   (Supposing the conclusion false for some a and b, let L consist of the real numbers l such that $na \geq l$ for some n.   Use the fact that $c - a/2$ is in L.)

*3.   Theorem 3-6 on assumption of the truth of Theorem 3-5.

9-15. Nests of Intervals.   The Bolzano-Weierstrass Theorem.

By a *nest of intervals* one means a denumerable set of finite, closed intervals $I_n: a_n \leq x \leq b_n$ such that all points of I_{n+1} are points of I_n for $n = 1, 2, \ldots$ and $b_n - a_n \to 0$ as $n \to \infty$.

THEOREM 9-4.   (Nested Intervals Theorem)   *There is one and only one point that lies in each interval of a nest of intervals.*

Proof.   The set of points $a_1, a_2, \ldots, a_n, \ldots$ is bounded on the right (in particular by b_1) and therefore has a least upper bound x_0.   Any number smaller than x_0 cannot lie in all of the I_n.   Similarly, the set of points $b_1, b_2, \ldots, b_n, \ldots$ is bounded on the left and therefore has a greatest lower bound x_0^*, and any number larger than x_0^* cannot lie in all of the I_n. Now x_0^* cannot be less than x_0, since there would then be some a_N greater than x_0^*, so that $b_n \geq a_N > x_0^*$ for all n. Thus $a_n \leq x_0 \leq x_0^* \leq b_n$ for all n. Since then $0 \leq x_0^* - x_0 \leq b_n - a_n$ for all n, and $b_n - a_n \to 0$ as $n \to \infty$, we must have $x_0^* = x_0$. Since x_0 clearly lies in each interval of the nest, the proof is complete.

It may seem evident to the student that a bounded infinite set of distinct points must have at least one limit point—or he may suspect that, with sufficient ingenuity, such a set might be constructed with no limit point. The truth of the matter is now set forth.

THEOREM 9-5.   (Bolzano-Weierstrass Theorem for Linear Sets) *A bounded infinite set S of distinct points x on the x axis has at least one finite limit point.*

Proof.   Let all of the points of S lie in the interval I_0: $a \leq x \leq b$. Then in one of the two intervals I_0': $a \leq x \leq (a + b)/2$ and I_0'': $(a + b)/2 \leq x \leq b$ (or both) lie infinitely many distinct points of S; let us pick one of these subintervals of I_0 for which this is the case (taking the left-hand one, for definiteness, if we have the choice) and call it I_1: $a_1 \leq x \leq b_1$. Then in one of the two intervals I_1': $a_1 \leq x \leq (a_1 + b_1)/2$ and I_1'': $(a_1 + b_1)/2 \leq x \leq b_1$ (or both) lie infinitely many distinct points of S; let us pick one of these subintervals of I_1 for which this is the case (taking as before the left-hand one if we have the choice) and call it I_2: $a_2 \leq x \leq b_2$. Continuing this process we generate a nest of intervals so that, according to Theorem 9-4, there is a point x_0 that is common to all the I_n. But in every neighborhood of x_0 lie intervals I_n of our nest, for sufficiently large n, whence in every neighborhood of x_0 lie an infinite number of distinct points of S, which means that x_0 is a limit point of S and therefore completes the proof.

If a real set S is not bounded on the right [left] one may say that "$+\infty$ [$-\infty$] is a limit point." With this terminology, then, *every* infinite set of distinct real numbers has a limit point.

9-16.   Extreme Limit Points of Real, Infinite Sets.

The Bolanzo-Weierstrass theorem for linear sets implies that the set S' of the finite limit points of a bounded infinite set S of distinct real numbers is not null.   Clearly, S' is itself bounded, whence it has a least upper bound and a greatest lower bound, say B and b, respectively. But B and b are themselves necessarily points of S', for if one of them were not, it would be a limit point of S', and S' is closed. Thus every bounded infinite set S of distinct real numbers has a greatest limit point (called the *upper limit* or *superior limit* and denoted by $\overline{\lim} \, S$ or lim sup S) and a least limit point (called the *lower limit* or *inferior limit* and denoted by $\underline{\lim} \, S$ or lim inf S).

The superior limit B of a bounded infinite set S of distinct real numbers is characterized by these properties:

> Given arbitrary $\epsilon > 0$, there are an infinite number of points x in S for which $x > B - \epsilon$ and at most a finite   (9-5) number of points x in S for which $x > B + \epsilon$.

The first property states that there is a limit point of S that is greater than $B - \epsilon$, and the second states that there is no limit point of S that is greater than B.

If a real set S is not bounded on the right [left], one may say that lim sup $S = \infty$ [lim inf $S = -\infty$], in accordance with the convention mentioned above.

EXAMPLE 1.   For the set S of all rational numbers x for which $0 < x \le 1$, we have lim sup $S = 1$ and lim inf $S = 0$.

EXAMPLE 2.   For the set S of the reciprocals of the positive integers, we have lim sup $S = $ lim inf $S = 0$.

EXAMPLE 3.   For the set S of all negative integers, we have lim sup $S = $ lim inf $S = -\infty$.

EXAMPLE 4.   For the set S of all numbers of the form $n^{(-1)^n}$, where n is a positive integer, we have lim sup $S = \infty$ and lim inf $S = 0$.

9-17. Extreme Limit Points of Real Sequences.

In §6-2 it was noted that the limit points of a sequence $\{z_n\}$, while including the limit points of the set S of the distinct values among the z_n, may be more extensive. The limit points of a real sequence $\{x_n\}$, like the limit points of the corresponding set S, have a maximum and a minimum, denoted respectively by $\overline{\lim}_{n \to \infty} x_n$ or lim sup$_{n \to \infty} x_n$ and $\underline{\lim}_{n \to \infty} x_n$ or lim inf$_{n \to \infty} x_n$ and including the "values" $+\infty$ and $-\infty$. The proofs are so similar to the proof of the Bolzano-Weierstrass theorem for linear sets and the argument in §9-16 that they are omitted here (though the student would do well to write them out in detail).

For a bounded sequence of real numbers $\{x_n\}$, $B \equiv \lim \sup_{n \to \infty} x_n$ is characterized by these properties:

> Given arbitrary $\epsilon > 0$, there are an infinite number of values of n for which $x_n > B - \epsilon$ and at most a finite number of values of n for which $x_n > B + \epsilon$. $\qquad$ (9-6)

EXAMPLE. Given the sequence

$$0, \frac{1}{2}, 0, \frac{3}{4}, 0, \ldots, \frac{1 - (-1)^n}{2} \frac{n}{n+1}, \ldots$$

and the set S of the distinct values among these numbers, we have $\lim \sup S = \lim \inf S = 1$ and

$$\lim_{n \to \infty} \sup x_n = 1, \qquad \lim_{n \to \infty} \inf x_n = 0.$$

9-18. Problems.

1. Find $\lim \sup S$ and $\lim \inf S$ for each of the sets S for which these quantities exist in problem 3 of §9-12.

2. Exhibit a denumerable set of finite, *open* intervals I_n: $a_n < x < b_n$ such that all points of I_{n+1} are points of I_n for $n = 1, 2, \ldots$, but such that there is no point that lies in each of the I_n. Where in the proof of Theorem 9-4 was the closedness of the I_n used?

3. Give a characterization of $\lim \inf S$, where S is a bounded infinite set of distinct real numbers, similar to the characterization of $\lim \sup S$ given by (9-5).

4. Give a characterization of $\lim \inf_{n \to \infty} x_n$, where $\{x_n\}$ is a bounded sequence of real numbers, similar to the characterization of $\lim \sup_{n \to \infty} x_n$ given by (9-6).

5. For each of the sequences $\{x_n\}$ below, find $\lim \sup_{n \to \infty} x_n$, $\lim \inf_{n \to \infty} x_n$, $\lim \sup S$, and $\lim \inf S$, where S is the set of distinct values among the x_n.

   (a) $1, \dfrac{1}{2}, 1, \dfrac{1}{4}, \ldots, 1 - \left[\dfrac{1 - (-1)^n}{2} \dfrac{n}{n+1}\right], \ldots$;

   (b) $0, 1, 0, 1, \ldots, \dfrac{1 - (-1)^n}{2}, \ldots$;

   (c) $0, 1, 0, \dfrac{1}{2}, \ldots, \dfrac{1 - (-1)^n}{n+1}, \ldots$;

(d) $\dfrac{1}{2}, \dfrac{1}{3}, \dfrac{2}{3}, \dfrac{1}{4}, \dfrac{2}{4}, \dfrac{3}{4}, \cdots, \dfrac{1}{k}, \dfrac{2}{k}, \cdots, \dfrac{k-1}{k}, \cdots;$

(e) $0, \dfrac{1}{2}, \dfrac{2}{3}, \dfrac{1}{4}, \cdots, \left[\dfrac{1-(-1)^n}{2} \dfrac{1}{n+1} + \dfrac{1+(-1)^n}{2} \dfrac{n}{n+1} \right], \cdots$

*6. Given two real sequences $\{x_n\}$ and $\{y_n\}$, such that
$$\lim_{n \to \infty} x_n = L > 0,$$

(a) show that $\lim \sup_{n \to \infty} x_n y_n = L \lim \sup_{n \to \infty} y_n$ (the usual convention being adopted in case $\lim \sup_{n \to \infty} y_n$ is not finite),

(b) decide whether also $\lim \inf_{n \to \infty} x_n y_n = L \lim \inf_{n \to \infty} y_n$.

7. Given two real sequences $\{x_n\}$ and $\{y_n\}$, such that $\lim_{n \to \infty} x_n = L < 0$, express the extreme limits of the sequence $\{x_n y_n\}$ in terms of L and the extreme limits of the sequence $\{y_n\}$.

8. Given two real sequences $\{x_n\}$ and $\{y_n\}$, is it necessarily true that

(a) $\lim \sup_{n \to \infty} x_n y_n = (\lim \sup_{n \to \infty} x_n)(\lim \sup_{n \to \infty} y_n)$?

(b) $\lim \sup_{n \to \infty} (x_n + y_n) = \lim \sup_{n \to \infty} x_n + \lim \sup_{n \to \infty} y_n$?

9-19. The Bolzano-Weierstrass Theorem for Plane Sets.

This theorem provides the first application of the preceding theory to the complex plane.

THEOREM 9-6. (Bolzano-Weierstrass Theorem for Plane Sets) *A bounded infinite set S of distinct points z in the plane has at least one finite limit point.*

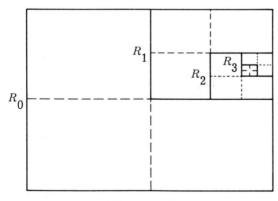

Figure 9-2

Proof. Let all of the points of S lie in the rectangle R_0: $a \leq x \leq b, c \leq y \leq d$ (Fig. 9-2). Then in one or more of the subrectangles

$$R_0': a \leq x \leq \frac{a+b}{2}, \qquad c \leq y \leq \frac{c+d}{2};$$

$$R_0'': \frac{a+b}{2} \leq x \leq b, \qquad c \leq y \leq \frac{c+d}{2};$$

$$R_0''': \frac{a+b}{2} \leq x \leq b, \qquad \frac{c+d}{2} \leq y \leq d;$$

$$R_0'''': a \leq x \leq \frac{a+b}{2}, \qquad \frac{c+d}{2} \leq y \leq d$$

lie infinitely many distinct points of S. Let us pick one of these subrectangles of R_0 for which this is the case (taking, for definiteness, the first in the sequence of the four subrectangles as listed) and call it $R_1: a_1 \leq x \leq b_1, c_1 \leq y \leq d_1$. Then in one or more of the subrectangles $R_1', R_1'', R_1''', R_1''''$, formed from R_1 exactly as the subrectangles $R_0', R_0'', R_0''', R_0''''$ were formed from R_0, lie infinitely many distinct points of S. Let us pick one of these subrectangles for which this is the case (following the same plan for definiteness decided upon before) and call it $R_2: a_2 \leq x \leq b_2$, $c_2 \leq y \leq d_2$. Continuing this process we generate two nests of intervals, $I_n: a_n \leq x \leq b_n$ and $J_n: c_n \leq y \leq d_n$. Denoting by x_0 the real number common to all the I_n and by y_0 the real number common to all the J_n, we see that the point $z_0 \equiv x_0 + iy_0$ is a limit point of S, for in every neighborhood of z_0 lie rectangles R_n of our sequence of rectangles for sufficiently large n, so that in every neighborhood of z_0 lie an infinite number of distinct points of S.

Hereafter the Bolzano-Weierstrass theorem for plane sets will be referred to simply as the Bolzano-Weierstrass theorem.

Clearly, the Bolzano-Weierstrass theorem may be phrased without the term "bounded" in the hypotheses provided that the term "finite" is omitted in the conclusion.

A companion to the Bolzano-Weierstrass theorem concerns sequences. A sequence $\{z_n\}$ is said to be *bounded* if the set of the points z_n is bounded.

THEOREM 9-7. *A bounded sequence $\{z_n\}$ has at least one finite limit point.*

Proof. If an infinite number of the z_n are distinct, it suffices to apply the Bolzano-Weierstrass theorem; and if only a finite number are distinct, then at least one number, say z_0, is infinitely often repeated.   The term "bounded" in the statement of Theorem 9-7 may be omitted if the term "finite" is also omitted.

Some applications of the Bolzano-Weierstrass theorem follow.
The *distance* of a point z_0 from a non-null set S is defined as inf $|z - z_0|$ for z in S.

EXAMPLE 1.   The distance of the point $z_0 = 1 + i$ from the set S: all points on the circle $|z| = 1$ is $\sqrt{2} - 1$; it is *assumed*: that is, there is a point z^* in S for which $|z^* - z_0|$ equals the distance of z_0 from S.   (The term "assumed" will be used in other connections and is there to be interpreted similarly.)

EXAMPLE 2.   The distance of the point $z_0 = 1$ from the set S: the points $n/(n + 1)$ for $n = 1, 2, \ldots$ is zero; it is not assumed.

THEOREM 9-8.   *The distance D of a point z_0 from a closed, non-null set S is assumed.*

Proof.   If D is not assumed, then D is a limit point of the real numbers $|z - z_0|$ for all z in S.   Hence there is a sequence of distinct points z_n in S for which $|z_n - z_0| \to D$.   Since $|z_n| \leq |z_0| + |z_n - z_0|$, this sequence is bounded and therefore has a limit point z_0' in the complex plane, by the Bolzano-Weierstrass theorem.   And, since S is closed, z_0' belongs to S.   Let $\{z_n'\}$ be a subsequence of the z_n such that $|z_n' - z_0'| \to 0$.   Then, since

$$|z_n' - z_0| - |z_n' - z_0'| \leq |z_0' - z_0| \leq |z_n' - z_0| + |z_n' - z_0'|,$$

we must have $|z_0' - z_0| = D$, contrary to the hypothesis.

By the *distance* between two non-null sets S and Σ is meant inf $|z - \zeta|$ for z in S and ζ in Σ.

EXAMPLE 3.   The distance between the set S: all real points x for which $x \geq 0$ and the set Σ: all points $z \equiv x + iy$ for which $y = 1/(x + 1)$ and $x \geq 0$ is zero; it is not assumed.

EXAMPLE 4.   The distance between the set S consisting of a single point z_0 and a non-null set Σ equals the distance of the point z_0 from the set Σ; it is assumed if Σ is closed.

Example 3 above proves that the distance between two non-null closed sets need not be assumed.   However, in problem 6 of §9-20, the student will prove the following theorem.

THEOREM 9-9.   *The distance between two non-null closed sets is assumed if one of these sets is bounded.*

The *diameter* of a non-null point set S is defined as the quantity sup $|z - \zeta|$ for z and ζ in S; it is written "diam S." For an unbounded set S, diam $S = \infty$.

EXAMPLE 5.   If S consists of the points of the circle $|z| = 1$ and the single additional point $z = 2$, then diam $S = 3$; it is assumed.

EXAMPLE 6.   If S consists of the interior of the circle $|z| = 1$ and the points z for which $|z + 2| \leq 1$, then diam $S = 4$; it is not assumed.

THEOREM 9-10.   *The diameter D of a non-null, closed, bounded set S is assumed.*

Proof.   If D is not assumed, then D is a limit point of the real numbers $|z - \zeta|$ for z and ζ in S. Hence there is a sequence of pairs of points (z_n, ζ_n) in S for which $|z_n - \zeta_n| \to D$. By Theorem 9-7, the sequence $\{z_n\}$ has a limit point z_0, and since S is closed, z_0 is in S. (Note that this is true even if z_0 is not a limit point of the set of the distinct values among the z_n.) Letting $\{z_n'\}$ be a subsequence of $\{z_n\}$ that converges to z_0, we now have $|z_n' - z_0| \to 0$ and $|z_n' - \zeta_n'| \to D$, where ζ_n' is that one of the ζ_n whose partner is z_n' in the original sequence of pairs (z_n, ζ_n). Hence the inequalities

$$|z_n' - \zeta_n'| - |z_n' - z_0| \leq |\zeta_n' - z_0| \leq |z_n' - \zeta_n'| + |z_n' - z_0|$$

show that $|\zeta_n' - z_0| \to D$. Applying Theorem 9-7 again, we deduce the existence of a subsequence $\{\zeta_n''\}$ of $\{\zeta_n'\}$ that converges to a limit ζ_0 in S. Thus we have $|\zeta_n'' - \zeta_0| \to 0$ and $|\zeta_n'' - z_0| \to D$, so that, as in the proof of Theorem 9-8, we may conclude that $|\zeta_0 - z_0| = D$, a contradiction that completes the proof.

9-20. Problems.

1. Find the distance of the point $z_0 = \sqrt{2}i$ from the set S consisting of the points below, and state whether it is assumed.

   (a) All points on the interior of the circle $|z| = 1$.
   (b) All points on the circle $|z| = 3$.
   (c) All points in the plane.

(d) All points in the plane whose ordinates are rational.

(e) The points $z = 1/n$ for $n = 1, 2, \ldots$.

(f) All points z for which $0 < a < |z| \leq b$.

2. Find the distance between the set S: all real points x for which $0 < x \leq 1$, and the set Σ, consisting of the points below, and state whether it is assumed.

(a) All real points x for which $x < 0$.

(b) All real points x for which $x \leq 0$.

(c) All points $z \equiv x + iy$ for which $y - 1 = x^2$.

(d) All points $z \equiv x + iy$ for which $y - 1 = (x - 1)^2$.

(e) All points z for which $|z - 2i| < 1$.

(f) The open half-plane $I(z) > 1$.

(g) All points z for which $0 < a \leq |z| < b$.

3. Find the diameter of the set S consisting of the points below, and state whether it is assumed.

(a) All points z for which $|z| \leq 1$ and $I(z) > 0$.

(b) All points in the first quadrant.

(c) All points $z \equiv x + iy$ for which $0 \leq x \leq 1$ and $0 \leq y < 1$.

(d) All points z for which $|z| < a$ and all points x on the x axis for which $|x| \leq b$.

(e) The points $z = 1/n$ for $n = 1, 2, \ldots$.

(f) The points $z = (-1)^n/n$ for $n = 1, 2, \ldots$.

4. State and prove the Bolzano-Weierstrass theorem for three dimensions, defining such terms as need to be carried over from two dimensions.

*5. Show that a path is a closed set of points.

*6. Prove Theorem 9-9.

7. Show that the distance of a point z_0 from a non-null set S equals the distance of z_0 from the closure of S.

8. Prove that the distance between two non-null, non-overlapping sets is not assumed if one of the sets is open.

9. Prove the following converse of Theorem 6-3 as rephrased in problem 10 of §6-11: *A function whose only singularities in the closed plane are poles is rational.*

10. (a) Show that, if a function $f(z)$ is regular throughout a closed and bounded region R except for isolated singularities, then the number of such singularities must be finite.

(b) Show by an example that the conclusion of part (a) does not necessarily follow if the closedness of R is omitted from the hypotheses.

*11. Prove the following extension of a part of Theorem 6-9. *If $w = f(z)$ is a non-constant regular function at a point z_0, $w_0 = f(z_0)$, and k is the order of the zero at z_0 of the function $\varphi(z) \equiv f(z) - w_0$, then there are two circles, $K: |z - z_0| = a$ in the z plane and $K': |w - w_0| = b$ in the w plane, such that the equation $w = f(z)$ is satisfied for each w on the interior of K' by exactly k values of z—each counted according to the multiplicity of the root—on the interior of K.* [Noting first that $f(z) - w_0 = (z - z_0)^k g(z)$, where $g(z)$ is regular at z_0 and $|g(z_0)| = B > 0$ (problem 8 of §6-13), choose a so small that $f(z)$ is regular and $|g(z)| > B/2$ for all z within or on K. If the conclusion of the theorem is false for the circle K as thus determined, then for every positive number b there is a point w_b on the interior of the corresponding circle K' such that the function $\varphi_b(z) \equiv f(z) - w_b$ vanishes for exactly k_b values of z—each counted according to the multiplicity of the root—on the interior of K, where $0 \leq k_b < \infty$ and $k_b \neq k$. Now proceed in a fashion suggested by the proof of the first part of Theorem 6-9.]

12. Using the theorem of problem 11 above, prove the Open Mapping Theorem: *The map T of an open region S by a function that is regular on S is itself open.*

13. State the real variable analogs of the theorems of problems 11 and 12 above, and show that they are false. [A real function $f(x)$ of the real variable x is said to be *regular* at a point x_0 if it is representable by a Taylor's series in powers of $x - x_0$ in the neighborhood of x_0.]

14. Given a non-null point set S, let us define
   (a) the *depth in S of a point* z in S as the distance of z from the complement of S,
   (b) the *depth of S* as the supremum of the depths in S of the points in S,
   (c) the *core of S* as the set of the points in S whose depths in S equal the depth of S.

   Examine the structure of the core K of a non-null set S, settling such matters as whether K may or must be null, consist of a single point, coincide with S, be open, be closed, and so on.

9-21. Nests of Plane Sets.

By a *nest of plane sets* is meant a denumerable set of non-null, closed, and bounded plane sets S_n such that all of the points of S_{n+1} are points of S_n for $n = 1, 2, \ldots$ and such that diam $S_n \to 0$ as $n \to \infty$.

THEOREM 9-11. (Nested Plane Sets Theorem) *There is one and only one point that lies in each set of a nest of plane sets.*

Proof. Let z_n be an arbitrary point in S_n for $n = 1, 2, \ldots$. Since the sequence $\{z_n\}$ is bounded, it has a finite limit point, say z_0. Now all of the z_n are in S_1, and S_1 is closed, so that z_0 is in S_1. Also, all of the z_n for $n > 1$ are in S_2, and S_2 is closed, so that z_0 is in S_2. And all of the z_n for $n > 2$ are in S_3, and S_3 is closed, so that z_0 is in S_3. And so on. Thus there is at least one point, z_0, that lies in each of the S_n. But there cannot be another, different point z_0' that lies in each of the S_n, for then diam $S_n \geq |z_0' - z_0| > 0$ for every n, contrary to the fact that diam $S_n \to 0$ as $n \to \infty$.

9-22. The Heine-Borel Theorem.
The Maximum Modulus Theorem.

A point z_0 is said to be *covered* by a set S if z_0 is an interior point of S.

THEOREM 9-12. (Heine-Borel Theorem) *If S is a closed, bounded, non-null set, every point z of which is covered by a set S_z, then every point of S is covered by one or another of only a finite number of the S_z, say $S_{z_1}, S_{z_2}, \ldots, S_{z_0}$.*
One says that S is *covered* by these of the S_z.

Proof. As in the proof of the Bolzano-Weierstrass theorem, let us start with a closed rectangle R_0 in which lie all of the points z of S. If the present theorem is false, then an infinite number of the S_z are necessary to cover these points z. The same must then be true of the points of S that lie in at least one of the closed subrectangles that we denoted by R_0', R_0'', R_0''', R_0'''' in the proof of the Bolzano-Weierstrass theorem; it must then be true of the points of S that lie in at least one of the closed subrectangles R_1', R_1'', R_1''', R_1''''; and so on. The single point z_0 that is common to all of the members of the nest of plane sets $R_0, R_1, \ldots$ is clearly a limit point of S and therefore belongs to S; it is covered by S_{z_0}.

But then so must be all of the points of S that lie in R_n for sufficiently large n, contrary to our deduction that it requires an infinite number of the S_z to cover all of the points of S in R_n for every n. This contradiction completes the proof.

The Heine-Borel theorem will now be used to prove the first in a sequence of three theorems that culminates in an improved form of the maximum modulus theorem.

THEOREM 9-13.   *A function $f(z)$ that is continuous with respect to a closed, bounded, non-null set S is bounded on S.*

Problem 1 of §9-14 is a special case of this theorem.

Proof.   The continuity with respect to S of $f(z)$ implies the existence of a neighborhood N_0 of each point z_0 in S such that $|f(z) - f(z_0)| < 1$ whenever z is in SN_0. By the Heine-Borel theorem, S is covered by a finite number of these neighborhoods, say $N_1, N_2, \ldots, N_k$. Hence for each z in S there is a j, $1 \le j \le k$, such that $|f(z)| \le |f(z) - f(z_j)| + |f(z_j)| < 1 + |f(z_j)|$, where z_j is the center of N_j, so that $|f(z)| < 1 + \sum |f(z_j)|$, which fact completes the proof.

THEOREM 9-14.   *The modulus of a function $f(z)$ that is continuous with respect to a closed, bounded, non-null set S attains a maximum value at some point z_0 in S.*

Proof.   By Theorem 9-13, the set of real numbers $|f(z)|$ for z in S is bounded. But then there is a point z_0 in S for which $|f(z_0)| = M$, where M is the least upper bound of this set of real numbers. For if there is no such point, then there is a sequence of points z_n in S such that $|f(z_n)| \to M$ and a subsequence of points z_n' of $\{z_n\}$ that converges to a limit z_0 that is in S; and then from the inequality

$$|f(z_n')| - |f(z_n') - f(z_0)| \le |f(z_0)| \le |f(z_n')| + |f(z_n') - f(z_0)|$$

we may conclude that $|f(z_0)| = M$, a contradiction that completes the proof.

The next theorem should be compared to Theorem 5-8, of which, together with Theorem 9-14, it is a consequence.

THEOREM 9-15.   (Maximum Modulus Theorem)   *If $f(z)$ is regular and non-constant in a closed, bounded, non-null region S, then*

$|f(z)|$ *attains a maximum value in S at, and only at, a point or points on the boundary of S.*

In problem 19 of §5-4 the student showed that an analytic function is not regular throughout the interior of a circle about a point z_0 that is larger than the circle of convergence of its Taylor series about z_0. A more precise statement may now be made.

THEOREM 9-16. *An analytic function $f(z)$ for which the Taylor expansion about a point z_0 has a finite circle of convergence K has a singularity on K.*

Proof. If $f(z)$ is regular at each point z' of K, then it is regular throughout the interior S' of a circle K' with center at z'. Let us take the radius of K' less than the radius of K. Since K is a closed, bounded set, it is covered by a finite number of these S', say $S_1, S_2, \ldots, S_k$, corresponding to circles K_j with centers z_j for $j = 1, 2, \ldots, k$. We may suppose that none of the S_j is contained in any other of the S_j, and that the z_j are numbered consecutively counterclockwise around K. If w_j is that intersection of K_j and K_{j+1} (K_{k+1} being defined as K_1) that lies outside of K, we put $R' = \min |w_j - z_0|$, whereupon it appears that $f(z)$ is regular for all z on the interior of the circle $|z - z_0| = R'$. This being impossible, since $R' > R$, we have a contradiction and the completion of the proof.

A theorem of central importance to the next section can easily be proved by means of techniques now available.

THEOREM 9-17. *If a function $f(z)$ is continuous with respect to a path k, then the function*

$$F(Z) \equiv \frac{1}{2\pi i} \int_{(k)} \frac{f(z)dz}{z - Z} \qquad (9\text{-}7)$$

is a regular function of Z for every Z that is not on k. Moreover,

$$F^{(n)}(Z) = \frac{n!}{2\pi i} \int_{(k)} \frac{f(z)dz}{(z - Z)^{n+1}}, \quad n = 1, 2, \ldots. \qquad (9\text{-}8)$$

The factor $1/2\pi i$ is introduced to call attention to the similarity between (9-7) and Cauchy's integral formula. Indeed, they are the same thing if k is a simple closed path, Z lies on the interior of k, and $f(z)$ is regular within and on k—a fact to be exploited in §9-24; under these circumstances $F(z)$ and $f(z)$ are the same for all z within k, and $F(z) = 0$ for all z neither within nor on k.   The similarity between (9-8) and the formula of Theorem 5-4 is also to be noted.

Proof.   Since k is closed (problem 5 of §9-20), and Z is not on k, the distance h of Z from k is positive; and since $f(z)$ is continuous with respect to k and k is bounded, $|f(z)|$ has a maximum M on k. Letting s represent the length of k and taking $|\varDelta Z| < h/2$, we have

$$\left| \frac{F(Z + \varDelta Z) - F(Z)}{\varDelta Z} - \frac{1}{2\pi i} \int_{(k)} \frac{f(z)dz}{(z - Z)^2} \right|$$

$$= \left| \frac{1}{2\pi i} \int_{(k)} \frac{f(z)dz}{(z - Z)(z - Z - \varDelta Z)} - \frac{1}{2\pi i} \int_{(k)} \frac{f(z)dz}{(z - Z)^2} \right|$$

$$= \frac{1}{2\pi} \left| \int_{(k)} \frac{\varDelta Z f(z)dz}{(z - Z)^2(z - Z - \varDelta Z)} \right| \leq \frac{M|\varDelta Z|s}{\pi h^3},$$

and the last expression in this inequality tends to zero as $\varDelta Z$ does so.   This establishes (9-8) for $n = 1$.   The proof for $n > 1$ can be made, using induction, in similar fashion (problem 9 of §9-23).

9-23.   Problems.

1.   If in the definition of a nest of plane sets either the closedness or the boundedness of the individual sets had not been required, then Theorem 9-11 would be false. Construct examples to show this.

2.   Find an explicit expression of the function $F(Z)$ of (9-7) in case k is the line segment $0 \leq x \leq 1$, $y = 0$ and $f(z) \equiv 1$ on k, and determine independently of the theory where $F(Z)$ is a regular function of Z.

3.   A real point x_0 is said to be covered by a real interval I if x_0 is an interior point (in the linear sense, of course) of I. State and prove the Heine-Borel theorem for the covering by real intervals of sets of real points.

4.   If $f(z)$ is non-constant and regular for $|z| < R$ and $M(r) \equiv \max_{|z| = r} |f(z)|$ for each non-negative r which is less than R, show that $M(r)$ is a strictly increasing function of r for $0 \leq r < R$.   (Compare problem 4 of §5-8.)

5.   Prove the last statement before the examples in §6-7.

6.   Prove that, if a function $f(z)$ is continuous with respect to a closed, bounded set S, then it is *uniformly continuous* with

respect to S; that is, given arbitrary $\epsilon > 0$, there is a $\delta > 0$ such that $|f(z) - f(z')| < \epsilon$ whenever z and z' are in S and $|z - z'| < \delta$. [With each point z' in S is associated a positive number R' such that $|f(z) - f(z')| < \epsilon/2$ whenever z is in S and $|z - z'| < R'$. The interior S' of the circle $|z - z'| = R'/2$ covers z'. Use the Heine-Borel theorem and put $\delta = \min R_j/2$ for a finite number of S_j from among the S' that suffice to cover S.]

7. Let S be the set of points $1, 1/2, \ldots, 1/n, \ldots$. Show that each point of S can be covered by the interior of a circle, no two of these covering sets having points in common. Is the same true of the closure $\bar{S}$ of S?

8. Show that the infinite point is a zero of the function $F(z)$ of Theorem 9-17.

*9. Assuming (9-8) established for $n = 1$, establish it for

   (a) $n = 2$,
   (b) n in general.

10. If $f(z)$ is regular and does not vanish for $|z| \leq R$, and if $|f(z)|$ is constant for $|z| = R$, then $f(z)$ is constant for $|z| \leq R$. Prove this.

11. Prove Schwartz's Lemma: *If $f(z)$ is regular and $|f(z)| \leq 1$ for z in $R: |z| < 1$, and if $f(0) = 0$, then $|f(z)| \leq |z|$ for z in R, equality for any particular z in R implying that $f(z) = e^{i\varphi}z$ for some constant φ and all z in R.* [Consider the function $F(z) \equiv f(z)/z$.]

12. Prove that, if $u(x, y)$ is a non-constant harmonic function in a closed, bounded, non-null region S, then $u(x, y)$ attains a maximum value and a minimum value at, and only at, a point or points on the boundary of S. [For the "maximum" part of the proof, consider the function $f(z) = e^{u+iv}$, where $v \equiv v(x, y)$ is a harmonic conjugate of $u \equiv u(x, y)$.]

9-24. The Continuous Differentiability of Regular Functions.

Crucial to the proof of Cauchy's theorem in Chapter 4—and hence to most of the derivations in Chapters 5 through 8—was the assumption that, as stated in §2-6, "regularity of a function $f(z) \equiv u + iv$ at a point implies the continuity of the first partials of u and v there." It is now possible for the first time to justify this assumption, or—what is equivalent—that a function that is regular at a point is continuously differentiable there. The plan of attack is, of course *without assumption that $f'(z)$ is continuous*, (1) to establish in a very special case the corollary to Cauchy's theorem expressed in Theorem 5-1, (2) to derive also in a special case Cauchy's integral formula, and (3) to arrive at the conclusion by applying Theorem 9-17 to this case of that formula. It is to be noted that the Cauchy deductions expressed in the generality of Theorems 4-14 and 5-2 become thus, by way of the developments in Chapter 4, consequences of the *particular* Cauchy deductions now to be proved.

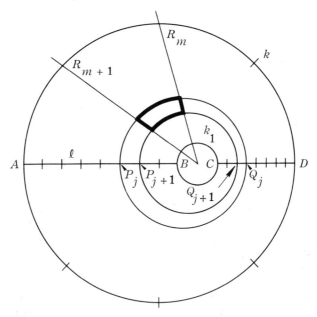

Figure 9-3

THEOREM 9-18. *Given two circles k and k_1, all points of k_1 being interior to k (Fig. 9-3), if a function $F(z)$ is regular in the closed region S between k_1 and k, then $\oint_{(k)} F(z)dz = \oint_{(k_1)} F(z)dz$.*

Proof. Given arbitrary $\epsilon > 0$, with each point z_0 in S, the differentiability of $F(z)$ assures the existence of a neighborhood $N_0: |z - z_0| < r_0$ such that

$$\left| \frac{F(z) - F(z_0)}{z - z_0} - F'(z_0) \right| < \epsilon$$

whenever $0 < |z - z_0| < r_0$. Defining

$$\eta_0(z) \equiv \begin{cases} 0 & \text{if } z = z_0, \\ \dfrac{F(z) - F(z_0)}{z - z_0} - F'(z_0) & \text{if } z \text{ is elsewhere in } N_0, \end{cases}$$

we therefore have

$$F(z) = F(z_0) + F'(z_0)(z - z_0) + \eta_0(z)(z - z_0)$$

with $\eta_0(z)$ continuous and numerically less than ϵ for z in N_0. By the Heine-Borel Theorem, S is covered by the interiors of a finite number of the circles $|z - z_0| = r_0/2$ thus determined for all z_0 in S. Let ρ be the least of the numbers $r_0/2$ among those of such a finite number of circles.

Letting l be the line of centers of k and k_1 (or any line through the common center if k and k_1 are concentric), let A be either intersection of l with k, D the other intersection of l with k, B the intersection of l with k_1 that is nearest to A, and C the other intersection of l with k_1. Let us divide AB into n equal segments P_jP_{j+1} by points $P_0 \equiv A, P_1, P_2, \ldots, P_n \equiv B$ and DC into n equal segments Q_jQ_{j+1} by points $Q_0 \equiv D, Q_1, Q_2, \ldots, Q_n \equiv C$ and construct the $n - 1$ circles, diameters of which are P_1Q_1, $P_2Q_2, \ldots, P_{n-1}Q_{n-1}$. Next, let us divide the circumference of k into n equal arcs R_jR_{j+1} by points $R_0 \equiv A, R_1, R_2, \ldots, R_n \equiv A$ and construct the n rays whose ends are the center of k_1 and that pass through the R_j. Thus upon S we lay a network of n^2 four-sided figures, of each of which two opposite sides are arcs of circles and the two remaining sides are linear segments. Ordering these in some fashion and calling their perimeters P_{nj}, we see, much as in the proof of Theorem 4-4, that

$$\oint_{(k)} F(z)dz - \oint_{(k_1)} F(z)dz = \sum_{j=1}^{n^2} \oint_{(p_{nj})} F(z)dz.$$

Letting p_{nj} now also denote the *length* of p_{nj}, we may suppose n so chosen that $p_{nj} < \rho$ for each j, whereupon we see that all points of p_{nj} lie within the neighborhood N_0, defined above, of one of the finite number of points z_0, mentioned at the end of the preceding paragraph, so that for these points z we have

$$F(z) = F(z_0) + F'(z_0)(z - z_0) + \eta_0(z)(z - z_0),$$

where $\eta_0(z)$ is continuous, $|\eta_0(z)| < \epsilon$, and $|z - z_0| < p_{nj}$. It follows first that

$$\oint_{(p_{nj})} F(z)dz = \oint_{(p_{nj})} \eta_0(z)(z - z_0)dz,$$

since Cauchy's Theorem is applicable to the function

$$F(z_0) + F'(z_0)(z - z_0),$$

whose derivative is surely continuous everywhere. But then we have

$$\left| \oint_{(k)} F(z)dz - \oint_{(k_1)} F(z)dz \right| < \sum_{j=1}^{n^2} \oint_{(p_{nj})} \epsilon |z - z_0| ds < \sum_{j=1}^{n^2} \epsilon(p_{nj})^2,$$

and since—with k now also representing the *circumference of k*— $p_{nj} < 4k/n$, this last expression is less than $16k^2\epsilon$. The arbitrariness of ϵ now establishes the conclusion of the theorem.

THEOREM 9-19. *If a function $f(z)$ is regular within and on a circle k, then, for each point Z within k,*

$$f(Z) = \frac{1}{2\pi i} \oint_{(k)} \frac{f(z)dz}{z - Z}.$$

Proof. As in the proof of Theorem 5-2, we see that, given arbitrary $\epsilon > 0$, there is a circle k_1 whose center is Z and all of whose points we may assume to be within k such that

$$\left| f(Z) - \frac{1}{2\pi i} \oint_{(k_1)} \frac{f(z)dz}{z - Z} \right| < \epsilon.$$

If then we put $F(z) = f(z)/(z - Z)$ and apply Theorem 9-18, we may conclude that

$$\left| f(Z) - \frac{1}{2\pi i} \oint_{(k)} \frac{f(z)dz}{z - Z} \right| < \epsilon,$$

which leads at once to the desired result.

THEOREM 9-20. *If a function $f(z)$ is regular at a point z_0, then its derivative is continuous there.* (Cauchy-Goursat)

Proof. Let k be a circle with center at z_0, within and on which $f(z)$ is regular. Then, by Theorem 9-19,

$$f(Z) = \frac{1}{2\pi i} \oint_{(k)} \frac{f(z)dz}{z - Z}$$

for each Z within k and, by Theorem 9-17, $f''(z_0)$ (in particular) exists, so that $f'(z)$ is continuous at z_0, as was to be proved.

9-25. Problems.

1. Let $F(z)$ be regular within and on a rectangle R. Using the Heine-Borel Theorem as in the proof of Theorem 9-18 and subdividing R into n^2 congruent subrectangles, prove without recourse to the continuity of $F'(z)$ that $\oint_{(R)} F(z)dz = 0$.

2. Let $F(z)$ be regular within and on a rectangle R and put $q = \oint_{(R)} F(z)dz$. Subdivide R as in problem 1, with $n = 2$, and deduce that $\left| \oint_{(R_1)} F(z)dz \right| \geq |q|/4$, where R_1 is some one (or another) of the four subrectangles of R. Subdivide R_1 similarly into four subrectangles and deduce that $\left| \oint_{(R_2)} F(z)dz \right| \geq |q|/4^2$, where R_2 is some one (or another) of the four subrectangles of R_1. Continuing in this fashion, set up a nest of closed interiors of rectangles R_n such that $\left| \oint_{(R_n)} F(z)dz \right| \geq |q|/4^n$ and $p_n = p/2^n$, where p is the perimeter of R and p_n is the perimeter of R_n. From the differentiability of $F(z)$ at the point z_0 that is common to the closed interiors of all the R_n, deduce finally that $q = 0$.

Some General Theorems Concerning Series

10

10-1. Cauchy's Convergence Criterion.

THEOREM 10-1. (Cauchy's Convergence Criterion) *A necessary and sufficient condition that a sequence $\{z_n\}$ converge is that $\lim_{m,n \to \infty} (z_m - z_n) = 0$.*

Proof. If $\{z_n\}$ converges, say to z_0, then, given arbitrary $\epsilon > 0$, there is a positive integer N such that $|z_n - z_0| < \epsilon/2$ whenever $n > N$. Hence

$$|z_m - z_n| \leq |z_m - z_0| + |z_n - z_0| < \epsilon/2 + \epsilon/2 \equiv \epsilon$$

whenever $m, n > N$. This proves the necessity of the condition.

To prove the sufficiency, let us first take $\epsilon = 1$ in the "ϵ–N" pattern. We know that there is a positive integer N such that, in particular, $|z_n - Z_{N+1}| < 1$ whenever $n > N$. Hence $|z_n| < |z_{N+1}| + 1$ for these values of n, and so

$$|z_n| < |z_1| + |z_2| + \cdots + |z_N| + |z_{N+1}| + 1$$

for *all* n. Thus $\{z_n\}$ is bounded and therefore, by Theorem 9-7, has a finite limit point z_0. Let $z_{n_1}, z_{n_2}, \ldots, z_{n_k}, \ldots$ be a subsequence of $\{z_n\}$ that converges to z_0. Now given arbitrary $\epsilon > 0$ there is a positive integer M such that $|z_m - z_n| < \epsilon/2$ whenever $m, n > M$. Letting z_{n_j} be one of the z_{n_k} for which both $n_j > M$ and $|z_{n_j} - z_0| < \epsilon/2$, we have

$$|z_n - z_0| \leq |z_n - z_{n_j}| + |z_{n_j} - z_0| < \epsilon/2 + \epsilon/2 \equiv \epsilon$$

whenever $n > M$. (Note that, though n_j "disappears" at this point, the *existence* of an appropriate z_{n_j} was essential to the argument.) But this simply means that $\{z_n\}$ converges to z_0 and therefore completes our proof.

10-2. A Formula for the Radius of Convergence of the General Power Series.

In §3-5 the existence of the circle of convergence of a power series was argued on the assumption of the existence of an interval of convergence of a real power series, and in problem 3 of §9-14 an independent proof was requested. Another independent proof is now given—the present proof providing an explicit formula for the radius of convergence of the series

$$\sum_0^\infty a_n(z - z_0)^n. \tag{10-1}$$

THEOREM 10-2. *If*

$$R = \frac{1}{\limsup \sqrt[n]{|a_n|}}, \tag{10-2}$$

where $\sqrt[n]{0}$ is to be interpreted as 0 and (10-2) is to be understood to mean that R is infinite if $\limsup \sqrt[n]{|a_n|} = 0$ and that $R = 0$ if $\limsup \sqrt[n]{|a_n|} = \infty$, then the series (10-1) converges absolutely for all values of z if R is infinite, converges only for $z = z_0$ if $R = 0$, and in the remaining case converges absolutely for all values of z for which $|z - z_0| < R$ and diverges for all values of z for which $|z - z_0| > R$.

Proof. Let us dispose of the extreme cases first. If

$$\limsup \sqrt[n]{|a_n|} = 0,$$

then $\lim \sqrt[n]{|a_n|} = 0$, so that $\lim \sqrt[n]{|a_n|} \, |z - z_0| = 0$ for every value of z, whence $\sqrt[n]{|a_n|} \, |z - z_0| < 1/2$ for $n > N$, say, so that the series (10-1) is dominated by the convergent geometric series $\sum 1/2^n$ and therefore converges absolutely. If $\limsup \sqrt[n]{|a_n|} = \infty$, then $\limsup \sqrt[n]{|a_n|} \, |z - z_0| = \infty$ for every $z \neq z_0$, whence $\limsup |a_n(z - z_0)^n| = \infty$, so that the series (10-1) converges only if $z = z_0$.

Suppose next that $L \equiv \limsup \sqrt[n]{|a_n|}$ is neither zero nor infinite. If $|z - z_0| < R \equiv 1/L$, we may write $|z - z_0| = 1/(L + 2\epsilon)$ for an appropriate positive number ϵ. But, by (9-6), there is a positive number N such that $\sqrt[n]{|a_n|} \le L + \epsilon$ whenever $n > N$. Hence $\sqrt[n]{|a_n|} \, |z - z_0| \le (L + \epsilon)/(L + 2\epsilon)$, or

$$|a_n(z - z_0)^n| \le \left[\frac{L + \epsilon}{L + 2\epsilon} \right]^n,$$

whenever $n > N$, so that the series (10-1) is dominated by a convergent geometric series and therefore converges absolutely. On the other hand, if $|z - z_0| > R \equiv 1/L$, we may write $|z - z_0| = 1/(L - \epsilon)$ for an appropriate positive number ϵ. But, again by (9-6), the inequality $\sqrt[n]{|a_n|} > L - \epsilon$ is satisfied for certain values n' of n, however large, so that $\sqrt[n']{|a_{n'}|} \, |z - z_0| > (L - \epsilon)/(L - \epsilon) \equiv 1$ and hence $|a_{n'}(z - z_0)^{n'}| > 1$, which means that the nth term in the series (10-1) does not tend to zero and therefore that the series diverges.

10-3. Problems.

1. Use Theorem 10-2 to find the radius of convergence of the series below.

   (a) $\sum_1^\infty n z^n$;

   (b) $\sum_1^\infty n^n z^n$;

   (c) $\sum_1^\infty z^n/n^n$;

   (d) $\sum_1^\infty n^{(-1)^n} z^n$;

   (e) $\sum_1^\infty (\ln n) z^n$;

   (f) $z/3 + z^2/2^2 + z^3/3^3 + z^4/2^4$
   $+ \cdots + z^{2k-1}/3^{2k-1} + z^{2k}/2^{2k} + \cdots$;

   (g) $\sum_0^\infty z^n/n!$, using the fact—from Stirling's approximation to $n!$ for large positive integers n—that

$$\lim \frac{n!}{(n/e)^n \sqrt{2\pi n}} = 1;$$

   (h) $z + z^2/2! + z^3 + z^4/4! + \cdots + z^{2k-1} + z^{2k}/(2k)! + \cdots$;

   (i) $\sum_0^\infty (n!)^{(-1)^n} z^n$.

2. Explain why the radius of convergence of the series

$$z^2 + 2z^3 + 3z^5 + \cdots + n z^{p_n} + \cdots$$

   is 1, where p_n is the nth prime.

3. Prove by means of Theorem 10-2 and problem 6 of §9-18 that, if P is a polynomial, then the radius of convergence of the series $\sum P(n) a_n z^n$ is the same as that of the series $\sum a_n z^n$. Can

you extend this result to $\sum R(n)a_n z^n$, where R is a rational function? (Compare the proof of Theorem 3-7.)

4. Letting z_1 and z_2 be any two different, fixed points, define the remaining elements of a sequence $\{z_n\}$ by the formula $z_n = (z_{n-2} + z_{n-1})/2$ for $n = 3, 4, \ldots$. Show directly that Cauchy's convergence criterion is satisfied by this sequence. Find the limit, if possible.

5. Show that, if none of the a_n in (10-1) is zero, and we put $L' = \limsup |a_{n+1}/a_n|$, then the series (10-1) converges absolutely if $|z - z_0| < R'$, where $R' = 1/L'$ if $L' \neq 0$ and R' is infinite if $L' = 0$. [Examine the ratio $|a_{n+1}(z - z_0)^{n+1}/a_n(z - z_0)^n|$ for large n.] What is the situation if L' is infinite?

6. The preceding problem shows that R' is not greater than the radius of convergence R of the series (10-1). Construct a series for which $R' < R$.

7. Cauchy's "ratio test," as given in the usual calculus course, shows that the radius of convergence R of the series (10-1) is given by $R = \lim |a_n/a_{n+1}|$ when this limit exists, all of the a_n presumed non-zero. Prove this independently by using Theorem 10-2 and showing that, if we put $R' = \lim |a_n/a_{n+1}|$, then

$$L \equiv \limsup \sqrt[n]{|a_n|} = \limsup \sqrt[n]{\left|\frac{a_n}{a_{n-1}}\right| \left|\frac{a_{n-1}}{a_{n-2}}\right| \cdots \left|\frac{a_2}{a_1}\right| |a_1|}$$

$$= \lim \left|\frac{a_n}{a_{n-1}}\right| \equiv \frac{1}{R'},$$

with the usual conventions as to infinite and zero values for R'. (Use logarithms and modifications of problem 9 of §9-2.)

8. Prove Mertens' Theorem, a "stronger" result than that stated in the first part of Theorem 3-4: *If $\sum w_k$ is (merely) convergent and $\sum z_k$ is absolutely convergent, then*

$$\left(\sum_0^\infty w_k\right)\left(\sum_0^\infty z_k\right) = \sum_0^\infty (w_0 z_k + w_1 z_{k-1} + \cdots + w_k z_0).$$

[Follow the proof of Theorem 3-4 through Equation (3-2).] Then, defining p as in that proof, observe that

$$|R_n| \leq \sum_1^p |z_k| \max_{1 \leq k \leq p} |w_{n-k+1} + w_{n-k+2} + \cdots + w_n|$$

$$+ \sum_{p+1}^n |z_k| \max_{p+1 \leq k \leq n} |w_{n-k+1} + w_{n-k+2} + \cdots + w_n|.$$

10-4. Uniform Convergence.

If a sequence of functions $F_1(z)$, $F_2(z)$, ..., $F_n(z)$, ..., each defined for all z in a set S, converges to a function $F_0(z)$ there, then for each z in S and for arbitrary $\epsilon > 0$, there is a positive number N such that

$$|F_n(z) - F_0(z)| < \epsilon$$

whenever $n > N$.

EXAMPLE 1.   Let S be the entire finite plane, and let $F_n(z) = 1/(n + |z|)$ for $n = 1, 2, \ldots$.   Then $F_0(z) = 0$ and

$$|F_n(z) - F_0(z)| < \epsilon$$

whenever $n > 1/\epsilon - |z|$.

EXAMPLE 2.   Let S be the entire finite plane except the origin, and let $F_n(z) = 1/n|z|$ for $n = 1, 2, \ldots$.   Then $F_0(z) = 0$ and $|F_n(z) - F_0(z)| < \epsilon$ whenever $n > 1/\epsilon|z|$.

There is an important difference between these two examples.   In the first, $|F_n(z) - F_0(z)| < \epsilon$ whenever $n > 1/\epsilon$ *for every z in S*; that is, there is an N of the sort required by the definition of convergence that is *independent* of z in S.   In the second example there is no such N, for $|F_n(z) - F_0(z)| < \epsilon$ *only if* $n > 1/\epsilon|z|$, so that such an N must satisfy the inequality $N \geq 1/\epsilon|z|$ for every z in S, and this is impossible whenever $|z| < 1/\epsilon N$.   One speaks of the convergence in Example 1 as *uniform* and of that in Example 2 as *non-uniform*.

Precisely, the sequence $\{F_n(z)\}$ *converges uniformly* to $F_0(z)$ on S if, given arbitrary $\epsilon > 0$, there is a positive number N such that $|F_n(z) - F_0(z)| < \epsilon$ *for every z in S* whenever $n > N$.   Correspondingly, one says that a series $\sum_1^\infty f_n(z)$ that is defined and convergent to a function $F_0(z)$ on a set S *converges uniformly* on S if the sequence $\{F_n(z)\}$ of the partial sums $F_n(z) \equiv \sum_1^n f_k(z)$ of the series converges uniformly to $F_0(z)$ on S.

EXAMPLE 3.   The *Dirichlet series* $\sum_1^\infty 1/n^z$, where by n^z is meant the principal value $e^{z \, \mathrm{Ln} \, n}$, is convergent for all z for which $R(z) \equiv x > 1$, since $\sum_1^\infty |1/n^z| = \sum_1^\infty 1/n^x$; it is *uniformly convergent* on S: $x \geq a$ for each real number a that is greater than 1 since, given arbitrary $\epsilon > 0$, if the positive integer N is so large that

$$\sum_{N+2}^\infty \frac{1}{n^a} < \epsilon,$$

then

$$|F_n(z) - F_0(z)| \equiv \left| \sum_{n+1}^\infty \frac{1}{k^z} \right| \leq \sum_{n+1}^\infty \frac{1}{k^a} < \epsilon$$

for every z in S whenever $n > N$.

A useful device that is frequently available to establish uniformity of convergence of a series is given in the next theorem.

THEOREM 10-3. *Let the functions* $f_0(z), f_1(z), \ldots, f_n(z), \ldots$ *be defined on a set S. If there is a convergent series* $\sum_0^\infty M_n$ *of positive numbers* M_n *such that* $|f_n(z)| \leq M_n$ *for* $n = 0, 1, \ldots$ *and every* z *in S, then* $\sum_0^\infty f_n(z)$ *is uniformly and absolutely convergent on S.*

Proof. First, the series $\sum_0^\infty f_n(z)$ is absolutely convergent for every z in S, being dominated by a convergent series of positive constants. Let $F_0(z) = \sum_0^\infty f_n(z)$. Next, given arbitrary $\epsilon > 0$ there is a positive integer N such that $\sum_{N+2}^\infty M_k < \epsilon$. Hence

$$\left| \sum_0^n f_k(z) - F_0(z) \right| \equiv \left| \sum_{n+1}^\infty f_k(z) \right| \leq \sum_{n+1}^\infty |f_k(z)| \leq \sum_{n+1}^\infty M_k < \epsilon$$

for every z in S whenever $n > N$.

The *uniformly dominating* series $\sum M_n$ of Theorem 10-3 is called a *Weierstrass M-series.*

THEOREM 10-4. *A power series* (10-1) *with positive radius of convergence R is uniformly convergent on* $S: |z - z_0| \leq R_1$ *for each positive number* R_1 *that is less than R.*

Proof. Since the point $z = z_0 + R_1$ is inside the circle of convergence of the series (10-1), the series

$$\sum_0^\infty |a_n| R_1^n \tag{10-3}$$

converges. But then the series (10-3) is a Weierstrass M-series for the series (10-1) with z in S, which leads at once to the conclusion of the theorem.

10-5.   Problems.

1. Show that the sequence in Example 2 of §10-4 converges uniformly on S_a for every positive number a, where S_a is the set of points z for which $|z| > a$.

2. Show that, if the set S of our definition of uniform convergence has only a finite number of points, the convergence is uniform.

3. The part of the Laurent series that was denoted by $f_-(z)$ in (6-7) is uniformly convergent on S: $|z - z_0| \geq r_2$ for each positive number r_2 that is greater than r_1. Prove this.

4. Show that the series

$$\frac{1}{|z|} - \frac{1}{2|z|} + \frac{1}{3|z|} - \cdots + (-1)^{n+1} \frac{1}{n|z|} + \cdots$$

is uniformly convergent on S: $|z| \geq a$ for each positive number a, but that this cannot be shown by means of a Weierstrass M-series.

5. Show that the series $\sum_1^\infty z^n/n^2$ is uniformly convergent on the set S consisting of the interior and the circumference of the circle of convergence.

6. Show that the series $\sum_1^\infty (-1)^n/(n + |z|)$ is uniformly convergent on the set S consisting of all points in the finite plane, but that there is no Weierstrass M-series by means of which one could prove this fact.

7. If the series (10-1) has finite radius of convergence and converges absolutely at any point on the circumference of its circle of convergence, then it converges uniformly on the set S consisting of the interior and the circumference of the circle of convergence. Prove this.

8. Show that no entire transcendental function has a power series expansion about any point z_0 that converges uniformly on the set S consisting of all points in the finite plane. Is the same true of polynomials?

9. If $\sum_0^\infty |f_n(z)|$ is uniformly convergent on a set S on which all of the $f_n(z)$ are defined, and if $\{M_n(z)\}$ is a sequence of functions defined on S that is bounded on S—that is, there is a positive number B such that $|M_n(z)| \leq B$ for $n = 1, 2, \ldots$ and every z in S—then $\sum_0^\infty M_n(z)f_n(z)$ is uniformly convergent on S. Prove this.

*10. Given a sequence of functions $\{F_n(z)\}$ defined on a set S. Show that this sequence converges uniformly on S if and only if, given arbitrary $\epsilon > 0$, there is a positive number N such that $|F_m(z) - F_n(z)| < \epsilon$ for every z in S whenever $m, n > N$.

11. A series $\sum f_n(z)$ is said to *converge uniformly at a point* z_0 if there is a neighborhood of z_0 throughout which $\sum f_n(z)$ converges uniformly. Show that, if a series $\sum f_n(z)$ converges uniformly at each point of a closed, bounded, non-null set S, it converges uniformly in S.

10-6. Applications of Uniform Convergence.

That uniformly convergent series of regular functions enjoy certain of the properties of finite sums of such functions is shown in the remaining theorems of this chapter.

THEOREM 10-5. *Let the functions* $f_0(z), f_1(z), \ldots, f_n(z), \ldots$ *be defined on a set* S, *let* $\sum_0^\infty f_n(z)$ *converge uniformly on* S *to* $F(z)$, *and let each of the* $f_n(z)$ *be continuous with respect to* S *at a point* z_0 *in* S. *Then* $F(z)$ *is continuous with respect to* S *at* z_0.

Proof. Given arbitrary $\epsilon > 0$, there is a positive integer N such that $|F(z) - \sum_0^N f_n(z)| < \epsilon/3$ for every z in S. Since $f_0(z)$, $f_1(z), \ldots, f_N(z)$ are continuous with respect to S at z_0, their sum is also continuous with respect to S at z_0, so that there is a $\delta > 0$ such that $|\sum_0^N f_n(z) - \sum_0^N f_n(z_0)| < \epsilon/3$ whenever z is in S and $|z - z_0| < \delta$. Hence

$$|F(z) - F(z_0)| \leq \left| F(z) - \sum_0^N f_n(z) \right| + \left| \sum_0^N f_n(z) - \sum_0^N f_n(z_0) \right|$$
$$+ \left| \sum_0^N f_n(z_0) - F(z_0) \right| < \frac{\epsilon}{3} + \frac{\epsilon}{3} + \frac{\epsilon}{3} \equiv \epsilon$$

whenever z is in S and $|z - z_0| < \delta$. This completes the proof.

THEOREM 10-6. *Let the functions* $f_0(z), f_1(z), \ldots, f_n(z), \ldots$ *be defined on a path* c, *let* $\sum_0^\infty f_n(z)$ *converge uniformly on* c *to* $F(z)$, *and let each of the* $f_n(z)$ *be continuous with respect to* c *at each point of* c. *Then* $F(z) \equiv \sum_0^\infty f_n(z)$ *is integrable on* c, *and*

$$\int_{(c)} F(z)dz \equiv \int_{(c)} \sum_0^\infty f_n(z)dz = \sum_0^\infty \int_{(c)} f_n(z)dz.$$

That is, the series is "*termwise integrable on* c."

Proof. Since $F(z)$ is continuous with respect to c at each point of c, $\int_{(c)} F(z)dz$ exists. Given arbitrary $\epsilon > 0$, there is a positive number N such that $|F(z) - \sum_0^n f_k(z)| < \epsilon/s$ for every z on c

whenever $n > N$, where s is the length of c.   Hence

$$\left| \int_{(c)} F(z)dz - \sum_0^n \int_{(c)} f_k(z)dz \right| \equiv \left| \int_{(c)} \left[F(z) - \sum_0^n f_k(z) \right] dz \right| < \frac{\epsilon}{s} s \equiv \epsilon$$

whenever $n > N$.   But this is to say that

$$\sum_0^\infty \int_{(c)} f_k(z)dz = \int_{(c)} F(z)dz,$$

as was to be proved.

THEOREM 10-7.   *Let the functions $f_0(z), f_1(z), \ldots, f_n(z), \ldots$ be regular in a neighborhood N of a point z_0 and let $\sum_0^\infty f_n(z)$ converge uniformly in N to $F(z)$.   Then $F(z)$ is regular in N,*

$$F^{(j)}(z) = \sum_0^\infty f_n^{(j)}(z), j = 1, 2, \ldots, \text{ for each } z \text{ in } N, \qquad (10\text{-}4)$$

and the convergence of the series in (10-4) is uniform in every neighborhood M of z_0 that is smaller than N.

Proof.   First, if c is an arbitrary closed path in N, then, by Theorem 10-6, $F(z)$ is integrable on c and

$$\oint_{(c)} F(z)dz = \sum_0^\infty \oint_{(c)} f_n(z)dz. \qquad (10\text{-}5)$$

Application of Cauchy's theorem to each term on the right-hand side of (10-5) now shows that $\oint_{(c)} F(z)dz = 0$, whereupon Morera's theorem assures us that $F(z)$ is regular in N.   We next let M be an arbitrary neighborhood of z_0 that is smaller than N.   To prove the rest of the theorem it will suffice to show that (10-4) holds at an arbitrary point Z of M and that the convergence of the series in (10-4) is uniform in M.   If R' and R'' are the radii of N and M, respectively, and we fix upon any number R between R'' and R', then $|Z - z_0| < R'' < R < R'$.   Putting $h = R - R''$, we therefore have $1/|z - Z| < 1/h$ for all z on the circle k: $|z - z_0| = R$, so that the series $\sum_{n=0}^\infty f_n(z)/(z - Z)^{j+1}$ converges uniformly on k for $j = 1, 2, \ldots$ to $F(z)/(z - Z)^{j+1}$ and hence

$$F^{(j)}(Z) \equiv \frac{j!}{2\pi i} \int_{(k)} \frac{F(z)dz}{(z - Z)^{j+1}} = \sum_{n=0}^\infty \frac{j!}{2\pi i} \int_{(k)} \frac{f_n(z)dz}{(z - Z)^{j+1}}$$

$$= \sum_{n=0}^\infty f_n^{(j)}(Z). \qquad (10\text{-}6)$$

Finally, the convergence of the last series in (10.6) is uniform for

Z (now regarded as variable) in M since—for such values of Z—

$$\left| \sum_{n=N+2}^{\infty} f_n^{(j)}(Z) \right| = \left| \sum_{n=N+2}^{\infty} \frac{j!}{2\pi i} \int_{(k)} \frac{f_n(z)dz}{(z-Z)^{j+1}} \right|$$

$$= \frac{j!}{2\pi} \left| \int_{(k)} \frac{\sum\limits_{n=N+2}^{\infty} f_n(z)}{(z-Z)^{j+1}} dz \right|$$

$$\leq \frac{j!}{2\pi} \frac{1}{h^{j+1}} \max_{z \text{ on } k} \left| \sum_{n=N+2}^{\infty} f_n(z) \right| 2\pi R.$$

10-7. Problems.

1. Let $f_n(z)$ be regular in an open set S for $n = 0, 1, \ldots$ and let $\sum f_n(z)$ converge uniformly in S to $F(z)$. Then the first two conclusions of Theorem 10-7 hold with "neighborhood N" replaced by "S," by that very theorem. Show, by means of the Heine-Borel theorem, that the third conclusion holds with "neighborhood M" replaced by "closed, bounded subregion of S."

2. Letting $F(z)$ represent the sum of the Dirichlet series exhibited in Example 3 of §10-4, find $F^{(j)}(z)$ for positive integral j and state for which values of z Theorem 10-7 guarantees that your answer is valid.

3. The series $\sum_1^{\infty} \sin n^3 x/n^2$ converges uniformly to a real function $f(x)$ of x for all real x. What does Theorem 10-7 tell us about the possibility of finding $f'(x)$ by termwise differentiation of the series?

4. What does Theorem 10-6 tell us about the possibility of finding $\int_a^b f(x)dx$ for arbitrary real a and b by termwise integration of the series of problem 3, if $f(x)$ is the function there defined?

5. Let a sequence of functions $\{F_n(z)\}$, each regular throughout an open set S, converge uniformly to a function $F(z)$ in S. Show how Theorem 10-7 guarantees that $F(z)$ is regular throughout S. Is it true that $F^{(j)}(z) = \lim_{n\to\infty} F_n^{(j)}(z)$ for positive integral j? [Consider the series $\sum_0^{\infty} f_n(z)$, where $f_0(z) \equiv F_0(z)$ and $f_n(z) \equiv F_n(z) - F_{n-1}(z)$ for $n = 1, 2, \ldots$.]

6. Weierstrass has shown that, given an arbitrary continuous real function $F(x)$ of the real variable x on the interval $a \leq x \leq b$, there is a series of real polynomials $\sum_0^{\infty} p_n(x)$ that converges

uniformly to $F(x)$ for $a \leq x \leq b$. Now the polynomials $p_n(z)$ are regular throughout the entire finite plane. Does not Theorem 10-7 then assert that every continuous real function of a real variable on a finite interval is, among other things, differentiable throughout that interval?

7. We know that $1 - x + x^2 - \cdots + (-1)^n x^n + \cdots = 1/(1 + x)$ whenever $|x| < 1$. Problem 10 of §10-5 shows that the convergence is not uniform here, but (x supposed real)

$$\int_0^1 \frac{dx}{1 + x} \equiv \ln 2 \equiv 1 - \frac{1}{2} + \frac{1}{3} - \cdots + \frac{(-1)^{n-1}}{n} + \cdots$$
$$= \int_0^1 dx - \int_0^1 x\,dx + \int_0^1 x^2\,dx - \cdots + (-1)^{n-1} \int_0^1 x^{n-1}\,dx + \cdots.$$

What is the relevance of this example of termwise integrability to Theorem 10-6?

On Connectedness of Sets

11

11-1. Connectedness of Sets in General.

In the earlier definition of a connected open region R (§4-6) it was required that, given any two points z_0 and Z in R, there exist in R staircase paths with all orientations joining z_0 and Z. But then it was stated parenthetically that this would later be shown to be automatically the case if there existed in R a staircase path with a *single* orientation joining z_0 and Z. Still more can now be said.

THEOREM 11-1. *If two points z_0 and Z of an open set S can be joined by any particular path k, all points of which are points of S, then z_0 and Z can be joined by a staircase path k' with any prescribed orientation φ, all points of which are points of S.*

Proof. First, let us observe that construction of the path k' is possible if S contains the interior of a circle within which z_0 and Z both lie. Let now a parameterization of k be $z = z(t)$, where $z_0 = z(t_0)$ and $Z = z(T)$, $t_0 < T$, and $z(t)$ is continuous. Let S_k be the real set of the values of t, $t_0 < t \le T$, for which every point $z(t')$ with $t_0 < t' \le t$ can be joined to z_0 by a staircase path with orientation φ, all points of which are points of S. Now S_k contains all points t greater than t_0 and sufficiently near t_0 and is therefore not null. It is also bounded (by T). So S_k has a least upper bound, T_0. If we can show that $T_0 = T$, then our proof is complete, by our first observation and the fact that Z is the center of a circle whose interior is contained in S and within which lie points $z = z(t)$ for t in S_k.

Suppose then that $T_0 < T$. The point $z = z(T_0)$ is the center of a circle whose interior is contained in S and within which lie all points $z = z(t)$ for which $T_0 - \delta \le t \le T_0 + \delta$ for some positive number δ. Again using our first observation, we conclude that $T_0 + \delta$ belongs to S_k and hence that T_0 is not the least upper bound of S_k, which is a contradiction.

Entirely equivalent to the earlier definition of a connected open set, then, is this:

> *A non-null open set S is said to be connected if it satisfies the*
> *condition that, given any two points z_0 and Z in S, there is a*   (11-1)
> *path k that joins z_0 and Z and all points of which are in S.*

Thus far the term "connected" has been applied only to open sets. More generally, any non-null set S is said to be *connected* if, for every pair of non-null subsets S_1 and S_2 of S for which $S = S_1 + S_2$ and $S_1 S_2$ is null, the set $S_1 \bar{S}_2 + \bar{S}_1 S_2$ is not null: that is, no matter how S may be split up into two non-overlapping, non-null subsets, at least one contains a limit point of the other. (Reflection will probably show that this definition is agreeable to the student's intuitive feeling as to what connectedness should mean.) If S consists of a single point, the condition for connectedness is said to be *vacuously satisfied*, and S is regarded as connected. In the next section it will be proved that this definition is consistent with that for open sets, which makes use of (11-1).

EXAMPLE 1.   The set S of the points on a line segment (including or excluding one or both end points) is connected, for the following reasons. Supposing, as we may, that S is a portion of the x axis, let it be separated into two non-null and non-overlapping subsets S_1 and S_2, and let x_0 be a point in S_1 and X a point in S_2. Let us assume for definiteness that $x_0 < X$. Denoting by x^* the least upper bound of the points x of S_1 for which $x \ge x_0$ and there are no points x' of S_2 such that $x_0 < x' \le x$, we need only observe that either x^* is a point of S_1—in which case it is a limit point of S_2, so that $S_1 \bar{S}_2$ is not null—or x^* is a point of S_2—in which case it is a limit point of S_1, so that $\bar{S}_1 S_2$ is not null.

EXAMPLE 2.   The points of a region S whose interior is the interior of a circle constitute a connected set. To show this, let us suppose S separated into two non-null and non-overlapping subsets S_1 and S_2, and let z_0 be a point in S_1 and Z a point in S_2. If T_1 and T_2 are the points of S_1 and of S_2, respectively, that lie on the line segment from z_0 to Z (z_0 and Z included), then, by Example 1 above, $T_1 \bar{T}_2 + \bar{T}_1 T_2$ is not null. But, since T_j and $\bar{T}_j$ are subsets of S_j and $\bar{S}_j$, respectively, for $j = 1$ and 2, this implies that $S_1\bar{S}_2 + \bar{S}_1 S_2$ is not null.

EXAMPLE 3. If T_1 is the set of points z for which $|z - 1| \leq 1$ and T_2 is the set for which $|z + 1| < 1$, then the set $S \equiv T_1 + T_2$ is connected, since $T_1\bar{T}_2$ contains the point $z = 0$ and no separation of S into non-null and non-overlapping subsets other than T_1 and T_2 needs to be considered, by Example 2 above.

11-2. Problems.

1. A *convex* point set is a non-null set S such that, for every pair of distinct points P_1 and P_2 in S, each point of the line segment between P_1 and P_2 is in S. Why is a plane convex set connected?

2. Let T_1 be the set of points z for which $|z - 1| < 1$ and T_2 the set for which $|z + 1| < 1$. Is the set $S \equiv T_1 + T_2$ connected?

3. Let T_1 and T_2 be the points in the open right half-plane $R(z) > 0$ and in the open left half-plane $R(z) < 0$, respectively. The set $S \equiv T_1 + T_2 + T^*$ will be connected if T^* is the set consisting of a single, appropriately chosen point z_0. Name such a z_0.

4. The set of points on a line that remain after removal of a single point from among them is not connected. Why?

5. Show that every point in a connected set S consisting of more than one point is a limit point of S.

6. Show by an example why connectedness of a set S is not equivalent to the property that, given any two non-null sets S_1 and S_2 such that $S = S_1 + S_2$ and $S_1 S_2$ is null, then $\bar{S}_1 \bar{S}_2$ is not null.

*7. Show that every path k is a connected set of points. [Work with the real sets T_1 and T_2 of values of t in a continuous parameterization $z = z(t)$ of k that correspond to the sets S_1 and S_2, respectively, into which the points of k are separated.]

*8. Is the set S that consists of the points on the curve $y = \sin(1/x)$ for $x \neq 0$ connected?   Is the set T connected if T consists of the points of S plus the origin?

9. Is the set S connected that consists of the points that lie on either of the loci, polar equations for which are

   (a) $r = 1/\theta$ and $r = 1/(\theta + 1), 0 < \theta < \infty$?
   (b) $r = 1/\theta$ and $r = 2/\theta, 0 < \theta < \infty$?

10. All points of the path k of Theorem 11-1 can be covered by the interiors k_j of a finite number of circles, all of the points of the k_j being points of S. (Why?) Use this fact to argue an alternative proof of Theorem 11-1.

11. Making use of the fact that the plane is a connected set, show that the only non-null plane set of points that is both open and closed is the entire plane.

12. Show that, if a set S is connected, a function $f(z)$ is continuous on S, and T is the map of S by $f(z)$, then T is also connected. This is a generalization of problem 7. How so?

11-3. Connectedness of Open and of Closed Sets.

In the following theorems the concept of connectedness assumed is that of the general definition, although ultimately it will be shown—among other things—that the definition involving condition (11-1) is equivalent in case the non-null set S is open.

THEOREM 11-2. *A sufficient condition that a non-null set S be connected is* (11-1).

Proof. We may assume S to contain more than one point. Suppose then that S_1 and S_2 are any pair of non-null subsets of S for which $S = S_1 + S_2$ and $S_1 S_2$ is null. Let z_0 be any point in S_1 and Z any point in S_2, and let k be a path of the sort specified in (11-1). Let T_1 be the set of the points of k that are in S_1 and T_2 that of those that are in S_2. Neither T_1 nor T_2 is null, their product is null, and their sum is the connected set k (problem 7 of §11-2). Hence $T_1\bar{T}_2 + \bar{T}_1 T_2$ is not null and, as in Example 2 of §11-1, it follows that $S_1\bar{S}_2 + \bar{S}_1 S_2$ is not null, which is what we set out to prove.

A concept that will appear in due time to be useful in characterizing connectedness of certain sets is that of an "ϵ-chain." Given two points z_0 and Z, not necessarily distinct, in a set S and a positive number ϵ, if there are points $z_1, z_2, \ldots, z_{n-1}$ in S for which $|z_j - z_{j-1}| < \epsilon$ for $j = 1, 2, \ldots, n$, where $z_n \equiv Z$, then the points $z_0, z_1, \ldots, z_n \equiv Z$ are said to constitute an ϵ-*chain in* S between z_0 and Z. Of immediate interest is the condition (referring to a non-null set S, though S may consist of a single point)

> *That, given any two points* z_0 *and* Z, *not necessarily distinct, in* S, *there is an* ϵ-*chain in* S *between* z_0 *and* Z (11-2)
> *for every* $\epsilon > 0$.

By means of this condition it is easy to phrase a companion to Theorem 11-2.

THEOREM 11-3. *A necessary condition that a non-null set* S *be connected is* (11-2).

Proof. Let z_0 be an arbitrary point of S and let $\epsilon > 0$ be arbitrary. Let S_1 consist of those points z of S between z_0 and which there is an ϵ-chain in S, and put $S_2 = S - S_1$. Then $S = S_1 + S_2$, and $S_1 S_2$ is null. Noting that S_1 is closed (so that $\bar{S}_1 S_2$ is null) and not null (since z_0 belongs to S_1), we may conclude from the connectedness of S that either S_2 is null or S_1 contains a limit point z' of S_2. But in the latter case there is a point z'' of S_2 for which $|z'' - z'| < \epsilon$, so that z'' belongs to S_1, contrary to the definition of S_2. Hence S_2 is indeed null: $S_1 = S$, and the proof is complete.

The next two theorems are concerned, respectively, with a necessity property of condition (11-1) and a sufficiency property of condition (11-2).

THEOREM 11-4. *A necessary condition that a non-null open set* S *be connected is* (11-1).

Proof. Let z_0 be an arbitrary point of S, let S_1 consist of those points z of S for which there is a path k that joins z_0 to z and all points of which are in S, and put $S_2 = S - S_1$. Then $S = S_1 + S_2$, and $S_1 S_2$ is null. Clearly, S_1 is open, so that $S_1 \bar{S}_2$ is null. Also, any limit point z' of S_1 that is in S is in S_1 (one describes this situation by saying that "S_1 is closed in S") so that $\bar{S}_1 S_2$ is null. Since S is connected, and S_1 is not null (all points in some deleted neighborhood of z_0 belong to S_1), we may conclude that S_2 is null, so that $S_1 = S$, as was to be proved.

THEOREM 11-5. *A sufficient condition that a non-null, closed, bounded set* S *be connected is* (11-2).

Proof. Supposing S_1 and S_2 to be any pair of non-null subsets of S for which $S = S_1 + S_2$, and $S_1 S_2$ is null, we must show that $S_1 \bar{S}_2 + \bar{S}_1 S_2$ is not null, so let us assume the contrary. But then $\bar{S}_1 \bar{S}_2$ is also null, for otherwise any point z' in $\bar{S}_1 \bar{S}_2$ would be a limit point of S_1 (and therefore also of S), which is not in S_1 (since $S_1 \bar{S}_2$ is null), nor in S_2 (since $\bar{S}_1 S_2$ is null), and hence not in S, contrary to the closedness of S. Since $\bar{S}_1$ and $\bar{S}_2$ are closed and bounded, the distance h between them is assumed: there are two points, z_0 in $\bar{S}_1$ and Z in $\bar{S}_2$ (whence both z_0 and Z in S), such that $|Z - z_0| = h$. It follows that $h > 0$. But then there is no ϵ-chain in S between z_0 and Z for which $\epsilon < h$, contrary to condition (11-2), for otherwise among the quantities $|z_j - z_{j-1}|$ for $j = 1, 2, \ldots, n$ ($z_n \equiv Z$) for the ϵ-chain would occur at least one with z_j in $\bar{S}_2$ and z_{j-1} in $\bar{S}_1$.

Justification for the definition following the proof of Theorem 11-1 from the standpoint of the general definition of connectedness (from which standpoint it must have been viewed as provisional) is asserted by an immediate corollary to Theorems 11-2 and 11-4.

THEOREM 11-6. *A necessary and sufficient condition that a non-null open set S be connected is* (11-1).

A similarly derived corollary to Theorems 11-3 and 11-5 follows.

THEOREM 11-7. *A necessary and sufficient condition that a non-null, closed, bounded set S be connected is* (11-2).

By Theorem 11-7, one may use condition (11-2) as a *defining* property of connectedness for a non-null, closed, bounded set S. This is, in fact, often done.

11-4. Problems.

1. For the set S of points x on the real axis for which $0 < |x| \leq 1$, condition (11-2) is satisfied. Yet S is not connected. Why is this example not in contradiction to Theorem 11-7?

2. Consider the set S of points $z \equiv x + iy$ for which either (a) $0 \leq x \leq 1$ and y is rational or (b) $0 \leq y \leq 1$ and x is irrational. Establish whether S is open, closed, connected.

3. Appealing directly to theorems in §11-3, give two reasons, for either one of which a path is a connected set of points.

4. Consider the set S consisting of the points $z \equiv x + iy$ for which $y = 1/x^2$ and $x \neq 0$, taking special note of the subsets S_1 and S_2 for which $x < 0$ and $x > 0$, respectively.

   (a) Show that S is closed.
   (b) Show that S is not connected.
   (c) Show that S satisfies condition (11-2).
   (d) Explain the relevance of this set S to Theorem 11-7.

5. Show that the set of points $z \equiv x + iy$ for which $0 \leq x \leq 1$ and $0 < y < 1$ is neither open nor closed and that condition (11-2) is satisfied by S. How do we know that S is connected?

6. Is the set S of problem 8 of §11-2 open? Closed? Does S satisfy condition (11-1)? Outline construction of an ϵ-chain in S between any two given points in S.

7. In both Example 2 of §11-1 and the proof of Theorem 11-2 we deduced connectedness of a set S from connectedness of a subset T of S that contained a point in S_1 and a point in S_2. Formulate a general theorem suggested by these cases.

Bibliography.

The following books will be of use in further study. Those listed in Part A are more or less general treatments of complex variable theory. Many of them are elementary, but some are rather advanced. More specialized and for the most part more advanced works are included in Part B.

A. General Works.

Ahlfors, L. V. *Complex Analysis*, McGraw-Hill Book Company, Inc., New York, 1953.

Burkhardt, H. *Theory of Functions of a Complex Variable*, D. C. Heath & Co., Boston, 1913.

Caratheodory, C. *Theory of Functions of a Complex Variable*, Vol. 2, Chelsea Publishing Company, New York, 1960. A somewhat advanced, topological approach.

Chevalley, C. *Introduction to the Theory of Algebraic Functions of One Variable*, American Mathematical Society, New York, 1951.

Churchill, R. V. *Complex Variables and Applications*, 2d ed., McGraw-Hill Book Company, Inc., New York, 1960. Very good on conformal mapping; mathematical, but oriented toward applications; contains bibliography.

Copson, E. T. *An Introduction to the Theory of Functions of a Complex Variable*, Oxford University Press, London, 1957. Large sections are devoted to special functions.

Courant, R. *The Theory of Functions of a Complex Variable*, New York University, Institute for Mathematics and Mechanics, New York, 1952.

Curtiss, D. R. *Analytic Functions of a Complex Variable*, Carus Mathematical Monographs, No. 2, Mathematical Association of America, 1926.

Deaux, R. *Introduction to the Geometry of Complex Numbers*, F. Ungar Publishing Company, New York, 1956.

Dienes, P. *The Taylor Series, an Introduction to the Theory of Functions of a Complex Variable*, Oxford University Press, Oxford, 1931. Has a large bibliography.

Durege, H. *Elements of the Theory of Functions of a Complex Variable with Especial Reference to the Methods of Riemann*, G. E. Fisher and I. J. Schwatt, Philadelphia, 1896.

Estermann, T. *Complex Numbers and Functions*, Athlone Press, London, 1962. Rather abstract, but assumes only real variable theory; contains a short bibliography.

Fiske, T. S. *Functions of a Complex Variable*, John Wiley and Sons, Inc., New York, 1907.

Forsyth, A. R. *Theory of Functions of a Complex Variable*, Cambridge University Press, Cambridge, 1900. An extensive treatment at a fairly advanced level.

Franklin, P. *Functions of Complex Variables*, Prentice-Hall, Inc., Englewood Cliffs, N.J., 1958. A class text at the upper class or graduate level; has a short bibliography.

Fuchs, B. A. *Theory of Analytic Functions of Several Complex Variables*, American Mathematical Society, Providence, R.I., 1963.

Fuchs, B. A., and V. I. Levin. *Functions of a Complex Variable and some of their Applications*, Addison-Wesley Publishing Company, Inc., Reading, 1961. Laplace transforms, differential equations, Hurwitz's problem for polynomials, etc.

Goursat, E. *A Course in Mathematical Analysis*, Part I of Vol. II: *Functions of a Complex Variable*, Ginn and Company, Boston, 1916.

Hille, E. *Analytic Function Theory*, 2 vols., Ginn and Company, Boston, 1959, 1962.

Knopp, K. *Theory of Functions*, 2 vols., Dover Publications, Inc., New York, 1945, 1962.

——————. *Elements of the Theory of Functions*, Dover Publications, Inc., New York, 1952.

Landau, E. *Foundations of Analysis*, Chelsea Publishing Company, New York, 1951. A very careful development of real and complex numbers from the beginnings.

LePage, W. R. *Complex Variables and the Laplace Transform for Engineers*, McGraw-Hill Book Company, Inc., New York, 1961.

MacRobert, T. M. *Functions of a Complex Variable*, The Macmillan Company, London, 1947. Emphasizes special functions.

Miller, K. S. *Advanced Complex Calculus*, Harper & Row, Publishers, New York, 1960.

Nehari, Z. *Introduction to Complex Analysis*, Allyn and Bacon, Inc., Boston, 1961. A chapter on physical applications.

Osgood, W. F. *Functions of a Complex Variable*, Chelsea Publishing Company, New York, 1936.

Pennisi, L. L. *Elements of Complex Variables*, Holt, Rinehart and Winston, Inc., New York, 1963.

Phillips, E. G. *Functions of a Complex Variable, with Applications*, Interscience Publishers, New York, 1957.

Pierpont, J. *Functions of a Complex Variable*, Ginn and Company, Boston, 1914. Emphasizes special functions.

Saks, S., and A. Zygmund. *Analytic Functions*, Nakladem Polskiego Tow, Matematycznego, Warszawa, 1952. Starts from set theory.

Sansone, G., and J. Gerrestsen. *Lectures on the Theory of Functions of a Complex Variable*, Vol. I: *Holomorphic Functions*, P. Noordhoff, Groningen (the Netherlands), 1960. At an intermediate level.

Scott, E. J. *Transform Calculus, with an Introduction to Complex Variables*, Harper & Row, Publishers, New York, 1955.

Stringham, I. *Uniplanar Algebra*, The Berkeley Press, San Francisco, 1893. A curious, geometric approach.

Thron, W. J. *Introduction to the Theory of Functions of a Complex Variable*, John Wiley and Sons, Inc., New York, 1953. A fairly high-level text.

Titchmarsh, E. C. *The Theory of Functions*, The Clarendon Press, Oxford, 1932.

Townsend, E. J. *Functions of a Complex Variable*, Henry Holt and Company, New York, 1915.

Whittaker, E. T., and G. N. Watson. *A Course of Modern Analysis*, Cambridge University Press, Cambridge, 1927. Perhaps the most popular book on analysis in English.

B. Specialized Works.

Abramov, A. A. *Tables of* Ln (z) *for Complex Argument*, Pergamon Press, London, 1960. Tables and an interesting introduction.

Bieberbach, L. *Conformal Mapping*, Chelsea Publishing Company, New York, 1953.

Bochner, S., and W. T. Martin. *Several Complex Variables*, Princeton University Press, Princeton, 1948. A group-theoretic approach; treats sub-harmonic functions; requires knowledge of the elements of Lebesgue integration.

Caratheodory, C. *Conformal Representation*, Cambridge University Press, Cambridge, 1952.

"Conference on Analytic Functions at the Institute for Advanced Study, Princeton, 1957," Princeton University Press, 1960. Advanced lectures on the theory of functions of several complex variables, conformal mapping and schlicht functions, Riemann surfaces, and automorphic functions.

"Conference on Functions of a Complex Variable, The University of Michigan, 1953," The University of Michigan Press, Ann Arbor, 1953.

Courant, R. *Dirichlet's Principle, Conformal Mapping, and Minimal Surfaces*, Interscience Publishers, Inc., New York, 1950.

Ford, L. R. *Automorphic Functions*, Chelsea Publishing Company, New York, 1951. A group-theoretic approach.

Forsyth, A. R. *Lectures Introductory to the Theory of Functions of Two Complex Variables*, Cambridge University Press, Cambridge, 1914.

Heins, M. *Selected Topics in the Classical Theory of Functions of a Complex Variable*, Holt, Rinehart and Winston, Inc., New York, 1962. Somewhat abstract.

Hervé, M. *Several Complex Variables, Local Theory*, Oxford University Press, New York, 1963. Advanced discussion of recent work in the theory of functions of several complex variables.

Jenkins, J. *Univalent Functions and Conformal Mapping*, Springer-Verlag, Berlin, 1958.

Kaplan, W., ed. *Lectures on Functions of a Complex Variable*, The University of Michigan Press, Ann Arbor, 1955. Lectures on various advanced topics given at a conference on functions of a complex variable.

Kober, H. *Dictionary of Conformal Representations*, Dover Publications, Inc., New York, 1952. A collection of conformal maps with diagrams and summaries of their properties.

Levin, B. J. *Distribution of Zeroes of Entire Functions*, American Mathematical Society, Providence, R.I., 1964.

Lewent, L. *Conformal Representation*, Methuen and Company, Ltd., London, 1925.

Marden, M. *The Geometry of the Zeroes of a Polynomial in a Complex Variable*, American Mathematical Society, New York, 1949.

Morse, M. *Topological Methods in the Theory of Functions of a Complex Variable*, Princeton University Press, Princeton, 1947.

Nehari, Z. *Conformal Mapping*, McGraw-Hill Book Company, Inc., New York, 1952.

Roberts, J. B. *The Real Number System in an Algebraic Setting*, W. H. Freeman, San Francisco, 1962. The development of the number system as far as complex numbers.

Siegel, C. L. *Analytic Functions of Several Complex Variables*, Institute for Advanced Study, School of Mathematics, Princeton, 1949.

Vekua, I. N. *Generalized Analytic Functions*, Pergamon Press, Oxford, New York, 1962. Advanced theory and applications.

Watson, G. N. *Complex Integration and Cauchy's Theorem*, Hafner Publishing Company, New York (originally published by the Cambridge University Press in 1914). ". . . a rigorous proof of Cauchy's theorem, together with a brief account of some of the application . . . to the evaluation of definite integrals" (quoted from the Introduction).

Index

A

Algebra:
  complex, 2–4
  functions, 39
  fundamental theorem, 93
  power series, 87–89
  sets, 174–176
Analysis techniques:
  Axiom of Continuity, 179–181
  Bolzano-Weierstrass theorem, 182,
    185–188
  boundary points, 172
  closed regions, 173
  complementary sets, 172–173
  continuous differentiability, 195–198
  cut number, 179
  Dedekind cut, 179
  epsilon-delta, 166–170
  extreme limit points, 182–184
  Heine-Borel theorem, 191–194
  isolated points, 172
  maximum modulus theorem, 192–194
  neighborhoods, 168–170
  nests of intervals, 181–182

Analysis techniques (*continued*):
  nests of plane sets, 191
  point sets, closed, null, and bounded,
    171
  region, defined, 173
  sets, *see* Sets
Analytic continuation:
  function with natural boundary, 135
  generation of function from ele-
    ment, 135–137
  line segments, 143
  multi-valued functions, 138–140
  open regions, 134–135
  persistence of functional relation-
    ships, 144–145
  Riemann surfaces, 140–141
Archimedes' theorem, 181
Associative operations, 2
Axiom of Continuity, 179–181

B

Basic elementary functions, 39
Bilinear transformation, 158–160, 161

Bolzano-Weierstrass theorem, 182, 185–188
Boundaries of sets, 171, 172

C

Casorati-Weierstrass theorem, 95–96
Cauchy-Riemann equations, 29–31
Cauchy's convergence criterion, 200–201
Cauchy's integral formula, 78–80
Cauchy's theorem, 63–64, 72
Circle of convergence, 46–48
Circular functions, 38
Closed sets, 171, 214–216
Commutative operations, 2
Complementary sets, 172–173
Complex algebra, 2–4
Complex numbers, history of, 1
Complex one (1, 0), 4
Complex reals, 5
Complex zero, 3
Components, real and imaginary, 7
Concepts, elementary, 1–15
Conformal mapping, see Mapping
Conjugates, 13
Connectedness of sets, 211–217
   (see also Sets)
Constants and differentiability, 18–19
Continuity, Axiom of, 179–181
Convergence of infinite series, 43–46
Counterparts, real, 5
Curves, equipotential, 155–157
Cut number, 179

D

Dedekind cut, 179
Dedekind, Richard, 179
Definite integrals, 57–58, 73–74
Difference, defined, 2
Difference theorem, 3
Differentiability:
   algebraic functions, 39
   basic elementary functions, 39

Differentiability (*continued*):
   Cauchy-Riemann equations, 29–31
   circular functions, 38
   conditions for, 28–31
   constants, 18–19
   continuity, 25–26
   e^z and ln z functions, 33–35
   elementary functions, 38–39
   functions, 18–19
   hyperbolic functions, 38
   identical vanishing of derivative, 33
   logarithmic functions, 34–35
   variables, 18–19
      limits of, 19–23
Differentiability of regular functions, continuous, 195–198
Differentiability to all orders, implied by regularity, 82
Dirichlet series, 204
Distributive operations, 2

E

e^z and ln z functions, 33–35
Epsilon-delta techniques, 166–170
Equality, defined, 2
Equipotential curves, 155–157

F

Fixed points in mapping, 161
   (*see also* Mapping)
Functions, and differentiability, 18–19

G

Green's theorem, 64

H

Heine-Borel theorem, 191–194
Hyperbolic functions, 38

I

i, defined, 1–2
Imaginary components, 7
"Imaginary," term, 1, 2
"Imaginary unit" (*i*), 1
Infinite series:
  absolute convergence, 43–46
  circle and radius of convergence, 46–48
  sequences, 41–42
  series, 42–43
    power, 46, 50–54
    product, 43–46
  term differentiation, 50–54
  Uniqueness Theorem, 53
Infinite sets, extreme limit points of, 182–183
Infinity, point at, 111–113
Integrals, residue theory in evaluation of, 125–129
Integration:
  bounding theorem, 59–60
  Cauchy's theorem, 63–64, 72
  continuous functions, 57–58
  equivalent paths, 77–78
  evaluation of integrals, 58, 73–74
  general properties of integrals, 59–60
  Green's theorem, 64
  line integrals, 57–58, 63–69
  Morera's theorem, 72
  open regions, 61–62
  regular functions, 71–72
  simple curves, class C_1, 56–57
Introduction to Complex Variables and Applications (Churchill), 164–165
Inverse functions, 129–132
Isolated points of sets, 172

L

Laurent expansion:
  analysis of isolated singular points, 109–111
  decomposition of rational functions into partial fractions, 109–111

Laurent expansion (*continued*):
  deleted neighborhoods, 101–102
  derivation of, 102–105
  inverse functions, 129–132
  limit points of sets and sequences, 99–100
  neighborhoods, 99
  point at infinity, 111–113
  principle of the argument theorem, 121–122, 123
  residue theory, 119–121, 125–129
  Rouché's theorem, 122–123
  singular points, 101–102
  uniqueness of, 105–108
  zeros, 115–117
Limit points of sets and sequences, 99–100
Line integrals, 57–58, 63–69
Liouville's theorem, 91–93
Loci, descriptions of, 13
Logarithmic functions and differentiability, 34–35

M

Maclaurin series, 83
Mapping:
  analytic functions, other mappings by, 162–165
  bilinear transformation, 158–160, 161
  conformal, 150–154
  fixed points of bilinear transformation, 161–162
  image, defined, 147
  inverse, 155
  limiting magnification, 153
  map, defined, 147
  Riemann surfaces, 162–163
  rotation, 153
  streamlines for harmonic equipotential curves, 155–157
  transformations, 147–150
Maximum modulus:
  principle in Taylor expansion, 89–90

Maximum modulus (*continued*):
  theorem, 192–194
Multiples, defined, 6–7

N

Negatives, defined, 3
Neighborhoods, 99, 168–170
Nests of intervals, 181–182
Nests of plane sets, 191
Notation, simplification of, 6–7
Null sets, 171 (*see also* Sets)

O

"On Two Theorems of Plane
  Topology" (Vaughan), 78
One (1, 0), 4
Open and closed sets, connected-
  ness of, 214–216
Open regions, 61–62
Order of approaching zero, defined, 115

P

Persistence of functional relationships
  (permanence of form), 144–145
Picard's theorem, 96
Plane, complex, 8–11
Plane sets, 185–188
Point at infinity, 111–113
Point sets, 171
Poles, relationship to zeros, 116–117
Power series:
  algebra of, 87–89
  defined, 46
  formula for radius of convergence,
    201–202
  term differentiation of, 50–54
Principle of the argument theorem,
  122, 123
Product, defined, 2
Product series, 43–46
Projection of solids on planes, 9

Q

Quadratic equations, 1, 5–6
Quotient, defined, 3
Quotient theorem, 3

R

Radius of convergence, infinite series,
  46–48
Rational functions, decomposition into
  partial fractions, 109–111
Real components, 7
Real counterparts, 5
Real numbers (complex reals), 5
Real sets, extreme bounds on,
  177–178
"Real," term, 1, 2
Reciprocal, defined, 4
Region, defined, 173
Regular functions, continuous differ-
  entiability of, 195–198
Regular functions, integrals of, 71–72
Residue theory, 119–121, 125–129
Riemann surfaces, 140–141, 162–163
Rouché's theorem, 122–123

S

Sequences, extreme limit points,
  183–184
Sequences, infinite, 41–42
Series:
  Cauchy's convergence criterion,
    200–201
  Dirichlet, 204
  infinite, *see* Infinite series
  power, *see* Power series
  radius of convergence, 201–202
  theorems, 200–210
  uniform convergence, 204–205,
    207–209
  Weierstrass M-series, 205
Sets:
  algebra of, 174–176

Sets (*continued*):
  Bolzano-Weierstrass theorem, 182, 185–188
  bounded, 171, 172
  closed, 171, 214–216
  complementary, 172–173
  connectedness, 211–217
  extreme bounds on real, 177–178
  Heine-Borel theorem, 191–194
  isolated points, 172
  limit points, 99–100, 182–183
  linear, 182
  nests of plane sets, 191
  null, 171
  plane, 185–188
Simple curves, class C_1, in integration, 56–57
Singular points, 101–102, 109–111
Sphere, complex, 9
Square root of minus one (i), 1
Sum, defined, 2

T

Taylor expansion:
  algebra of power series, 87–89
  Casorati-Weierstrass theorem, 95–96
  Cauchy's integral formula, 78–80
  entire functions, 91–93
  equivalent paths of integration, 77–78
  fundamental theorem of algebra, 93
  identity theorems, 86–87
  Liouville's theorem, 91–93
  Maclaurin series, 83

Taylor expansion (*continued*):
  maximum modulus principle, 89–90
  Picard's theorem, 96
  regularity and differentiability to all orders, 82
  transcendental entire functions, 95–96
Taylor's series, 80–83 (*see also* Taylor expansion)
Transcendental entire functions, 95–96
Transformations, *see* Mapping
Triangle inequality, 13–15
Trigonometric form, 10–11

U

Uniqueness theorem, infinite series, 53

V

Variables, differentiability and, 18–19
Variables, limits of, 19–23

W

Weierstrass M-series, 205

Z

Zero, 3, 115–117